AFGHAN AIR WARS

OSPREY
PUBLISHING

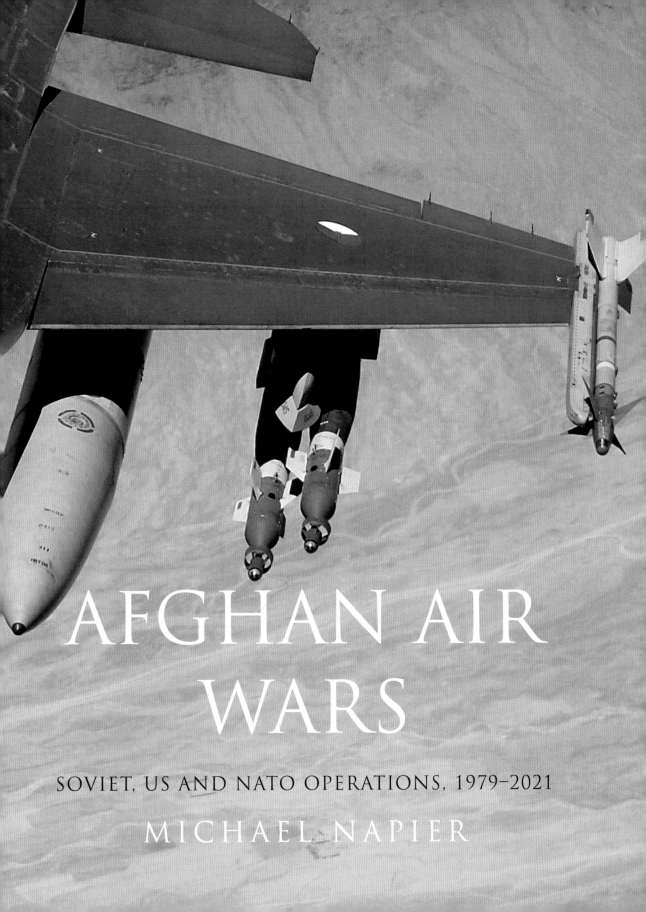

AFGHAN AIR
WARS

SOVIET, US AND NATO OPERATIONS, 1979–2021

MICHAEL NAPIER

OSPREY PUBLISHING
Bloomsbury Publishing Plc
Kemp House, Chawley Park, Cumnor Hill, Oxford OX2 9PH, UK
29 Earlsfort Terrace, Dublin 2, Ireland
1385 Broadway, 5th Floor, New York, NY 10018, USA
E-mail: info@ospreypublishing.com
www.ospreypublishing.com

OSPREY is a trademark of Osprey Publishing Ltd

First published in Great Britain in 2023

ISBN: PB 9781472859013;
eBook: 9781472859020;
ePDF: 9781472859037;
XML: 9781472859044

23 24 25 26 27   10 9 8 7 6 5 4 3 2 1

Cover, page design and layout by Stewart Larking
Title page image: An F-16AM Fighting Falcon of the RNLAF over
Afghanistan. (USAF)
Image on this page: A USAF F-15E Strike Eagle over Afghanistan on
28 May 2008. (USAF)
Maps by Nicki Averill
Index by Alan Rutter
Originated by PDQ Digital Media Solutions, Bungay, UK
Printed and bound in India by Replika Press Private Ltd.

MIX
Paper from
responsible sources
FSC® C016779

Osprey Publishing supports the Woodland Trust, the UK's leading
woodland conservation charity.

To find out more about our authors and books visit
www.ospreypublishing.com. Here you will find extracts, author
interviews, details of forthcoming events and the option to sign up for
our newsletter.

CONTENTS

AUTHOR'S NOTE

Part of the 'Hippy Trail' in the 1960s and 1970s, Afghanistan dominated the headlines in the next decade and again in the first two decades of this century. Unfortunately, the reason was not 'love and peace in the world' as the hippies may have hoped, but a series of brutal wars, in which airpower played an important role. This book records and explains the critical role of airpower in Afghanistan not only over the last 20 years but also during the ten-year occupation by the USSR in the 1980s, drawing the parallels between the experiences of both NATO and the Soviet Union.

As with my previous books, this volume is intended to provide a chronological and complete overview of the air campaigns with enough detail for readers to identify any areas for further research or reading, if they are so interested and inclined. In the last chapter I have also offered my own brief assessment of the events that I have described, but I leave it to the reader to draw their own conclusions, which of course may differ from mine.

The US-led occupation between 2001 and 2021 was supported by many other countries. These were in the main members of NATO, but also included Australia, New Zealand, Austria, Sweden and Switzerland as well as others such as Azerbaijan, Armenia, Georgia, Mongolia and Ukraine. For this reason, I have frequently used the term 'Coalition' in referring to non-US forces of that period, where I know or suspect that non-NATO personnel were involved.

The maps show as much detail as possible, but I have omitted some of the locations that are very close to others in order to reduce clutter. In these cases, I have given the position relative to a location that does appear on the map.

A NOTE ON UNITS OF MEASUREMENT

In aviation we use different measuring units for different things. For example, speeds are measured in knots, whereas visibility is measured in kilometres; altitude is measured in feet, but fuel quantity is measured in kilogrammes; gun and rocket ranges are measured in metres, but bomb weights are measured in pounds. I have retained this mixed system because that is how the quantities are described by those who were there; also, there is no standard alternative – US measures differ from the Imperial system and while the metric system offers some advantages, it is only used consistently in the context of aviation in Russia and China. For the Soviet experience in Afghanistan, I have retained the metric units that were used by aircrews at the time.

I have therefore used the following convention:

Distance – statute miles
Altitude – feet (except in direct quotes from Soviets, in which case metres – multiply by three for rough conversion to feet)
Speed – knots (except in direct quotes from Soviets, in which case kph – divide by two for rough conversion to knots)
Weights (including fuel) – kg (multiply by two for rough conversion to lb)
Weapons – weights in lb for US/British bombs, but kg for Soviet bombs

ACKNOWLEDGEMENTS

I am very grateful to Melvin G. Deaile, Michael Vizcarra and 'Cab' Townsend for allowing me to quote from their personal reminiscences and to Albert Grandolini and Chris Stradling for letting me use images from their collections. Thank you to Nicki Averill for drawing the maps. Thank you, too, to my editor, the redoubtable Jasper Spencer-Smith, and to Marcus Cowper from Osprey.

The high mountains of the Hindu Kush in Afghanistan, as seen from a USAF Lockheed C-130 Hercules transport aircraft en route to Bagram Air Base in December 2002. The mountainous terrain complicated air operations and made those on the ground particularly arduous. (USAF)

CHAPTER 1

AN INTRODUCTION TO AFGHANISTAN

When you're wounded and left on Afghanistan's plains,
And the women come out to cut up what remains,
Jest roll to your rifle and blow out your brains
An' go to your Gawd like a soldier

Rudyard Kipling

Just before midnight on 30 August 2021, Major General Chris T. Donahue, commander of the US Army 82nd Airborne Division, walked up the cargo ramp of a USAF Boeing C-17 Globemaster III transport aircraft at Hamid Karzai International Airport in Kabul, Afghanistan. He was the last US soldier to leave Afghanistan, marking almost 20 years of US military presence in the country. At precisely 23:59hrs Kabul time, the final C-17 lifted off from the runway and as the aircraft disappeared into the distance, Taliban official Hekmatullah Wasiq commented: 'Afghanistan is finally free.' Perhaps a similar sentiment had been expressed 30 years earlier when Colonel General Boris V. Gromov, the last Soviet soldier to leave Afghanistan, crossed the Friendship Bridge over the Amu-Daria River to return to the USSR, marking the end of nearly ten years of Soviet occupation. For by 2021, Afghanistan had endured four decades of internal conflict while first the USSR, and then a US-led Coalition, attempted to establish some sort of stability in the country.

Against a backdrop of the mountains of central Afghanistan, an RAF Panavia Tornado GR4 refuels from a USAF McDonnell Douglas KC-10 Extender tanker. (Stradling)

During that time, both the geography of Afghanistan and the military situation in the region meant that airpower would play a vital role in all of the various campaigns. In fact, aircraft had been involved in Afghanistan since 1919, but it was the Soviet invasion of the country in 1989 that brought with it the large-scale use of helicopters and fighter-bomber aircraft. The Afghan terrain also dictated that the Soviets rely on air transport to keep their army supplied and reinforced. However, even the Soviet efforts were surpassed by the massive deployment of US-led Coalition air forces in the 2000s. With 20 years of improved technology compared to the Soviets in the 1980s and with recent combat experience in Iraq and the Balkans, Coalition airpower was a formidable force: an extensive intelligence gathering capability was backed by delivery platforms for precision guided munitions. However, despite wielding this impressive firepower, the Coalition presence in Afghanistan still came to an ignominious end with an evacuation airlift – repeating the experience of the British just over 100 years earlier.

GEOGRAPHY

Approximately the same size as Texas, Afghanistan lies in southwest Asia between Pakistan, Iran and the former Soviet territories that are now Turkmenistan, Uzbekistan, and Tajikistan. Once an important part of the historic Silk Road, in the 19th century it became a buffer zone between the British and Russian empires; more recently it has found itself at the meeting point between the Western and Soviet, and later the Western and Islamic, spheres of interest.

The country is dominated by the mountains of the Hindu Kush which run from the 22,000ft peaks in the northeast of the country to form a central massif, the Hazarajat, which reaches around 14,000ft. The major cities of Afghanistan form a ring around the base of the mountains, from the capital Kabul clockwise around the Hazarajat through Kandahar, Herat, and Mazar-e-Sharif to Kunduz. In turn, Kunduz and Kabul are linked by the Salang Pass and Salang Tunnel. Kabul is at an elevation of nearly 6,000ft, while Kandahar and Herat are at 3,000ft and Mazar-e-Sharif and Kunduz are at approximately 1,000ft. To the southwest of the mountains, the Dasht-e Margo desert stretches 300km from Lashkar Gah to the Iranian border.

The contrasting terrain of Afghanistan – desert, mountains, towns and farmland all in close proximity. This view shows the Arghandab River and the edge of the red Registan Desert in the southwest of the country. This region, comprising Kandahar and Helmand provinces, was the centre of Taliban influence in the early 2000s. (Stradling)

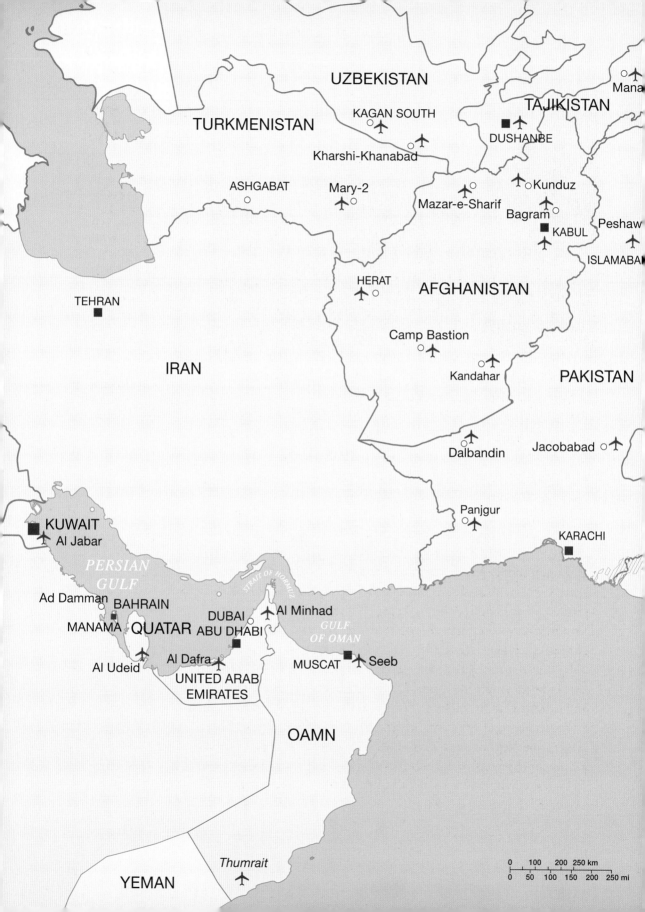

The Arghandab River which runs through Kandahar, the Hari River which runs through Herat, the Helmand River which runs through the southwest red Registan Desert and the Kunduz River which flows north from Kunduz into the Amu-Daria River are all surrounded by 'green zones' of dense vegetation. Here, complex irrigation networks support extensive agricultural activity alongside the rivers. Outside these fertile areas, the terrain is generally arid although, except for the desert regions, it does support subsistence farming. The rural communities are often small villages or hamlets made up of solidly built compounds known as *kishlaks*. Constructed of mud bricks with walls over a metre thick and perhaps 6m high, the kishlaks were typically built in a 'U' shape, with the living accommodation along the southerly (warmest) wall. Some of these buildings are also fortified.

Afghanistan enjoys a semi-arid climate, with cold winters (temperatures of around minus 7°C in Kabul and 0°C in Kandahar) and hot summers (typically 32°C in Kabul and 40°C in Kandahar). Summers, between May and September, are dry but there is some rain on about ten days a month during the winter, between October to April; this precipitation falls as snow on the mountains. In the summer, the frequent strong winds often kick up dust storms which reduce visibility to 300m or less.

HISTORY

Although it boasts its own flag and a seat at the United Nations (UN), Afghanistan is not a monocultural nation in the Western understanding of nationhood – rather, it is an expanse of territory that is occupied by a number of disparate and mutually hostile groups. These groups do, however, share a deeply conservative culture rooted in fundamentalist Islam, with medieval views on blood feuds, honour, and the treatment of women. They also share a distrust of outsiders and are prepared to bury their differences, albeit temporarily, to expel foreign influences. Afghanistan is defined at the UN as a low income, least developed country (LDC)[1]. Reliable statistics are hard to come by, and estimates of the population vary, but in 2000 it was thought to be around 26 million and had risen to almost 39 million by 2020. The largest ethnic group of these is Pashtun, making up some 40 percent of the total. The Pashtuns, also called Pathans, straddle the border with Pakistan and family loyalties often lie in both countries. The second largest group in Afghanistan, the Tajiks, account for 20 percent of the total population, while the Uzbeks and Hazaras make up 19 percent and six percent respectively. Three quarters of the Afghan population lives in rural communities and the literacy in the country rate is less than 50 percent. Life expectancy in Afghanistan in 2000 was just 56 years[2], but by 2020 it had risen to 65 years.

A Royal Aircraft Factory BE2c of 31 Sqn RAF in flight over northwest India. Although the type was truly obsolete, it played an important role in defeating the Afghan army in the third Anglo-Afghan War of 1919. (Jarrett)

Afghanistan became important to both Britain and Russia in the 'Great Game' of the 19th century, during which the Russian Empire sought to advance southwards towards the Indian Ocean, while the British Empire sought to secure the borders of its Northwest Frontier of India. The British were keen to keep Afghanistan as a buffer between India and any possible expansion towards it by Russia or Persia. In many ways, the First Anglo-Afghan War fought between 1839 and 1842 set the tone for foreign involvement in Afghanistan. Concerned with the relationship of the Amir of Afghanistan, Dost Mahommed Khan Barakzai Amir, with Persia and the possibility of an Afghan invasion of India, the British decided to replace the Amir with his deposed predecessor, Shah Shuja Durrani.

The British plan was to invade the country with a limited military contingent in order to enforce a regime change to a better pro-British prospect, then establish stability in the country and withdraw. It was estimated that such an operation would take a year or so at most. In reality the task was not completed by the time the British were ejected two years later, and the installed government did not survive after the British withdrew.

The British invaded the country in early 1839 and obtained the surrender of Dost Mahommed after the capture of Kandahar in July of the same year. Most of the British troops were withdrawn, but the

The Handley Page V/1500 'Old Carthusian' which bombed the Amiri palace in Kabul on 24 May 1919 and persuaded the Amir Amanullah Khan both to seek an armistice and establish his own air force. (Jarrett)

government of Shah Shuja was dependent on the 8,000 remaining troops to maintain power against an increasing insurgency. Finally, an uprising by Afghan rebels in November 1841 forced the withdrawal of British troops who were then massacred as they tried to reach the Khyber Pass in January 1842. Legendary stories of how the Afghans had defeated the British were still part of Afghan culture 160 years later. The Second Anglo-Afghan War of 1878 to 1880 was more successful than the previous conflict, but even so, the British withdrew quickly from the country once they had set up their client government. The borders of Afghanistan were not properly defined until the end of the century: an attempted invasion by Russia in 1885, in which it successfully annexed Pandjeh, led to the delimitation protocol of 1885, but the border between Russia and Afghanistan was only fully established in 1895. The border between Northwest India (now Pakistan) and Afghanistan was settled along the Durand Line in 1893. However, while the northern boundary is well defined by the Amu-Daria River, the Durand Line through the Spin Ghar mountains is simply a line on the map: in reality it is neither obvious and nor is it particularly enforceable, so it remains a porous boundary that is not recognized by the Pashtun groups who live on either side of it.

In 1919, the Third Anglo-Afghan War between Great Britain and Afghanistan saw the first use of aeroplanes over Afghanistan. In April that year, the Amritsar Massacre marked the end of a period of relative calmness in India, and civil unrest erupted. Taking advantage of this distraction, the Amir Amanullah Khan of Afghanistan saw an opportunity to invade Northwest India and recapture the city of Peshawar, which had once been part of Afghanistan. The Afghan army captured Bagh on 3 May, but British and Indian troops managed to hold them there. Meanwhile, the two resident Royal Air Force (RAF) units, 31 Squadron (Sqn) and 114 Sqn, had been put on standby for operations. They were still equipped with the Royal Aircraft Factory BE2, an obsolete type that had long been withdrawn from front-line service elsewhere. A reconnaissance flight

The RAF squadrons in India also flew the BE2e, which was very similar to, and as just as obsolete as, the BE2c variant. This particular aircraft was operated by 31 Sqn in northwestern India in 1918.

on 6 May by 31 Sqn reported the disposition of the Afghan troops as well as local tribesmen, who had crossed into India via the Khyber Pass to support them. Three days later, 16 aircraft carried out bombing attacks on the main Afghan encampment at Dakka while the Indian army carried out a counter-attack at Bagh; although this action was unsuccessful, a second counter-attack on 11 May drove the Afghans back across the border, hotly pursued by aircraft and the Indian army. The aircraft of 31 Sqn also bombed Jalalabad. Meanwhile the Handley-Page V/1500 bomber, named 'Old Carthusian', which had been flown from Great Britain a few months earlier, was pressed into service. On 24 May, the 'Old Carthusian' was flown by Capt R. Halley from Risalpur (near Peshawar) to bomb the Amiri palace in Kabul. Not only did his bombs cause physical damage to the palace when four of them destroyed a wall of the harem, but they also had a significant personal and psychological effect on the Amir himself, who hastily sought an armistice. Four days later, the Afghans launched a counter-attack against British and Indian forces, laying siege to their camp at Thal. RAF aircraft played an important role in the relief of Thal on 1 June when they carried out bombing attacks against Afghan positions and directed the artillery fire from the relief force. The Third Afghan War ended in an armistice on 3 June, and the peace treaty was signed on 8 August.

The ungainly lines of a Vickers Victoria transport aircraft of 70 Sqn RAF, seen in flight over Iraq. The aircraft, which could carry 22 passengers, made the long journey from Iraq to India to conduct the evacuation of Kabul in 1928–29. (Jarrett)

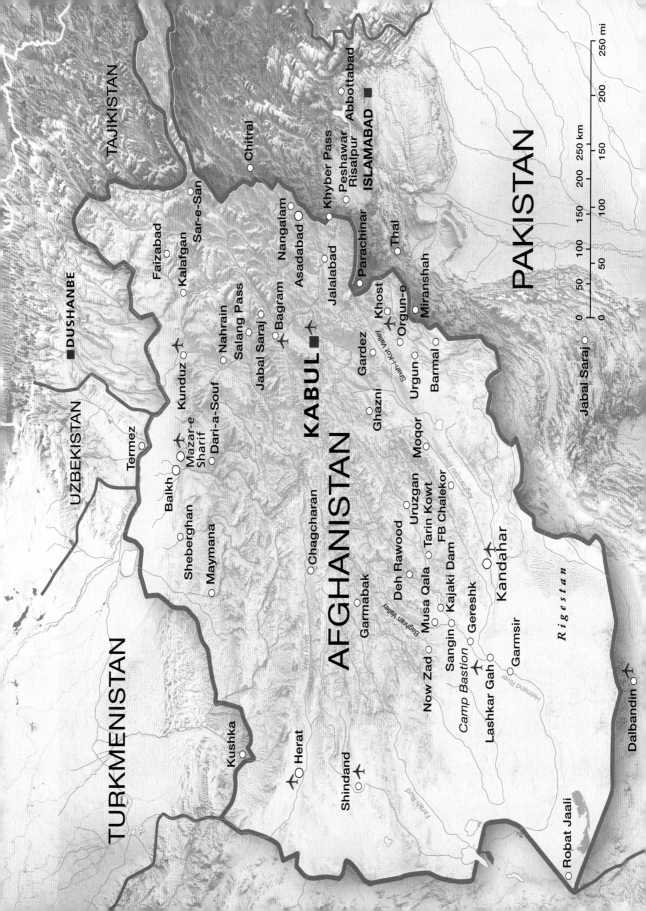

Having seen at first hand the effectiveness of airpower during the short war, the Amir Amanullah Khan decided that he should have an air force of his own. Thus in 1920 he formed the small Royal Afghan Air Force, a small service comprising a handful of Soviet-built aircraft flown by Soviet contract pilots.

Eight years later, aviation was again called to play an important role in another event. In November 1928, an uprising by rebels who opposed the introduction of liberal 'western' customs into Afghan life by (the now) King Amanullah led to civil war. After seizing Jalalabad, the rebels advanced on Kabul and by 14 December fighting between the rebels and forces loyal to the king raged around the British Legation on the western outskirts of the city. As well as the British and Indian staff and their families, a number of European civilians also took refuge in the Legation building. Contingency plans to evacuate women and children from Kabul had already been sketched out in early December, when it became apparent that the rebellion was gaining support, and the Vickers Victoria transport aircraft of 70 Sqn, based at Hinaidi near Baghdad, in Iraq, were earmarked for the task. When direct land communication between the British Legation in Kabul and the Indian government was interrupted, the plans for evacuation were put into action. On 15 December a Victoria flown by Sqn Ldr R.S. Maxwell was dispatched to India from Iraq and after covering a distance of over 2,000 miles, the aircraft arrived at Risalpur on 19 December.

The prototype Handley Page Hinaidi, a converted Hyderabad bomber with more powerful engines, was undertaking tropical trials in India when it was sent to assist with the Kabul airlift. The aircraft is seen here on the ground at Sherpur airfield, Kabul. (Jarrett)

A Victoria takes off from
Kabul in the snow. The
airlift to evacuate civilians
from Kabul was beset by
the winter weather and
freezing conditions
through December 1928
and January 1929.
(Jarrett)

Meanwhile, on 17 December, in response to a faint 'SOS' message
received by radio from Kabul, Fg Off C.W.L. Trusk and LAC G.A.
Donaldson from 27 Sqn flew a reconnaissance of the city in a DH9A.
They were also tasked with dropping a Popham panel signalling
device at the British Legation. On reaching Kabul, they flew over the
Legation building where the residents had used sheets to spell the
message 'All Well – Fly Very High – Do Not Land.' Although Trusk
and Donaldson saw the message, they could see no sign of life in the
building and therefore decided to carry out a low-level flypast in
order to see if anyone was there. They also dropped the Popham panel
into the Legation grounds. Perhaps unsurprisingly, since the Royal
Afghan Air Force was using the Polikarpov R-1, an exact copy of the
DH9A, to bomb the rebels, Trusk and Donaldson came under heavy
fire as they flew past the Legation building. Their aircraft was hit in
the engine oil sump, and with engine failure imminent, Trusk
managed to land at the nearby airfield at Sherpur. On each of the
next five days, a DH9A reconnaissance sortie was flown over Kabul
to monitor the messages on the Popham panel at the legation, but no
change was seen in the messages. However, on 22 December, shortly
after the reconnaissance by Fg Off Prendegast, the rebel forces were
forced back and, reconnected to the city once more, the British
Legation staff were able to establish telephone contact with the British
administration in India and also to establish a route from the legation
building to Sherpur airfield.

The air evacuation commenced the next day, 23 December. While 23 women and children made the hour-long journey walking through the snow from the British Legation to the Italian Legation near to the airfield, five aircraft were making their way through the winter skies towards Kabul. They were led by Sqn Ldr Nicholas in a Westland Wapiti, one of two such aircraft which were being trialled in India; the remainder of the formation comprised three DH9As flown by Fg Off Prendegast, Fg Off Pelly and Fg Off Fullergood and the Victoria flown by Sqn Ldr Maxwell and Fg Off Beasley. After all of the aircraft had landed at Sherpur, the evacuees were driven the short distance from the Italian Legation to the airfield. The passengers were flown out from Kabul in the Victoria, while the DH9As were used to carry their luggage. The next day the Victoria returned, this time accompanied by a Wapiti and 11 DH9As. On the same day, two more Victorias set off from Iraq to join the airlift operation. There were no evacuation flights planned for Christmas Day, but the airlift continued on 26 December. Over the previous few days RAF aircraft had transported 71 dependents, including 18 Germans, ten French, nine Persians, six Turks, three Italians, one Swiss and one American national, from Kabul through the mountains of the Himalayan foothills to Risalpur. Unfortunately, heavy snow closed the airfield at Sherpur on 27 and 28 December, but by the time that flights restarted on 29 December, the airlift fleet had been enlarged with the arrival of the prototype Handley Page Hinaidi (not to be confused with the airfield of the same name) and now comprised a total of three Victorias, as well as the Hinaidi, two Wapitis and two squadrons of DH9A.

As well as the Hinaidi, two Westland Wapiti army co-operation aircraft were also undergoing trials in India and took part in the airlift.

A Vickers Victoria from 70 Sqn RAF arriving at Risalpur carrying evacuees from Kabul. By 25 February 1929, when the airlift was completed, 586 people had been flown out of the city. (Jarrett)

The intensely cold winter weather took its toll of the Hinaidi on its first flight, as the engine oil almost froze and the starboard Jupiter engine stopped as soon as the aircraft landed at Sherpur. It took the crew, led by Flt Lt D.F. Anderson, four days on the ground at Kabul using coal braziers to heat the engine oil sufficiently for them to restart the engines. The evacuation continued steadily through January 1929, but by then the rebels had gained the upper hand. On 14 January, King Amanullah abdicated in favour of his brother Inayatullah and left the country. Three days later, Inayatullah also abdicated, and he was replaced in turn by the rebel leader, Habibullah Kalakani. But throughout these events, the evacuation continued unchallenged. There was a lucky escape from disaster on 29 January 1929, when a Victoria flown by Flt Lt R. Ivelaw-Chapman and Fg Off A.R.S. Davies suffered a double engine failure en route to Kabul. Water had collected in the fuel tanks, causing the filters to freeze up. Luckily, the pilots skilfully managed to glide the aircraft and make a forced landing onto a small plateau surrounded by a 2,000ft precipice. The two officers were then captured by the rebels who held them as hostages until 18 February when they were released. By early February there were eight Victoria transports flying between Risalpur and Kabul, including aircraft from 216 Sqn which had flown from

Heliopolis in Egypt. The airlift continued with daily flights until it was completed on 25 February 1929. By that time 586 individuals of eleven different nationalities had been flown from Kabul to India. This operation was the first ever large-scale airlift.

SOVIET INTERVENTION

The Soviet-Afghan Treaty of Friendship was signed in 1921, marking a long association between Afghanistan and the Soviet Union. Over the next decades, the USSR became the most important commercial and political partner for Afghanistan. The USA also courted Afghanistan in the 1950s and 1960s, including funding the work of the Helmand and Arghandab Valley Authority, which built the Kajaki dam and constructed much of the canal system that provided irrigation in the green zones. It was during the early 1960s that the airfield at Kandahar was built to support US Lockheed U-2 reconnaissance operations over the USSR. Nevertheless, the USSR was the favoured partner and not only were the Afghan armed forces equipped and trained by the USSR, but many Afghanis were educated at universities in the Soviet Union. Throughout the 1960s, a tolerant and relatively liberal society flourished in the cities of Afghanistan, although rural areas still clung to their more conservative way of life. In 1965, the communist People's Democratic Party of Afghanistan (PDPA) was formed in Kabul university. Unfortunately, the early 1970s brough dissent and dissatisfaction with the monarchy, leading to a military *coup d'etat* in 1973, starting a series of events which would eventually lead to anarchy, foreign invasion and civil war. After the coup, the monarchy was abolished and a republic was proclaimed, but five years later another coup put the PDPA into power. Unfortunately, chaos ensued, since the PDPA was obsessed by intellectual argument rather than practical measures and was riven by deep ideological disagreements. Rural Afghans who still held to their Islamic lifestyle disapproved of the communist ideology that was being forced upon them and there were a series of revolts, centred around Herat. Facing anarchy in the country, the Afghan government asked the

The Tajbeg palace in Kabul in 2013: Once the residence of the Amir and King of Afghanistan, it was where Soviet troops assassinated Hafizullah Amin, the leader of the Democratic Republic of Afghanistan on 27 December 1979. The building also served as the headquarters for the Soviet 40th Army in Afghanistan. (US Army)

USSR for support. For its part the Politburo in the USSR was reluctant to intervene, but, nervous of possible US interference, it decided to take action.

The Soviet plan was to invade the country with a limited military contingent in order to enforce a regime change to a better pro-Soviet prospect, then establish stability in the country and withdraw. It was estimated that such an operation would take a year or so at most. In reality, the task was not completed by the time the Soviets withdrew nearly ten years later, and the installed government did not survive long after the Soviets withdrew.

On the orders of the Soviet Politburo, the Soviet 40th Army invaded Afghanistan in December 1979 and deposed the government. Throughout their ten-year occupation, Soviet forces were supported by the armed forces of the Democratic Republic of Afghanistan (DRA), which comprised the Soviet trained and equipped DRA Army and DRA Air Force (DRAAF). In the late 1970s, the DRA Army numbered 100,000 troops, but the Soviets found the army to be politically unreliable and did not encourage recruitment. As a result of casualties and defections, by 1983 the DRA Army numbered just 40,000 troops, most of whom were conscripts. In contrast, the DRAAF proved to be more reliable and reasonably combat effective and its strength was therefore increased slightly over the same period.

Afghan resistance to the Soviet occupation started soon after Soviet troops arrived in the country and was carried out by various local militias, known collectively as 'the Mujahideen'. These separate groups were formed around tribes and religious sects, reflecting local loyalties, and by the mid-1980s were thought to number about 90,000 fighters. During the 1980s many of the independent groups coalesced into loose alliances, the largest group of which was the Tajik-dominated Jamiat-e Islami, which was led by Burhanuddin Rabbani and Ahmad Shah Massoud. Another major group, the Hizb-e Islami, led by Gilbuddin Hekmatyar, was a confederation of Pashtun groups and it enjoyed generous funding from the Pakistani Inter-Services Intelligence (ISI) and from the US Central Intelligence Agency (CIA), as well as other western agencies.

After the Soviet withdrawal in 1989, the DRA was governed by President Mohammed Najibullah, but the country remained unstable. The plethora of mujahedeen groups which had been united in their fight against the Soviet occupation now had no common enemy, so they turned against the government and one another. The Afghan government survived the Battle of Jalalabad in 1989, when elements of the mujahideen led by Gilbuddin Hekmatyar attempted a frontal assault to capture the city but were defeated. Even so, the Najibullah regime lasted only another three years, for after the fall of the USSR, Russia withdrew its support and Afghanistan descended into civil war. On the one side, the Tajik and Uzbek groups coalesced into the Northern Alliance, in which the major player was Massoud, while the predominant group on the other side was the Taliban led by

A bomb-armed Soviet Air Force Sukhoi Su-17M4 waits on ground alert in Afghanistan during the 1980s. The terrain and conditions in the country made the Soviet ground forces in the country reliant on tactical air power. (Grandolini)

Mullah Muhammad Omar. The Taliban was made up of young Afghan men chiefly recruited from the madrassas (Islamic religious schools) in Pakistan, where they had lived most of their lives as refugees. Under the leadership of Mullah Omar, the Taliban was closely tied to the Pakistani ISI agency, which provided weapons, fuel and military advisers from 1994. With no real link to or experience of Afghan culture and having been indoctrinated with a militant and extreme interpretation of Islam, the Taliban fought bravely and mercilessly. In 1996 it seized control of Kabul from the Northern Alliance and became the de facto government of Afghanistan. At this point the former Afghan Army general Abdul Rashid Dostrum, who had been fighting with the Taliban, changed sides and joined the Northern Alliance.

THE AMERICAN INTERVENTION

By 1998, the Taliban had become heavily influenced by the Saudi Arabian-born terrorist Osama bin Laden, whose Islamist-terrorist organization Al Qaeda had established training bases in Afghanistan. From there it started to wage a terrorist campaign against the USA, culminating on 11 September 2001 with the hijacking of airliners which were used to carry out suicide attacks against the World Trade Center in New York and the Pentagon in Washington. On 4 October, NATO announced that this attack was considered to be an attack on all members of the alliance, under Article 5 of the Washington Treaty. Other friendly nations, including Australia and Uzbekistan, also pledged their support. Three days later, the US administration invoked its right to use military force in self-defence under Article 51 of the UN Charter and declared war on Al Qaeda and its host the Taliban.

The American plan was to invade the country with a limited military contingent in order to enforce a regime change to a better pro-Western prospect, then establish stability in the country and withdraw. It was estimated that such an operation would take a couple of years or so at most. In reality the task was not completed by the time the Americans withdrew nearly 20 years later, and the installed government did not survive after the Americans withdrew.

ABOVE Two General Dynamics F-16C Fighting Falcons of the 174th Fighter Wing of the Air National Guard (ANG) over Afghanistan, equipped with laser target designator pods and laser guided bombs in 2003. Just like the Soviets before them, US and Coalition troops became increasingly dependent on air support. (USAF)

LEFT Equipped by the US and Pakistan, Afghan and Arab muhajideen fighters carried out a vicious guerrilla war against the Soviet occupation. Some 20 years later, US and Coalition Forces also faced an intense campaign against them by well-trained and well-equipped insurgents. (Library of Congress)

In their first offensive against the Taliban in December 2001, US Special Operations Forces (SOF) worked closely with fighters from the Northern Alliance. Northern Alliance guerrillas supported by US airpower attacked Taliban garrisons in the north of the country. By the time US troops arrived in Afghanistan, both the Afghan army and air force had ceased to exist. With no indigenous troops to support them, the US forces relied instead on other Coalition members, principally NATO, to provide troops. Security in Afghanistan was therefore delegated, albeit temporarily, entirely to foreign personnel. In late 2001, the new Afghan government of Mohammad Karzai, supported by the US administration, established the Afghan National Army (ANA), which was to have an initial strength of 70,000 and would be trained, equipped and organized along Western lines. Five years later, the Afghan Air Force (AAF) was also re-established.

Just as the Soviet invasion had been stoutly opposed by the mujahideen, so the US-led invasion was contested by the Taliban and Al Qaeda. Amongst the other groups who also opposed the US and Coalition involvement of the country were the Haqqani Network, the Hizb-e Islami Gilbuddin (HIG) and later the Islamic State of Iraq and Syria – Khorasan Province (ISIS-K). The Haqqani Network, led by Jalaluddin Haqqani, was based in North Waziristan, Pakistan and was mainly involved in cross-border insurgency. The HIG, a splinter group from the original Hezb-e Islami, was a virulently anti-Western insurgent group, while ISIS-K, a particularly violent sect based in Nangarhar province, was closely linked to the Haqqani Network. During the insurgency all of these groups fought under the banner of the Taliban.

AFGHAN INSURGENTS

In the years of Soviet occupation, most of the mujahideen fighters fought in the terrain in which they had lived all their lives and which they knew intimately. Fieldcraft came naturally to them and, having used firearms from an early age, they were well versed in using weapons. Thus, with minimal training they became extremely effective guerrillas and years of practice against the Soviet forces had enabled them to perfect the art of the ambush. The struggle against the Soviets attracted not only Western funding but also a number of Arab fighters, who also brought military skills with them. By the time that the Soviet troops had left Afghanistan, the mujahideen groups that they had faced were well-trained and well-equipped combat-hardened soldiers.

The civil war that followed the Soviet occupation had enabled the older generation of mujahideen to pass on their skills to younger fighters and by the time the US and Coalition Forces arrived in Afghanistan, the Taliban had access to thousands of guerrillas with an excellent appreciation of basic infantry tactics. The organization of the Taliban comprised a number of layers. At the centre were Mullah Muhammad Omar and other religious-military leaders, who made policy and planned strategy. Outside that inner circle

A US Marine on patrol in a green zone in Afghanistan. In these areas high crops could reduce the visibility to a few metres, leaving Coalition troops vulnerable to ambushes and making it difficult for them to co-ordinate air support. (USMC)

were a larger number of hard-line ideologically driven activists, who put the policies and strategies into effect. In this they used an outer layer of locally recruited fighters, who were probably not so much inspired by religious ideology as by tribal loyalty, monetary reward, or fear of reprisal, and who might fight for just a few days before returning to their normal everyday life. In addition to fighters, the Taliban made good use of a network of local 'spotters' (known colloquially to British troops as 'dickers') who reported the movement of Coalition personnel, vehicles and aircraft.

In setting up an ambush, the Taliban often worked at night, so that they could move around freely, unarmed, during daylight. Ambush points were carefully planned to give the insurgents a safe line of retreat by which to disengage, for they often fought for just 15 to 20 minutes before withdrawing. Ambushes were often planned to be hit-and-run affairs, pulling back before airpower could be used against them. The insurgents also worked in small, dispersed groups to make it difficult for Coalition aircraft to locate and attack them. Often ambushes were triggered by improvised explosive devices (IED) and sometimes they were very complex, in some cases being strung out over 10km. The Taliban also used IEDs to harass Coalition troop patrols and as a means of besieging Coalition static positions. Apart from being adept hit-and-run guerrillas, they were also capable

May 2014: A sandstorm engulfs Camp Bastion; such conditions would bring flying operations to a standstill. (Crown Copyright/MoD)

of constructing complex defensive positions using local materials (such as wood beams in the Panjwayi valley or rocks in more mountainous regions). Forts and caves were used, often with tunnels connecting them to other fortified positions. The Taliban rarely fought traditional pitched battles, preferring to melt away in the face of overwhelming force: the local recruits would revert to their normal lives while their leaders laid low. However, once Coalition or government forces had withdrawn or reduced their numbers sufficiently, the Taliban would move back. Thus, the Taliban insurgents faced by US and Coalition troops were capable and effective soldiers.

However, while the insurgents against both the Soviet and US occupations claimed allegiance to strict Islamic faith, they also encouraged a narco-economy based on the production of opium as a means of funding themselves. In 1970, the annual production of opium poppies in Afghanistan stood at 90 tonnes, but after the expansion of the drugs trade in the 1980s, annual production had reached 1,800 tonnes in the 1990s and was still increasing. In 2007 annual production peaked at 4,200 tonnes, which represented 93 percent of world opium production. During the 1980s the increase in opium poppy growing was supported logistically by the Pakistani ISI and protected politically by the CIA. Revenue gained from the sale of opium gave the mujahidin groups, and in particular the Pashtun Hizb-e Islami, a steadily increasing source of income with which to buy weapons and pay fighters. Poppies were cultivated in Afghanistan but processed into heroin in factories in Pakistan. After the collapse of the post-Soviet government and the ending of funding from both the former USSR and from the West, all of the factions involved in fighting the civil war turned to opium as the easiest source of money, and the whole opium poppy trade became a commercialized business. For example, the Taliban derived an estimated US$ 45 million in taxes alone from the opium trade in 1999. For farmers there were great benefits in cultivating poppies, which needed little water at a time when many of the irrigation channels had been damaged in the fighting. Not only were poppies far more resistant to drought than wheat, but they commanded a much higher price. It therefore took little persuasion for them to grow poppies and approximately ten per cent of the population became involved in opium growing. In 2000, the Taliban leader Mullah Omar had a change of heart and banned the cultivation

Bagram Air Base served as the main operating base for aircraft of both the Soviet and US air forces. This image was taken in February 2002, shortly after US forces were deployed to the area. (NARA)

of poppies, so that the annual production figure for 2001 plummeted to just 170 tonnes. However, a year later the production figures had recovered to their previous level, and they continued to rise year on year. As Afghanistan overtook Myanmar to become the number one opium producer in the world, corrupt politicians and government employees within the Karzai government were happy to take their own levy from the trade. Subsequent Western-backed initiatives to reduce the drug trade made little difference, although some farmers did abandon opium poppies – to grow marijuana instead.

AVIATION IN AFGHANISTAN

Even in the late 1970s, the transport infrastructure in Afghanistan was almost non-existent, apart from the airfields. With no rail or water transport, the poorly maintained roads were the only means of surface transport. However, these routes were extremely vulnerable to ambushes, and later to IEDs, and were by no means secure. In addition, the long distances involved over rugged terrain made the road network unsuitable for moving the vast quantities of supplies that were needed to feed and equip large armies. Thus, in the 1980s and 2000s, it was on air transport that the burden of supplying first the Soviet, and then the US and Coalition Forces, fell. Without large-scale air transport by cargo aircraft and helicopters, neither sets of forces could have sustained their ground operations in Afghanistan. The speed, reach and firepower of offensive airpower delivered by helicopter gunships and fighter-bombers also became a vital part of ground operations, because it was the only way quickly to reinforce ground troops if they came under enemy fire in remote areas.

However, from the aviation perspective, Afghanistan presents a number of challenges to air operations. Firstly, because of the mountainous Hazarajat in the centre of the country, the major airfields, like the main cities, are situated in the plains at the foot of the mountains – at Kabul, Bagram (40km north of Kabul), Shindand (130km south of Herat) and Kandahar. All of these runways are at a significant altitude above mean sea level (AMSL): Kabul is at almost 6,000ft AMSL, Bagram approximately 5,000ft AMSL, Shindand

some 4,000ft AMSL and Kandahar just over 3,000ft AMSL. At these altitudes the air is somewhat rarefied in comparison to sea-level runways, which degrades the performance of both engines and wings. This effect is further exacerbated by the high temperatures during the summer months, which make the air even thinner. Thus, in practice the Soviets found that their aircraft could rarely carry their theoretical full weapon load because the take-off performance was severely restricted, particularly in the summer. For example, the take-off run for a Mikoyan-Gurevich MiG-21bis under sea level conditions was around 850m, but in the heat of summer in Afghanistan it could increase to 1,500m. Furthermore, like the fixed wing aircraft, the performance of the helicopters was also limited by the air density at high altitudes amongst the mountains, and in the heat of the Afghan summer their load carrying capability was also severely restricted: for example, the Mil Mi-8, which could carry 24 fully armed troops at sea level, would only accommodate 12 soldiers over Afghanistan and sometimes the conditions would allow even fewer than that.

Kandahar Air Base was the second major centre for air operations in Afghanistan during both the 1980s and 2000s. It was expanded significantly during the early 2000s and is seen here as it was in 2010. (Stradling)

The airfields at Bagram and Kandahar were originally constructed by the Americans in the early 1960s, whereas Kabul and Shindand were built by the Soviets some years later. Nevertheless, all of the airfields in Afghanistan were in poor shape during the Soviet occupation in the 1980s and they had deteriorated even further by the time that US and Coalition aircraft arrived in the early 2000s. During the US and NATO occupation, numerous small airstrips were also built at remote forward operating bases (FOB), which were, by their very nature, of basic construction. Operating from rough or poorly maintained airstrips brought further risks, for example from damage to aircraft caused by loose stones and rocks on the runway being blown against the aircraft structure or being ingested by an engine. The all-pervading dust also clogged filters and eroded engine parts.

Strong winds and air currents amongst the mountains made flying conditions unpredictable; for example, local wind effects could make it challenging for helicopters trying to land on small landing zones (LZ)

at altitudes close to their ceiling. Even high-performance jet fighter-bombers were adversely affected by high altitude: the thin air generates higher groundspeeds than at lower levels, adding to the workload of the pilot, and also makes the aircraft less manoeuvrable at height than at low level. Navigation, target acquisition and weapon delivery were also difficult in mountainous terrain where ridges obscured the forward view and targets might be hidden in the depths of a ravine. Moreover, the well camouflaged caves or rock shelters used as fire bases for insurgent groups amongst the mountains were difficult to pinpoint from the cockpit of a fast-moving jet.

A line of MiG-21bis (NATO: Fishbed L/N) fighters of the 322nd IAP armed with FAB-250 bombs at Bagram in the late 1980s. (Grandolini)

In some respects, the green zones were even more difficult for aircrews attempting to support ground troops: here the dense vegetation provided cover to insurgents hiding from air patrols and the strongly constructed kishlaks, which often served as rebel strongholds, also proved to be impervious to all but the largest weapons. The interconnected maze of irrigation ditches provided insurgents with a means of moving swiftly and unseen through the terrain, while crops, both opium poppies and marijuana, growing as high as 2m meant that the visibility for ground troops was less than 100m. Under these conditions, firefights were at close range, making it difficult for supporting aircraft and helicopters to intervene without risking endangering the very troops they were trying to support.

THE AFGHAN AIR FORCE (AAF)

One casualty of the uprising and civil war of 1928 was the Royal Afghan Air Force: most of its aircraft were destroyed by the rebels and the Soviet pilots hurried back to the USSR. After some years without a viable air force in the country, the Royal Afghan Air Force was regenerated in the mid-1930s, this time equipped with the British-built Hawker Hind and the Italian-supplied Meridionali Ro.37. During World War II, the air force was largely grounded once again, this time by logistical problems experienced during the conflict. In 1955, the air force was completely modernized and re-equipped by the USSR with MiG-17 fighters, Ilyushin Il-28 bombers, Ilyushin Il-14 and Antonov An-24 transport aircraft, as well as helicopters and training aircraft. By 1960, the air force possessed 100 combat aircraft. In the mid-1960s, MiG-21 fighters and Mil Mi-8 helicopters formed the mainstay of the service. By the time of the Soviet invasion in 1979, the Democratic Republic of Afghanistan Air Force (DRAAF), as it had now become, had a strength of some 200 aircraft including MiG-21s, Sukhoi Su-7BM fighter-bombers and An-26 transport aircraft. Thanks to Soviet support in the next years, the Afghan combat force grew to some 230 aircraft, with a helicopter force of some 150 Mi-8 transports and Mi-24 gunships. The DRAAF worked closely with their Soviet counterpart during the 1980s and was reasonably effective in combat.

MiG-21 pilots from 322 IAP of the Democratic Republic of Afghanistan Air Force pose by one of their aircraft, late 1980s. (Grandolini)

In the aftermath of the Soviet withdrawal, the air force, like the Afghan Army, was split up between the various factions. Ahmad Shah Massoud absorbed about 200 aircraft (mainly helicopter transports and gunships, but including some MiG-21 fighters), which were under the command of Mohammed Dawran, while Abdul Rashid Dostrum took 120 aircraft (including MiG-21s, Su-7s, An-12s, and Mi-8s) to form the rival Dostrum-Gilbuddin Militia Air Force (DGMAF) based at Mazar-e-Sharif. The two air forces occasionally fought each other and in January 1994, MiG-21s from the air element commanded by Dawran shot down two DGMAF Su-7s and a MiG-21. The Taliban also had an air element, and their capture of Kabul was supported by Su-22Ms. They also acquired some 30 MiG-21s at Kabul airport, but the aircraft were mostly unflyable after years of neglect. It was after the Taliban take over that Dostrum changed sides and joined the Northern Alliance, bringing his air force with him. By the time of the US-led invasion, only a few of the fixed-wing transport aircraft and some helicopters belonging to the Northern Alliance were still serviceable.

The sad end that befell most of the aircraft of the Democratic Republic of Afghanistan Air Force (DRAAF): the hulk of a MiG-21 lies abandoned at Bagram Air Base in the summer of 2002. (NARA)

Civil aviation in Afghanistan had started in 1955 with the formation of the state-owned Ariana Airlines. Beginning services with three Douglas DC-3 Dakotas, the airline flew international routes around the region with a relatively modest fleet of aircraft which now included a Douglas DC-4 Skymaster. By 1979, the fleet included a McDonnell Douglas DC-10 and two Boeing 727s. A state-owned domestic airline, Bakhtar Airlines, was formed in 1967, and it absorbed Ariana Airlines in 1985 to form Bakhtar Afghan Airlines equipped with two Tupolev Tu-154M.

A Soviet Air Force MiG-21bis over the mountains of Afghanistan. This
aircraft appears to be armed with a FAB-250 bomb. (Grandolini)

CHAPTER 2

THE SOVIET EXPERIENCE 1979–1989

I am asked if I think the war was a just war ... how can I
answer? I was a boy born and raised in beautiful Leningrad,
a boy who loved his parents and went obediently to school.
A boy who was yanked out of that life and dumped in a
strange land where life followed different rules

Vladislav Tamarov, *Afghanistan: A Russian Soldier's Story*

The 108th Motorizovannyy Strelkovaya Diviziya (MSD – Motorized Rifle Division) of the Soviet 40th Army entered Afghanistan from the Uzbek Soviet Socialist Republic (SSR) on the evening of 25 December 1979. After crossing the Amu-Daria River at Termez, the division advanced in a clockwise direction around the central massif via Kunduz and the Salang Pass towards Kabul. On the same day, the 103rd Aviadesantnaya Gvardeyskaya Diviziya (AGvD – Guards Airborne Division) landed at Kabul and Bagram to seize the key political and military installations around Kabul. They were ferried by a fleet of Antonov An-12, An-22 and Ilyushin Il-76 transports drawn from across the Voyenno-Vozdushnye Sily (VVS – Soviet Air Force). The first aircraft loss of the campaign occurred during this phase when an Il-76

ABOVE An Antonov An-22 (NATO: Cock) transport aircraft of the Soviet Air Force being unloaded at Kabul airport on 11 January 1980. (Bettmann/Getty Images)

RIGHT Soviet troops boarding a Mil Mi-8 (NATO: Hip) transport helicopter as it hovers on a precarious mountain landing zone. (Grandolini)

commanded by Capt V.V. Golovchin flew into a hillside, killing the crew and 37 paratroopers.

Two days later, a second MSD entered northwestern Afghanistan from the Turkmen SSR near Kushka, taking an anti-clockwise route via Herat and Shindand. The troops were told that they were acting to protect the Afghan people from an imminent US invasion. The ground forces were supported by helicopters and tactical aircraft from the 49th Vozdushnye Sily (VS – Air Force) based in the Turkmen SSR, with the helicopters patrolling ahead of the ground convoys to check that villages on the route were clear of rebel forces. The first clash between Soviet aircraft and Afghan rebel forces was on 30 December when a Mil Mi-8 flown by Col V.K. Gainutdinov, deputy commander of the 181st Otdel'nyy Vertoletnyy Polk (OVP – Independent Helicopter Regiment) received multiple hits from small arms while carrying out a reconnaissance sortie and had to make a forced landing because of the damage. The next day Mi-8s from the 302nd Otdel'nyy Vertoletnyy Eskadril'ya (OVE – Independent Helicopter Squadron) fired rockets at targets on the road near Kushka, to the west of Mazar-e-Sharif. They were in action again a day later, clearing the way for the convoys to clear the Rabati–Mirza pass to the north of Herat.

Two MiG-21 squadrons provided air cover for the invading forces, patrolling over northern Afghanistan. However, they had little intelligence on the state of the Afghan air defences and one pair of MiG-21s were surprised by an apparent missile launch; it was only after they had carried out defensive manoeuvres that the pilots realized that what they had actually seen was a dust cloud generated by a light aircraft taking off from a small airstrip north of Mazar-e-Sharif.

Soon after the airfields had been secured by the airborne troops, aviation units started to deploy forwards. The 302nd OVE and one squadron from 280th OVP, both of which were equipped with the Mi-8 and based at Kagan-South, deployed to Shindand in western

A MiG-21PFM (NATO: Fishbed F) of the Democratic Republic of Afghanistan Air Force (DRAAF) over Afghanistan. (Grandolini)

Afghanistan and to Kandahar respectively. A heavy lift capability was provided by the 181st OVP, which operated the Mi-6, Mi-8 and Mi-10 types, when it transferred to Kunduz in the first 14 days of January. They were joined there by a Mi-24 attack helicopter regiment, the 292nd OVP. Meanwhile, the Su-17M3-equipped 217th Aviatsionnyy Polk Istrebiteley-Bombardirovshchikov (APIB – Fighter-Bomber Regiment) had deployed from Kzyal-Arvat to Shindand and one squadron from the 115th Gvardeyskiy Istrebitel'nyy Aviatsionnyy Polk (GvIAP – Guards Fighter Regiment) at Kokaydy moved to Bagram with 12 MiG-21bis fighters to fulfil the air-defence role. The unit also had two twin-seat MiG-21UMs, colloquially known as 'Sparkys'. The 136th APIB flying the obsolescent MiG-21PFM in the ground-attack role initially continued to operate from Kokaydy, before transferring one squadron to Kandahar in early January.

In the mountainous terrain, aerial reconnaissance took on a special importance. Eight Yakovlev Yak-28R reconnaissance crews from the 39th Otdel'nyy Razvedyvatel'nyy Aviatsionnyy Polk (ORAP – Independent Reconnaissance Regiment) deployed from Balkhash to Mary-2 to carry out missions over Afghanistan. Usually, one crew would be stood down for the day, leaving seven to fly the missions that had been planned the previous evening. Alexander Zhibrov[3], a Yak-28R pilot, recalled:

> We got up at 06:00hrs, and at 08:00hrs the first plane took off. The others followed it with an interval of 20 minutes, and by 12:00hrs everyone was already returning. If the weather permitted, we carried out two flights a day … During visual search, flights in the target area were performed at low altitude. If, after solving a specific problem, the remaining fuel allowed, the crews 'improved their low-flying skills', dropping over the flat terrain [mainly roads and villages] to between 5m and 10m. The tasks of our group included: performing photo reconnaissance … of settlements, roads, airfields, passes, terrain sections, fortified areas, fortresses; searching for caravans and rebel bands, photographing them and transmitting coordinates when approaching the airfield; clarification of intelligence reports, identification of areas with strong air defence; detection of aircraft crash sites, etc … Very often there were simply

stupid tasks, for example, work in the southeast of the DRA. There was enough fuel to fly there and back at an altitude of 10,000m, and yet it was still necessary to conduct reconnaissance at ground level! When performing such tasks, it was necessary to save fuel, and all the same, the aircraft returned to their airfield with its dangerously small reserves. Repeatedly I had to land at forward airfields in Afghanistan. Twice they wanted to transfer our group to Kandahar, but for take-off from this airfield, located at an altitude of 1,200m, the Yak-28R required the use of afterburner, which had been prohibited … back in 1976.

The photo-recce missions of the terrain in the vicinity of Faizabad, Kabul, Jalalabad, etc were particularly difficult and dangerous. These mountainous regions with peaks of more than 3,500m abounded in narrow and dark gorges, and we had to fly there at low altitude and low speed, which required accurate piloting technique … Very often I had to work in difficult weather conditions, because January to February in that region is characterized by unstable weather … I must say that us pilots always tried to complete the mission, often breaking all the rules and regulations. We flew in thunderstorms, entered the gorges under the lower edge of the clouds, descending 2,000m to 2,500m below the mountain peaks. If it was dangerous to break through the clouds, we looked for a 'window' within a radius of 40km to 50km, and then, flying close to the ground, went out into the reconnaissance area. The strong turbulence was especially annoying. When you fly at a speed of 900kph, the impression is as if someone is hitting the fuselage with a sledgehammer.

Two Su-7BMK (NATO: Fitter A) of the DRAAF taxiing out for a mission. In 1980, the DRAAF had 24 of these aircraft, allotted to the 355th Fighter Bomber Regiment (APIB) at Bagram airfield. (Grandolini)

Three Mi-24D (NATO: Hind-D) gunships and two Mi-8 transports on the dispersal at a base in Afghanistan, possibly Herat. Soviet helicopters frequently operated in mixed formations of Mi-24 and Mi-8s. (Grandolini)

On 9 January a motor rifle regiment column moving from Termez to Faizabad was ambushed by rebels as it passed Talukan. After suffering extensive losses, the ground troops called for air support. A pair of MiG-21PFMs from the 136th APIB led by Capt A. Mukhin responded, firing 57mm S-5 rockets to drive off the rebel band. On the same day, the 186th MSD moved to suppress a mutiny by the 4th Artillery Regiment of the Afghan Army at Nahrain, some 160km north of Kabul. An attempt to bomb the weapon storage areas by fighter-bombers based in the USSR failed when the pilots were unable to identify the targets amongst the snow-covered hills. The task was taken by the MiG-21s from Bagram, and the mutineers were dispersed the following day by armed Mi-8 helicopters.

The first Soviet aircraft combat loss occurred on 13 February when a Mi-24 flown by Capt S.I. Khruleva of the 292nd OVP was shot down by rebel forces. The following week, hundreds of Afghans were killed and several thousand arrested during anti-Soviet protests in Kabul; a riot was also put down by Soviet troops in Shindand. On 22 February, MiG-21PFMs from a squadron of the 136th APIB arrived at Bagram. Almost immediately, a section led by Capt Tomin was tasked to refuel and carry out a strike near Asmar, close to the Pakistani border to the northeast of Jalalabad. The aircraft were loaded with two 250kg FAB-250 bombs and a ventral fuel tank to give them the range to reach the target, which was a fortress at the entrance to the Kunar Valley. Still unfamiliar with operating techniques in mountainous terrain, the pilots did not bomb accurately, but the Kunar Valley was to become a regular target over the coming months. The next day, 23 February, which was also 'Soviet Army Day', a pair of Mi-8T helicopters from the 280th OBP flown by Capt Lyamtsev and Capt Vakulenko went to investigate a convoy of Toyota pick-ups that had been reported near Kandahar. As the helicopters approached the convoy fired on them with a DShK heavy machine gun, scoring hits on the No.2 helicopter, which was forced to land. The lead helicopter neutralized the DShK with a salvo of rockets and the crew of the No.2 aircraft was able to make sufficient repairs to their helicopter to return to Kandahar.

Meanwhile Soviet Army Day also saw a MiG-21 squadron from the 115th GvIAP arriving at Bagram. A reconnaissance squadron equipped with MiG-21R, the 64th ORAP, also deployed there for a short detachment. By now Bagram had become a major base for jet aircraft, including three MiG-21 squadrons and a Su-7BMK squadron from the DRAAF. The task of the Bagram aircraft was to cover the central and eastern regions.

In 1980, the AAF had 22 Mi-17 (NATO: Hip-H) helicopters in service. The aircraft could be armed – note the triple weapons pylons on either side of the fuselage. (Grandolini)

Capt V. Shevelev[4], who was among the first Soviet pilots to arrive there, wrote:

> They issued us with a weapon, but told us nothing more, expecting us to figure it out on the spot. The first impressions as we climbed out of the aeroplane were how close the mountains were. There was steppe all around, but mountains on all sides – it was like being in a bowl made of rock. The sunshine reflecting off the bright snowclad peaks hurt our eyes, but it was beautiful, just like a postcard. Then on the apron we saw a Mi-24 with a bullet hole in the pilot's windshield. Wow. Everyone carried guns. Nearby, coffins were being loaded onto a plane. This did not add to the mood – it turns out that they are killing here. I had to live in the hut up on the outskirts of the airfield, because there was not enough space for all the new arrivals. A chilling wind whistled through cracks in the windows despite attempts to plug them with plywood. A potbelly stove provided some warmth when it was lit, but the hut was cold again as soon as the fire went out. At night-time there is shooting, and everyone wakes up, jumps out of bed, firing randomly at any lights.

At the beginning of March 1980, the MiG-21PFM squadron was redeployed from Kandahar to Kabul, where it joined the helicopters of the 50th Otdel'nyy Smeshannyy Aviatsionnyy Polk (OSAP –

A Soviet Air Force Su-17M3 (NATO: Fitter-H) of the 156th APIB is refuelled and rearmed in readiness for another combat mission over Afghanistan. Underwing fuel tanks were necessary for sorties flown from Mary-2 Air Base in the Turkoman SSR. (Grandolini)

Independent Mixed Aviation Regiment) to support ground operations in and around Kabul, where there was growing unrest. The jet aircraft performed a series of low-level 'shows of force' over the city, before the unit was withdrawn from the country on 13 March to re-equip with the MiG-21SM. By March there was widespread open hostility and resistance to the Soviet presence in Afghanistan and Soviet and Afghan government forces commenced a campaign against the rebels. Given the terrain, airpower would clearly play a critical role both in supporting ground forces and in striking enemy groups in isolated areas that would be hard for ground forces to reach. For this reason, all aviation units in the country were transferred to the command of the Ogranichennyy Kontingent Sovetskikh Voysk v Afganistane (OKSVA – Limited Contingent of Soviet Forces in Afghanistan), as the 40th Army was now known, and an aviation command post was established within HQ OKSVA at Kabul. In this first phase of hostilities, the rebel forces comprised small, scattered and poorly armed bands, and jet aircraft were able to operate with impunity against them. On occasions a supersonic flypast at low level was sufficient to scatter the enemy, but on other occasions pilots dropped bombs or fired rockets and cannons at their targets, often pressing into close range to ensure the accuracy of their attacks.

A product of the mid-1960s, the MiG-21PFM (operated initially by the 136th APIB) lacked an internally mounted gun and had only one weapons hardpoint under each wing. As such it was vastly inferior

A Soviet Air Force Su-17M4R (NATO: Fitter-K). The bat marking of the 886th ORAP based at Bagram Air Base. The aircraft is equipped with a KKR-1 (Konteyner Kompleksnoy Razvedki – integrated reconnaissance system) pod mounted under the fuselage. (Grandolini)

in the Afghan theatre to the more modern MiG-21bis (flown by the 115th GvIAP) which had a more powerful engine, mounted an internal twin-barrel 23mm GSh-23-2L cannon and had a total of four underwing hardpoints. However, both types could carry bombs of up to 500kg or 57mm S-5 rockets (usually carried in 32-round pods) on each underwing pylon; both could also carry a centreline fuel drop tank to increase their range. The MiG-21SM variant (with which the 136th APIB was re-equipped) was very similar in configuration to the MiG-21bis but had a slightly less powerful engine. Fighter-bomber tactics over Afghanistan in the early days of the conflict were very simple: aircraft would make sequential runs in line astern or set up an orbit above the rebels and dive on them from different directions. The most challenging aspects for pilots were the identification of targets in areas where rocks, caves and vegetation provided plenty of cover and also in finding their way over mountainous or desert terrain. Navigation while flying amongst 12,000ft mountains was not straightforward and it was not unusual for pilots to be unable to pinpoint exactly where they had dropped their weapons. Radio contact was also often lost while flying between the ridges.

The MiG-21R (NATO: Fishbed-H) reconnaissance variant used by the Soviet Air Force in Afghanistan was derived from MiG-21PFS, modified to carry the Type D (Dnevnaya Fotorazvedka – day photoreconnaissance) pod. (Grandolini)

In March, Soviet forces commenced operations in the Kunar Valley, which runs northeastwards from Jalalabad along the border with Pakistan. Offensive sweeps of the Kunar Valley would be carried out almost monthly by Soviet forces during 1980. The aim of this first operation was to relieve the Afghan Army post at Asadabad which was blockaded by rebels. The advance by a motor rifle regiment

was supported by MiG-21 fighter-bombers flying from Bagram, but the difficulty of navigating among the mountainous terrain with outdated and inaccurate maps made it difficult to locate enemy firing points hidden amongst the rocks. As a result, there were cases when aircraft mistakenly attacked friendly forces. Meanwhile, the two squadrons from the 136th APIB which had already converted to the MiG-21SM were sent to Afghanistan: one deployed to Shindand and the other to Kandahar.

At the end of March, the helicopters were operating in Badakhshan in the far northeast of Afghanistan. On 30 March, a Mi-8 flown by Capt Y. Vlasov of the 181st OVP made an emergency landing in hostile country in the Fayzabad Valley. Two helicopters attempted to rescue the crew. Maj V. Gainutdinov tried to land next to the damaged helicopter but had to break off when he came under fire which killed the flight engineer; however, Capt V. Obolonin managed to extract the downed crew from the midst of the firefight. In a similar incident the following day, another Mi-8 flown by Maj V. Kopchikov was hit by ground fire and made a forced landing in the middle of a rebel-held village. This time, two helicopters circling overhead, led by Obolonin, laid down covering fire from their door-mounted machine guns, while Maj V. Shcherbakov landed to pick up the crew.

Because of the difficulties in co-ordinating fast-jet aircraft with ground troops, only helicopters were used to support the first offensive by three Soviet and two Afghan battalions into the Panjshir River Valley in April. The need for better armament and protection for the

The Soviet Navy trialled the use of the Yakovlev Yak-38 (NATO: Forger) at Shindand in April 1980, but the aircraft proved to be unsuitable for operations over Afghanistan due to its short range and limited payload. (Grandolini)

Three Soviet Mi-24 gunships during a mission amongst the Afghan mountains. (Grandolini)

Mi-8T had been quickly recognized and by April most helicopters had been armed with multiple machine guns firing through the doors and blister windows, as well as a 30mm ATS-17 grenade launcher mounted in the doorway. Additional armament included a forward-firing Kalashnikov PKT which was originally designed for tanks, while on its stub wings the Mi-8 could also mount four rocket pods with 57mm S-5 rockets or four 250kg bombs. The Mi-8MT variant was even better armed, with six hardpoints for weapons under its stubs. Extra armour was also added to the aircraft. Soviet helicopters generally operated in pairs to provide each other with cross-cover. The OKSVA used helicopters extensively during ground operations, either for direct fire support or to carry out airborne assaults. In the case of an airborne assault, a strike group of Mi-24 gunships and MiG-21 or Su-17 fighter-bombers would neutralize the LZ before a small formation of armed Mi-8MTs inserted the first troops to secure the LZ. These troops would include a forward air controller (FAC). A larger wave of Mi-6 and Mi-8s would then deliver the main body of troops. Their landings would be covered by two to four Mi-24 which could suppress enemy fire. A follow-up group of helicopter gunships would then provide direct air support for the ground assault. Helicopters were also used to place smaller groups of troops onto high ground during cordon operations or to place others in position for ambushes. Finally, convoy escort would involve positioning soldiers into observation posts (OP) ahead of the convoy to deny the area to the enemy; on these missions the helicopters also performed armed overwatch of the convoy, ready to respond to ambushes.

The recently modified Mi-8s of the 280th OVP had an opportunity to use their new weaponry on 11 June, when a pair of Mi-8Ts led by Capt E. Surnin of the 280th OVP came across a band of horsemen amongst the foothills during a search of the area south of Ghazni (which lies 130km south of Kabul). Flight Engineer M. Kehl[5] recalled:

They rode beautifully, like something out of the films about the Civil War, in turbans and cartridge belts, with *beshmets* flowing behind them. They galloped towards a palm grove, but the pilot turned sharply ahead of them, cutting off their path. I covered

LEFT A Su-25 (NATO: Frogfoot) loaded with external fuel tanks and B8M pods for 80mm S-8 rockets. The type was first used in combat over Afghanistan by the 200th OShAP in July 1980. (Grandolini)

BELOW A MiG-23MLD with a full load of 250kg bombs, ready for a combat mission over Afghanistan. The lack of flare-dispenser strakes above the fuselage dates this image to the early 1980s. (Grandolini)

the whole group with a short burst of from the grenade launcher. The target was in the sights at close range, so the plumes from the explosions were clearly visible, and horses and riders collapsed in a heap.

Because of the slow forward speed of a helicopter, the aircraft was very vulnerable to self-damage from the blast debris when dropping bombs. The debris from a 500kg bomb could reach up to 3,000ft and even the smallest weapons might send fragments as high as 2,000ft when the weapon exploded. For this reason, helicopters were usually armed with delayed-action bombs, but even these need to be treated with respect, as a pair of Mi-8s found on 26 July. Bombing from a height of 50m (150ft) the leader was safe from self-damage, but his wingman following close behind flew straight through the debris. Fortunately, the fragments missed the pilots, but the machine, including its fuel tanks, was peppered with holes and the helicopter flew out of the blast in a white cloud of vapourized fuel and force landed immediately. The flight leader held back the rebels with machine gun fire until the crew managed to patch up the holes in the fuel tank.

One of the most formidable aircraft in the Soviet inventory was the Mi-24 gunship, which equipped six squadrons in Afghanistan by the end of 1980. Armament for this helicopter included an internally mounted 12.7mm Yakushev-Borzov (Yak-B) rotary cannon and six weapons pylons that could mount GSh-23 cannons and S-5 rockets. The Mi-24, known as the 'crocodile' to Soviet troops and as 'Satan's chariot' to Afghan rebels, was very effective in its role and could remain on station for much longer than jet fighter-bombers. In addition, because of the slower speed of the helicopter, the Mi-24 crews found it easier to locate targets than did the jet pilots. The Mi-24 was based on the Mi-8 design but being 1,500kg heavier, it was more severely performance restricted by the hot and high conditions in Afghanistan. At the other end of the scale, even in the summer months the Mi-6 could lift between two or three times the load of the Mi-8. The fuselage of the Mi-6 was also large enough to accommodate artillery pieces or armoured cars. In order to maximize their lifting performance, the Mi-6 crews would carry out rolling take offs using about 350m of runway, much like a fixed-wing aeroplane. In addition

LEFT A pair of AAF MiG-21PFMs in flight. Both aircraft are carrying UB-16 rocket pods for the 55mm S-5 rockets. (Grandolini)

BELOW LEFT A MiG-23MLD of the 120th IAP configured for the air-defence role. It carries Vympel R-23R (NATO; AA-7 Apex) radar-guided air-to-air missiles (AAM) under the wings and Vympel R-60 (NATO: AA-8 Aphid) infra-red seeking AAM under the fuselage. (Grandolini)

to troop transport, the Mi-6 was used to resupply remote outposts, including daily runs to the garrison at Bamiyan (130km west of Kabul), as well as to Lashkar Gah, Chagcharan (almost halfway between Kabul and Herat) and Turghundi (north of Herat on the Turkmen SSR border].

April 1980 saw a short deployment by four Yak-38 naval aircraft to Shindand to evaluate their effectiveness. Missions were flown typically as a pair of Yak-38s accompanied by a Su-17. After a total of 107 sorties, the trial concluded that with a war load of two 250kg bombs and a maximum endurance of just 40min, the aircraft was deemed unsuitable for operations over Afghanistan. Unfortunately, one aircraft was lost in a take-off accident during this deployment.

In the summer of 1980, the bombers of the Voyenno-Vozdushnye Sily Dal'naya Aviatsiya (VVS-DA – Soviet Air Force Long-Range

Aviation) were called in to strike a rebel stronghold in the remote mining village of Sar-e San on the far northeastern border with Tajik SSR. Lapis Lazuli stones were being exported by the rebels from here to Pakistan in exchange for weapons and supplies. The first attempt to reach the village by Mi-8 helicopters of the Soviet Border Force was driven off by heavy anti-aircraft fire. Because the location of the settlement, which lay at the foot of one of the highest peaks in the Hindu Kush, was beyond the range of tactical aircraft operating from Afghan airfields, the VVS-DA was given the task. The attack was carried out on 10 June, but since the bombing was carried out from altitudes in excess of 30,000ft it seems unlikely that any significant damage was caused.

Mindful of the increased risks in combat operations and the relative inexperience of many young pilots, the Soviets introduced a pre-deployment training scheme for pilots selected for tours of Afghanistan. Firstly, they would spend two or three months at their home base following a pre-deployment syllabus before moving to the Turkmen SSR for two to three weeks of more specific tactical training. Once in Afghanistan there was a further ten days of in-theatre training before the pilot was considered combat ready. Later in the conflict, the lessons from Afghanistan had already been incorporated into routine training, so pilots were posted directly to the country, where the in-theatre training consisted simply of a familiarization sortie in a two-seat Su-17UM.

A young MiG-21bis pilot, Lt Mikhail Pravdivets[6], remembered his first combat mission:

In the spring of 1980, there were not enough pilots in the regiment, and it was necessary to bring the squadrons in Afghanistan to full strength by transferring from other units. When I arrived in Afghanistan, I had no experience ... and we never even dropped training bombs. I only had a vague idea about the theory of bombing and piloting techniques during strikes ... Such were the 'aces' who strengthened the combat squadrons! After several training flights, Komesk included me in the combat pair. We were tasked to strike in the Parma gorge near Bagram. The aircraft were loaded with four OFAB-250-270 bombs each. After the briefing, I asked the leader:

'And how do I drop bombs?' He explained to me that the main thing is to keep in battle formation and watch him. As soon as his bombs come off, then I have to drop with a delay. So, for the first attack in my life, I still won't see where to aim, especially since we have to strike at 'suspected' firing points. And the delay is necessary for the bombs to be dispersed: there is no point in putting all eight weapons in one place, let these two tons cover a large area, it's more reliable.

The sortie was carried out on 8 August in the early morning. We took off at dawn, while it was cooler, otherwise taking off in summer in the daytime heat with four loaded pylons is very difficult. With a load of four bombs, the plane really took an unusually long time to unstick. A FAC was contacted over the place, he suggested landmarks and the slope on which to work. It was still a little dark in the gorge in the early morning. Following the leader, we dived somewhere into the darkness. His bombs came off, and I also pressed the weapon release button. For the first time in my life, I felt how the plane trembled when the bombs were released. Recover. The FAC says where the gaps lay and corrects. We switched to inner pylons and made another pass. Press the weapon release button again. Recover. From the ground we are asked to 'give it one more time', but the leader reports that there are no more bombs, the mission is complete, and we are returning to base.

A MiG-21bis of the Soviet 927th IAP which overran the runway at Bagram in the mid-1980s (Grandolini)

ABOVE Armed with a chin-mounted turret mounting a four-barrelled 12.7mm Yakushev-Borzov (Yak-B) rotary canon and six hardpoints for rockets or bombs, the Mi-24V (NATO: Hind-E) was a powerfully armed gunship. (Grandolini)

RIGHT A MiG-21R over Afghanistan. The aircraft is carrying outboard fuel tanks, a configuration exclusive to the MiG-21R variant. The Type D reconnaissance pod incorporated seven cameras. (Grandolini)

A year later, Pravdivets was an experienced combat pilot and had flown 380 combat sorties.

A MiG-21bis pilot was lost during an operation at Jabal Saraj at the mouth of the Panjshir Valley on 1 August. Senior Lt V. Cheshenko was No.3 in the leading formation, in which each MiG was armed with two OFAB-250-270 bombs and two 240mm S-24 rockets. Cheshenko did not recover from a dive attack and when the wreckage of his aircraft was recovered, there was evidence of multiple small arms hits around the cockpit. An Afghan prisoner confirmed that all the rebels had fired into the air to create a wall of fire when they saw the aircraft commence its dive attack. Rebels, by now organized into loosely affiliated groups of Islamic 'mujahideen' fighters, became better equipped and more daring. Armed with GShK machine guns and 14.5mm KPV anti-aircraft guns, they began to target aircraft as they took off or landed. On 26 August a MiG-21bis was hit by seven rounds as it departed from Bagram.

In September, Soviet forces carried out operations around Herat, the Panjshir Valley and the Kunar Valley, with further operations in October and November in the Panjshir Valley and Kunar Valley respectively. Kandahar and Herat also remained as trouble hotspots with significant mujahideen activity. Both of these cities were close to 'green zones' – areas intersected by numerous irrigation canals and with dense vegetation which gave cover to rebel groups – so convoys or troop movements had to be protected by armed helicopters. Apart from direct support of the ground forces, helicopters were routinely tasked with locating and checking the caravans that criss-crossed the country and also with minelaying on suspected rebel trails. Caravan inspection was carried out by a pair of Mi-8s carrying the search teams, working with a pair of Mi-24s as cover. Once a caravan was spotted, one Mi-8 would land ahead of it and the other at the rear. If the search team found weapons, they would arrest the members of the caravan and destroy the vehicles and equipment. Mining was carried out using Mi-8s equipped with the VSM-1 aerial mine system, which was capable of sowing over 8,000 PFM-1 'butterfly' anti-personnel mines as a strip 2km wide. Again, the Mi-8 was typically escorted by a pair of Mi-24 gunships during these missions.

Increasingly, fighter-bombers were used to subdue remote areas which were difficult to reach in force with ground troops. The weapons inventory now included the 240mm S-24 unguided rocket, which was far more effective against the thick-walled buildings and compounds in Afghanistan. With the increased threat from rebel anti-aircraft fire, airstrikes were usually preceded by an air-defence suppression flight of two or four rocket-armed MiG-21s or Su-17s. Once the area had been sanitized, a pair of Mi-8s would mark the target with smoke rockets for

ABOVE Two Su-17M4 of
the 886th ORAP on
ground alert at Bagram
Air Base. Both are
armed with bombs for a
ground-attack mission.
(Grandolini)

BELOW Armourers load a
500kg FAB-500M62
bomb onto a MiG-
23MLD. (Grandolini)

the main strike group of four to eight jets. A post-strike reconnaissance would then be flown by a MiG-21R. Aerial reconnaissance continued to play a vital role in shaping ground operations. The MiG-21R and Yak-28R were replaced by the Su-17M3R, which carried the KKR-1 pod with both visible spectrum and infra-red (IR) sensors. Night reconnaissance missions were also routinely flown, using SAB photo-illumination flares to illuminate the target.

Heavy fighting continued around Kandahar and Herat during early 1981 and there were offensive sweeps into the Panjshir Valley in April and August. The summer months also saw operations in Nangahar province on the border with Pakistan to the south of Jalalabad. Outside these concerted efforts, routine tasks continued. Early in the morning of 24 June, six Mi-8s from the 181st ORAP carried out an airstrike near Gulkhana, at the northeasterly reaches of the Panjshir Valley in response to mujahideen attacks. The helicopters dropped eight FAB-500M62 onto the mountain passes and scattered anti-personnel mines to stop the infiltration of fighters from Pakistan. Two days later an Mi-8T was lost during a similar operation while attacking a village on the Arghandab River near Kandahar. The bomb fused instantaneously and exploded just under the helicopter. Capt G. Govtvian and his crew were injured, but they were rescued by other helicopters in their flight. In late July, a flight of Mi-8s was tasked to lay mines on the

A pair of FAB-500M62 bombs loaded on a tandem beam on the inner wing pylon of a Su-24 (NATO: Fencer) for a ground-attack sortie. The Su-24 first saw combat over Afghanistan in 1984. (Grandolini)

road close to the Pakistan border, but unfortunately, they made a navigation error and mined the road 5km into Pakistani territory. A similar error was also made by a flight of Mi-24s in December when they dropped their mines near the Pakistani town of Torkhum in the Khyber Pass.

In mid-July 1981, the 200th Otdelnyy Shturmovoy Aviatsionnyy Polk (OShAP – Independent Assault Aviation Regiment) was deployed to Shindand to evaluate the new Su-25 in the close air support (CAS) role. The unit took part in operations near Herat during the summer, including conducting strikes on individual buildings in the city that were being used as strongpoints by mujahideen, as well as enemy positions in the green zone of the Harirud River valley. The Su-25s also participated in the offensive around Kandahar that commenced in September 1981. Operations in mountainous terrain, and particularly in the Black Mountains (some 10km north of Kandahar) illustrated the excellent manoeuvrability, especially the turning radius, of the Su-25 in comparison to the MiG-21 and Su-17. During one mission, other aircraft types had failed to hit a firing position at the end of a winding canyon by bombing from above, but the Su-25 was able to enter the canyon and destroy the target. The aircraft also soon won the respect of its pilots because of its robust construction and the armour protection around the cockpit.

A Tupolev Tu-22M3 (NATO: Backfire-C) loaded with FAB-500M62 bombs. The type could carry 28 such weapons or fewer, larger weapons including 3,000kg bombs. (Grandolini)

Mujahedeen fighters loyal to the local tribal leader Jalaluddin Haqqani besieged Khost in July 1983, beginning a siege that was to outlast the Soviet presence. Entirely cut off from land links, the Soviet garrison was reliant on resupply by air.

Capt V. Goryachev[7], an An-12 captain, described the routine operations to support Khost:

From Bagram airfield, we carried out the transportation of personnel, weapons and other cargo in the interests of the Afghan army. In the summer, we flew mainly to the surrounded Khost [twice a week]. They usually transported soldiers [both there and back], ammunition, flour, sugar, and other products. These flights were very important for the Khost garrison blocked by the rebels. This is evidenced at least by the fact that the An-12 is designed for a maximum of 90 paratroopers. In reality then, there were sometimes up to 150 Afghans 'crammed' into planes there. And they often had to fly standing up. Nevertheless, the commander of the Khost garrison was very grateful for such flights. The possibility of changing personnel had a positive effect on both the physical condition and the morale of his subordinates.

The work of the OKSVA was also supported by the Soviet border forces, and on 17 October 1981 Border Force Mi-8s were tasked to insert an assault force in the Kuf Ab region on the border between the Tajik SSR and northeastern Afghanistan. As they landed, the

ABOVE A MiG-23MLD landing at Bagram Air Base. The braking parachute was vital at the hot and high airfields in Afghanistan. (Grandolini)

LEFT An Afghan mujahideen fighter with a FIM-92 Stinger man-portable air defence system (MANPADS) near a remote rebel base in the Safed Koh Mountains south of Jalalabad in February 1988. The missiles, which were first used in combat in Afghanistan during September 1986, had a fundamental effect on the air campaign in the country. (Photo by Robert Nickelsberg/ Liaison/Getty Images)

helicopters were ambushed. In one helicopter the pilot, Senior Lt A.N. Skripkina, was hit in the chest, but his navigator Capt V.P. Romanov managed to take control and land the aircraft, although it was destroyed on the ground. Most of the helicopters were hit and 19 people were killed during this operation. The following month there was a more successful operation by OKSVA helicopters near Bagram. Eight Mi-8s carried out simultaneous landings before dawn near to Estalef, in the mountains 10km to the southwest of Bagram. The mission was to insert a reinforced reconnaissance company to block the mujahideen withdrawing from the main assault being made against them from the direction of Bagram. In the end some 250 rebel fighters were caught in the trap.

In 1982, the 9M17M Falanga-M anti-tank guided missile (ATGM) became available for use on the Mi-8. This weapon was particularly useful for attacking pinpoint targets, such as cave openings, which were often used by mujahideen as firing positions. Later in the year, the Mi-8s and Mi-24s of the 302nd OVE pioneered night interdiction tactics against insurgents crossing the border from Iran. The first attempts, firing S-5 rockets from a height of around 6,000ft under the light of a SAB parachute flare, were not particularly successful, but a tactic perfected by Capt Khorev proved more effective. The helicopters continued to patrol at altitude, but once the headlights of a caravan were spotted, they dropped to low level and approached from downwind, so that the insurgents believed them to be further away.

Another attempt to close the Iranian border to insurgents had been made in April. A detachment of eight MiG-23M fighters deployed to Shindand, from where they were to provide air-defence cover for an air assault on a rebel encampment near Robat Jaali on the border in the far southwest of Afghanistan. Defence suppression would be by Su-17s from Shindand, after which Mi-8TV helicopters from the 280th OVP would insert the assault troops. The whole operation was co-ordinated from an An-30 airborne command and control aircraft. Unfortunately, the helicopters landed inside Iranian territory and a pair of Iranian F-4E Phantoms came to investigate; because of gaps in the Soviet defensive air cover the Phantoms were able both to damage many of the helicopters and drive off the An-30.

In the first half of May, another operation to secure the Kuf Ab region was carried out by Soviet Border Force helicopters. This included a nine aircraft attack on the stronghold at Mushtiw. Over a 17-day period, one Mi-8 crew fired 1,845 rounds of 7.62mm ammunition, 500 PKT grenades and 646 S-5 rockets. Another Mi-8TV flown by Senior Lt I.A. Ephraim was shot down, but its crew was rescued. On 15 May, three Soviet divisions opened the fifth operation – 'Panjshir V' – into the Panjshir Valley where the main mujahideen force of some 5,000 fighters was concentrated. This was the largest ground operation by Soviet forces to date and was in retaliation for a rebel attack on Bagram Air Base. During the first week of May, Su-17s carried out detailed photo reconnaissance survey of the entire valley, so that the most up to date information was

available for the army commanders. On 15 and 16 May there was a diversionary attack into Gorband before the main offensive started on 17 May with a mass airstrike by Su-17, Su-25 and MiG-21s along the length of the valley. An hour later, a battalion each of Soviet and Afghan troops had been air landed by helicopter near the towns of Rokha and Bazarak to secure the high ground and LZs nearby, which had already been subjected to massive airstrikes with preparatory bombing and strafing runs. During the first phase of the operation, Soviet helicopters landed six battalions, a total of 1,200 troops, up to 50km into the valley. Helicopter gunships accompanied the advancing infantry. On the second day two battalions were air landed at Mata, a further 25km up the valley, and by the end of the fourth day of the offensive, helicopters had inserted 65 battalions into the valley. The objective of the offensive was to seize Evim, at the junction of two valleys approximately 95km along the Panjshir Valley, which was a

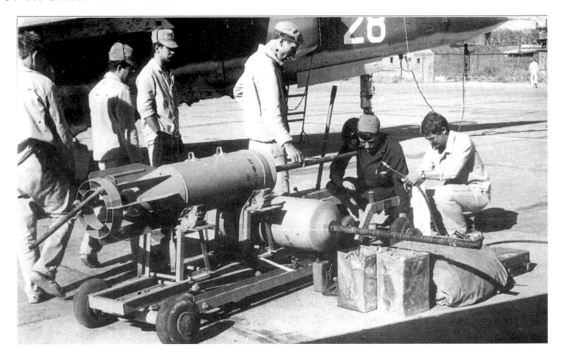

Soviet Air Force armourers fitting rods to FAB-500 bombs, so that they detonate just above the ground, making them more effective against personnel. (Grandolini)

route for supplies and equipment from Pakistan. The Evim LZ was prepared over a period of 14 days and 130 sorties were carried out against it. The landings took place on 24 May, with the helicopters approaching the landing zones at altitudes of 15,000ft, right at the ceiling limit of the Mi-8. For this reason, all the air support for the landings and subsequent operations in this area was carried out by MiG-21bis and Su-25s. Throughout the offensive, a force of 30 transport helicopters were flying three lifts per day moving 180,000kg of ammunition and 30,000kg of rations and supplies into the operational area. Having completed the assault, the combined Soviet and Afghan force withdrew from the valley over the next four days.

In February 1983, Soviet specialists working at a fertilizer plant near Mazar-e-Sharif were kidnapped and murdered by a rebel band. In retaliation, their stronghold in the village of Vakhshak was cordoned off by a force of six Mi-8 supported by a section of Mi-24s to ensure that no-one could leave, and the village was attacked by four Su-25s. The aircraft delivered two ODAB-500P 1,000lb bombs, a further 10,000kg of smaller bombs and 40 rockets, destroying much of the village. Targets were not always easy to locate, however, and as the mujahideen obtained more anti-aircraft weapons, pilots had to be careful not to loiter in the target areas for too long. In the summer of

1983, a Su-17 was shot down as it made a sixth pass over a target. In comparison to the previous years, 1983 was relatively quiet, especially as the Soviets had agreed a ceasefire in the Panjshir Valley after a further expedition there in the previous autumn. However, many routine operations continued, during which aircrews faced real dangers. On 9 September, two Mi-8s from the 181st OVP were shot down simultaneously while carrying out a mine-dropping mission to the south of Faizabad. The aircraft were flying at an altitude of 12,000ft in a valley between mountains reaching up to 10,000ft when they came under fire. One pilot, Maj V.N. Balobanov and his navigator, Senior Lt V.V. Burago, were killed when their helicopter crashed, but the other crew members survived and were subsequently rescued.

The Soviets reneged on their ceasefire agreement in the Panjshir Valley in 1984 and the 'Panjshir VII' offensive was launched in April. The operation also included pushes into the Andarab Valley and Alishang Valley. At 04:00hrs on 19 April, Tupolev Tu-16s from the 200th Gvardeyskiy Tyazhelyy Bombardirovochnyy Aviatsionnyy Polk (GvTBAP – Guards Heavy Bombing Regiment) and Tu-22M2s from the 1225th TBAP carried out carpet bombing in the Panjshir Valley,

The crew of an Il-76 (NATO: Candid) releases infra-red decoy flares, to minimise the threat from MANPADS, as it climbs steeply after take-off. (Photo by Robert Nickelsberg/Liaison/ Getty Images)

ABOVE The dorsal strakes containing the BVP-50-60 flare dispensers are clearly visible on this MiG-23MLD, as it prepares to taxi for an air defence sortie from Bagram Air Base. (Grandolini)

RIGHT A Su-25 from the 378th OShAP taxies out for a sortie over Afghanistan. The aircraft is finished in a new camouflage scheme that was introduced in the summer of 1987. (Grandolini)

dropping heavy bombs, including the 9,000kg FAB-9000 weapons. They were followed by a force of 60 Su-24s dropping from 30,000ft through the clouds. Operating from Kharshi-Khanabad in the Uzbek SSR, the heavy bombers continued the bombardment for three days. Not surprisingly, this 'carpet bombing' achieved little in sparsely populated mountainous terrain, except in destroying some Afghan Army units that were already deployed in the valley. 'Panjshir VIII' followed in the September.

The main development in aerial tactics, however, was not the use of the heavy bomber by the Soviets, but the use of increasing numbers of man-portable air defence systems (MANPADS) by the mujahideen. Ironically the first of these to arrive in Afghanistan were the Soviet 9K32 Strela-2 IR seeking surface-to-air missiles (SAM), which were supplied by Egypt. In 1984 there were 50 SAM launches, of which six hit their target, but in 1985 there were over 460 launches. Soviet authorities had to reconsider what countermeasures were needed to address this new threat when a civilian Il-76 was shot down near Kabul on 27 October 1984. Viktor Isakov[8] recalled:

> This happened in front of my crew, as we were unloading our cargo. The crew of our second aircraft, also unloading at the time, managed to record the last words and shouts of these people on the onboard tape recorder. The commander of the stricken aircraft pressed the transmit button, and all the intercom communications went live. Then we listened to this recording ... The terrible event made a very strong impression on everyone, our guys returned from Kabul depressed. At first, no one could tell whether it was shot down by a missile or crashed due to a pilot error.

Departures were flown as steep climbs and arrivals as steep-angle descents. In addition, aircraft began to be fitted with IR flare dispensers and deploying flares became a regular tactic by Soviet aircrew. As an interim measure, the SAB parachute flare, normally used for night photography, was employed as decoys. The first loss of a Su-25 occurred on 16 January 1984 when Lt Col P.V. Ruban was shot down over Urgun. Unfortunately, the pilot was unable to eject. Another Su-25 pilot was more fortunate when the warhead of a SAM did not detonate, and he landed with the missile embedded in the engine.

A line up of MiG-23MLD (NATO: Flogger-K) air-defence fighters from the 120th IAP at Bagram Air Base with a pair of Su-25 offensive support aircraft taxiing in the background. (Grandolini)

A Soviet tactical reconnaissance pilot carries out the pre-flight checks in his Su-17M4R (NATO: Fitter-K) at Bagram Air Base, in preparation for a combat sortie over Afghanistan. (Grandolini)

Meanwhile, night-time search and destroy missions continued. On 24 April 1985, Mi-24V pilot Lt Col Savinkov, flying a patrol on moonless night, discovered a mujahideen caravan consisting of 14 Toyota pick-up trucks. He managed to follow the caravan unobserved and the mujahideen only started to fire in random directions after the first volley of S-5 rockets struck the lead vehicle. All of the rebel vehicles were subsequently destroyed. The Su-25 also took part in night patrols, generally making use of moonlight to avoid the high ground and the convoy headlights to locate their targets. It was demanding flying and at least one pilot, Capt L.A. Baranov, was killed in the winter of 1985 when he flew into a mountainside in the darkness.

In daylight, the Su-25s provided overwatch for resupply convoys, searching possible ambush points ahead of the vehicles and attacking any mujahideen groups that were found. Su-25 pilot Capt A. Pochkina[9] reported: 'operating a pair along the road north of the city of Gardez, I found a rocket launcher on the top of the hill that was preparing to fire at the convoy of tankers, and I destroyed it with a single bombing strike.'

In the high threat environment, convoy protection was a major undertaking and, for example, a convoy of 250 trucks bringing supplies to Chagcharan in August 1985 was escorted by four motorized rifle battalions and 32 aircraft, including both helicopters and fixed wing types. The heavy tasking, particularly for the Su-25s

THE SOVIET EXPERIENCE 1979-1989 **69**

which were flying at three times the rate of the Su-17s, took its toll of aircraft, using up much of their fatigue life.

Recognising the possibility of intervention by the Pakistani or Iranian air forces, the Soviet air force had deployed MiG-23ML fighters to three airfields in Afghanistan. MiG-23 regiments were detached to Afghanistan for a 12-month period. Aircraft based at Bagram provided air defence against Pakistan, while those at Kandahar and Shindand covered the Iranian border. At each base two aircraft were maintained on air-defence quick reaction alert (QRA), while another pair, loaded with air-to-ground weapons, was kept at readiness to provide emergency CAS for ground troops.

The crew of a Soviet Mi-24 gunship walk back to debrief after a combat sortie over Afghanistan. (Grandolini)

The largest Soviet offensive after Panjshir VII commenced in August 1985, with the aim of regaining control of the provinces of Paktia and Khost. This operation, which continued into the next year, included actions against mujahideen bases close to the Pakistan border, some of which were within Pakistani territory. As cross-border raids increased, so did the efforts of the Pakistan Air Force (PAF) to defend its airspace. On 11 February 1986, two Chinese-built Shenyang F-6 fighters of the PAF which were on patrol near Parachinar were vectored towards four MiG-23s which had entered Pakistani airspace. In this instance, the MiG-23s swiftly returned to Afghanistan. However, as Soviet forces targeted mujahideen supply bases along border area near Khost, incursions into Pakistan became more regular. Several waves of Afghan Air Force Su-22s, escorted by Soviet MiG-23MLDs, bombed Pakistani border posts and on 10 April Su-24s and Su-25s attacked the supply base at Tani in Afghanistan. Two days later, three PAF F-6s, led by Gp Capt Shahid Kamal, intercepted a formation of Su-25s over Pakistani territory. Kamal fired two AIM-9P air-to-air missiles (AAM) but missed as they were out of range, and another AIM-9 fired by Sqn Ldr Chaudry also missed its target. PAF Dassault Mirage IIIs of No.18 Sqn PAF were more successful on 16 April when they managed to shoot down a DRAAF MiG-21.

A two-seat MiG-23UB 'Sparky' leads a MiG-23MLD, both from the 120th IAP, over Afghanistan. The two-seat aircraft were often used to assist in locating a target and for directing an air attack. (Grandolini)

No.9 Sqn PAF, equipped with the General Dynamics F-16 Fighting Falcon, also began to operate in the Afghan border area, but on 14 May neither Sqn Ldr Ras Qamar Suleman nor Flt Lt Nawaz could achieve a firing solution against Soviet helicopters. Three days later, Su-17s attacked a mujahideen camp in Pakistan, but were intercepted by a pair of F-16s flown by Sqn Ldr Hameed Qadri and Sqn Ldr Mohamed Yousef who were patrolling near Parachinar. An AIM-9 fired by Qadri missed, but Yousef fired a second missile and claimed the destruction of a Su-17.

Pilots from the 168th IAP pose in front of a MiG-23MLD at Bagram Air Base in the summer of 1988. Note the falcon emblem of the regiment on the engine air intake. (Grandolini)

New, more effective weaponry was introduced in Afghanistan by both sides during 1986: the Soviet air force units began to receive the Kh-25ML and Kh-29 laser guided AAM. These were first used by Su-25s from the 378th OShAP in April against cave entrances near Khost. The missiles could be guided by the firer or by another aircraft, using the on-board Klen-PS designator, although the most successful results were obtained when the target was illuminated by ground forces. For the mujahideen fighters, the introduction of the US-made FIM-92 Stinger MANPADS in late 1986 gave them a powerful weapon against Soviet aircraft. The Stinger had greater IR discrimination and longer range than previous missiles, and during the first week that they were used, they accounted for four Su-25, killing two pilots. By the following autumn, Stingers had shot down

ABOVE A Soviet Mi-24P gunship taxiing. On this variant the chin-mounted 12.7mm minigun was replaced with a fixed twin-barrel 30mm GSh-30K autocannon on the side of the nose. (Grandolini)

the equivalent of an entire squadron of Su-25s. Alexander Koshkin[10], a Su-25 pilot, later wrote:

> with these new-fangled 'Stingers' that the mujahideen suddenly began to get in huge quantities, the odds are stacked up against a ground-attack pilot. The only thing that can save you is a carefully planned attack – when you know exactly how you will go to the target, so that, for example, the sun shines in the eyes of the Stinger operator, where you will go after the first attack, where after the second and how to manoeuvre so that all your movements become unpredictable to the enemy air defence.

Practice over the years meant that helicopter-borne operations had become more effective. On the evening of 21 July 1986, a force of four Mi-8TVs inserted a company-sized ambush party to intercept a mujahideen convoy. The helicopters flew at very low level to the

RIGHT The Soviet Air Force deployed four Tu-22PD (NATO: Blinder-E) electronic-support aircraft to Mary-2 in late 1988 to jam Pakistani air-defence radars while heavy bombers attacked targets close to the Afghan-Pakistan border. (Grandolini)

ABOVE Groundcrew push a loading trolley carrying two 500kg FAB-500M54 bombs in front of a line-up of MiG-23MLDs being re-armed after a mission over Afghanistan. (Grandolini)

drop-off point some 5km away from the ambush site, before setting down at another extraction LZ. The ambush was supported by four Mi-24 gunships which were held on the ground until they were required. The ambush, carried out in the small hours of the following morning, successfully destroyed a convoy of six trucks. Other raids were carried out regularly, often around noon when mujahideen were eating or engaged in religious rituals, to destroy enemy weapons dumps, command posts, training centres and strongpoints. Over the winter months Mi-24s and Su-25s hunted convoys at night, when vehicles were more easily visible against the snow on moonlit nights.

From the summer of 1986, Soviet long-range bombers were once again involved in operations over Afghanistan. Unlike the tactical fighter-bombers based within the country, the Tu-16s of the 251st TBAP flying from Mary-2 could cover the whole of Afghanistan and carry a substantial bomb load. In particular, the Tu-16s employed the 2,600kg FAB-1500-2600TS deep penetration bomb against the cave complexes that were being used by the mujahideen. At their bombing

Soviet troops wait near a Soviet Mi-8MT (NATO: Hip-H). The three weapons pylons on the side of the fuselage are clearly visible. (Grandolini)

ABOVE The An-26 (NATO: Curl) tactical transport aircraft played a vital role in delivering personnel and supplies from Kabul to Soviet garrisons in the outlying areas. (Grandolini)

RIGHT A MiG-23MLD from the 120th IAP, configured for the air-defence role, on final approach to landing after a mission over Afghanistan. (Grandolini)

height, the Tu-16s were immune from the threat of MANPADS, but the bomber formations were routinely escorted by MiG-21bis of the 115th GvIAP in case of interception by PAF fighters.

Despite a ceasefire at the beginning of 1987, the mujahideen began to use Stingers near to Soviet airfields and in January at least one Mi-24 was shot down near Kabul. At dusk on 21 January, a Su-25 was brought down after take-off from Bagram and although the pilot Lt K. Pavlyukov ejected successfully, he was killed on the ground during a firefight with the mujahideen. The security situation had deteriorated significantly during 1987, which saw major Soviet operations in the areas of Kandahar in the southwest of the country, Kalafgan in the north, and the Khost and Paktia regions bordering Pakistan in the east. In addition, tensions mounted on the border with Pakistan. On 29 April 1987, four MiG-23MLDs of the 190th IAP led by Lt Col A. Pochitalkin took off from Bagram to drop cluster bomb units (CBU) in the area of a fortified strongpoint, known as Javara, near Khost. As they dropped their weapon load, the MiG-23s were intercepted by a pair of F-16s from No.9 Sqn PAF. One F-16 fired an AIM-9L but rather than hitting a MiG-23, the missile homed onto the other F-16, flown by Flt Lt Shahid Sikander, destroying the aircraft.

Many of the Soviet operations in this stage of the conflict were carried out by helicopter-equipped Desantno Shturmovaya Brigada (DShB – Air Assault Brigade) troops. For example, at the end of August a force of 14 Mi-8s landed some 1,700 DShB troops near the Salang tunnel over a four-hour period in which each aircraft made 12 sorties. Such landings were typically supported by Su-25s. In November 1987, the large-scale Operation *Magistral* commenced to retake the Khost area which was still under mujahideen control. Some 20,000 ground troops were supported by intensive airstrikes carried out each day by around 90 Su-17, MiG-23 and Su-25 fighter-bombers. In addition, the MiG-23 units based in Shindand supported operations in the 'green zone' near Herat. In the two months of Operation *Magistral*, the fighter-bomber pilots flew more hours than they would routinely have flown in an entire year at their home base. Deployed initially as an air-defence fighter, the MiG-23 was very much a last resort if no helicopters or Su-25s were available.

Maj M. Oger[11], a MiG-23 pilot from the 168th IAP described a sortie in February 1988 when he was called in to support an army unit that was pinned down in a village near Gardez:

The 'ghosts' [Soviet troops referred to their elusive guerrilla opponents as 'ghosts'] pinned down paratroopers on the outskirts of the village, and they asked for air support. But they did not have a FAC with them, and we were orbiting with three sections above them. No one could point out the target to us and trying to locate these machine gunners from height was a hopeless task. We couldn't even make out where the firefight was going on, as the village was a big one. In the end, our leader ordered one pilot to drop bombs directly into the centre of the village, so that the soldiers could give their position in relation to the bomb strike. However, the troops could not even raise their heads and did not even notice the explosions. Then their commander mentioned that a bus was burning nearby and there was a plume of black smoke coming from the tyres – you could see it a mile away. We headed for the smoke plume and each pair worked along the line of cover, where the 'ghosts' nested. The explosions from the bomb strikes formed a screen, behind which the troops managed to extricate themselves from the trap.

On 14 April 1988, the Geneva Accords were signed and included, amongst other arrangements, the Soviet undertaking to withdraw from the country by 15 February 1989. However, hostilities between the various mujahideen groups and Soviet forces continued unabated – as did cross-border tensions with Pakistan, especially when Soviet aircraft were supporting ground offensives in the Kunar Valley. In the evening of 4 August 1988, a pair of F-16s from No.14 Sqn PAF led by Sqn Ldr Ather Bokhari were scrambled to intercept unidentified aircraft that were approaching Miramshah. Bokhari fired an AIM-9L which shot down a Su-25 flown by Col A. Rutskoi. In another engagement in the early morning of 12 September, a pair of F-16s were vectored towards six MiG-23MLDs from the 120th IAP which were bombing a target close to the border to the east of Asadabad. Sqn Ldr Khalid Mahmood fired two AIM-9Ls at the attackers and claimed two kills before he and his wingman were chased off by Lt

A Soviet Mi-24 provides air cover for ground forces, including an artillery battery, on the Salang highway some 15km north of Kabul, as Soviet forces prepare to withdraw from Afghanistan in January 1989. (Photo by Robert Nickelsberg/Getty Images)

Col Bunin and Maj N. Golosienko, who were trailing the other six MiGs. In fact, only one missile fired by Mahmood found a target and it damaged, rather than destroyed, the MiG-23 flown by Capt S. Privalov, who managed to recover his aircraft to Bagram.

Two MiG-27-equipped regiments, the 129th and 134th APIB, deployed to Shindand to replace the Su-17s units there in October. From Shindand the MiG-27 units took responsibility for missions around Kandahar and in the western part of the country around Herat. Despite this deployment, the withdrawal of Soviet forces from Afghanistan was well under way by January. The remaining aircraft took part in Operation *Typhoon* between 23 January and 25 January to neutralize enemy forces in the northern and central regions of the country. Over 600 sorties were flown before the tactical support aircraft were withdrawn from bases in Afghanistan by the end of the month. Meanwhile, one squadron of Tu-16s from the 251st GvTBAP and two squadrons of Tu-22M1 from the 185th GvTBAP deployed to the Mary-1 and Mary-2 airfields to carry out long-range bombing over Afghanistan in support of the withdrawal. The bombers flew

pre-emptive raids against known mujahideen bases and positions until the last Soviet troops left Afghanistan on 15 February 1989.

During the Afghan conflict, Soviet military transport aircraft, including An-12, An-26, An-30 and Il-76, had flown over 27,000 flights into Afghanistan. These sorties had carried more than 880,000 troops and 430,000 tonnes of cargo. A total of 16 transport aircraft were lost in action either from anti-aircraft fire or through operational accidents. The tasking had also included the 'Black Tulip' flights, repatriating the bodies of servicemen killed in Afghanistan. On these flights an An-12 would typically carry between eight and 15 coffins accompanied by an officer from the unit of the dead personnel. However, the air war over Afghanistan was predominantly fought by helicopters and this was reflected in the high losses: 329 helicopters were lost, including 127 gunships, 174 armed-transport types and 28 heavy lift machines.

Seen between two DRAAF Mi-17 helicopters, a Soviet Il-76 transport aircraft lands at Kabul airport during the evacuation of Soviet troops in February 1989. (Photo by Eric BOUVET/Gamma-Rapho via Getty Images)

A USAF C-17A Globemaster III transport seen in flight during a
mission in support of Operation *Enduring Freedom* on 22 May 2002.
(NARA)

CHAPTER 3

US AND NATO INTERVENTION 2001–2005

God told me to smite Osama bin Laden,
so I invaded Afghanistan

attributed to George W. Bush, 2005

Just 15 days after the terrorist attacks of 11 September, as the US government considered how to respond to the atrocity, a five-man team from the CIA deployed into Afghanistan in a Mi-17 helicopter for Operation *Jawbreaker*. Of their Soviet-built aircraft, the CIA team leader Gary Schroen[12] later said, 'it's an awkward looking piece of machinery, but don't be fooled – the Russians built it for utility and service, rather than looks and style.' With them the *Jawbreaker* team carried US $3 million in cash, with which to buy over the Northern Alliance into the US camp and to persuade them to destroy the Taliban and Al Qaeda. The contacts made by the team paved the way for the success of the subsequent offensive air and land operations by Coalition Forces by arranging the integration of US SOF teams into the various Northern Alliance factions. At the same time, CIA operatives began using AGM-114 Hellfire-armed RQ-1B Predator remotely piloted air system (RPAS) flying from Uzbekistan to patrol Afghanistan, searching for the Al Qaeda leadership.

A USAF Boeing B-52 Stratofortress, flown by Capt Will Byers and Maj Tom Aranda from the 2nd Bomb Wing (BW) during a combat mission over Afghanistan. Six joint direct attack munition (JDAM) bombs can be seen on the underwing pylons. This was a typical load for a mission in late 2001, but this image was taken in February 2006. (USAF)

For the USN and USAF one of the main problems to be overcome was how to gain access to a landlocked country, which is separated from established US bases in the Gulf region by Iran. An agreement was reached with Pakistan to allow military aircraft to transit through Pakistani airspace via a corridor in the west of the country, paving the way for USN Lockheed P-3C Orions as well as English Electric Canberra PR9s and a British Aerospace (BAe) Nimrod R1 of the RAF, to fly reconnaissance and intelligence gathering sorties over Afghanistan. It also opened the way for USN aircraft flying from carriers in the Arabian Sea and for USAF long-range bombers flying from the island of Diego Garcia. Similarly, aircraft could fly long-range missions from the Gulf around Iran to enter Afghanistan via Pakistan. However, all of these options relied heavily on air-to-air refuelling (AAR), making the provision of adequate tanker aircraft a high priority. Apart from the USAF AAR assets based in the Gulf, the RAF provided ten Vickers KC-10 and Lockheed TriStar tankers based at Seeb in Oman. Meanwhile, a strike force of eight Rockwell B-1B Lancers and ten Boeing B-52 Stratofortress bombers was established at Diego Garcia and the Northrop Grumman B-2 Spirit stealth bombers were also readied for operations from their home base in Missouri. The aircraft carrier USS *Enterprise* (CVN-65), which was approaching the end of a cruise to support Operation *Southern Watch* over Iraq with Carrier Air Wing (CVW)-8 embarked, was re-tasked into the north Arabian Sea. McDonnell Douglas F/A-18C Hornets of VFA-15, flying from USS *Enterprise*, began flying CAPs over Pakistan from 4 October, while Grumman F-14B Tomcats equipped with the tactical airborne reconnaissance pod system (TARPS) were also flying missions into Afghanistan. A second aircraft carrier, USS *Carl Vinson* (CVN-70), was near the southerly tip of India en route to relieve USS *Enterprise* of her responsibility for Operation *Southern Watch*.

Operation *Enduring Freedom* commenced on 7 October 2001. That night at 21:00hrs local time, US and British forces carried out strikes against 31 targets near Kabul, Herat, Shindand, Sheberghan, Mazar-e-Sharif and Kandahar. The aim of the first phase of the operation was to destroy the Taliban air-defence capability and thereby achieve complete air supremacy over Afghanistan. US planners realized that the AAF presented negligible threat to US aircraft, but the feared that the Taliban might pack explosives into the aircraft and use them for suicide attacks on US military bases. For this reason, the airfields which were thought to be bases for the MiG-21 and Su-22 units were hit on the first night. Other targets attacked on the first night included radar sites and SAM sites, as well as the Taliban headquarters in Kandahar and terrorist training camps. The attack was opened by 50 BGM-109 Tomahawk land attack missiles (TLAM) fired from two Aegis-equipped Arleigh-Burke-class destroyers, USS *McFaul* (DDG-74) and USS *John Paul Jones*

A JDAM-armed Grumman F-14 Tomcat of VFA-102, operating from USS *Theodore Roosevelt* (CVN-71) over Afghanistan in November 2001, after refuelling from an RAF Vickers VC-10K tanker. (Roxburgh)

Replenishment at sea (RAS): aircraft carrier USS *Carl Vinson* (CVN-70) takes on fuel and other supplies from USS *Sacramento* (AOE-1), a fast combat-support ship, in the Indian Ocean on 12 October 2001. Aircraft from the ship carried out combat operations over Afghanistan between October and December against terrorist training camps and Taliban military installations. (USN)

(DDG-53), a Spruance-class destroyer, USS *O'Brien* (DD-975), the Ticonderoga-class cruiser USS *Philippine Sea* (CG-58), and three nuclear attack submarines, USS *Providence* (SSN-719), HMS *Trafalgar* (S107) and HMS *Triumph* (S93). The TLAMs were followed by long-range bombers: two B-2 Spirit stealth bombers flew direct from Whiteman AFB, Missouri, while five B-1B Lancer and ten B-52H Stratofortress flew from Diego Garcia. The next wave that night consisted of 25 carrier-based aircraft from the USS *Carl Vinson* and USS *Enterprise*, which were now sailing in the Arabian Sea.

The mission flown by the two B-2 Spirits of the 509th Bomb Wing (BW) took the record for the longest manned bomber mission ever flown. The aircraft, each loaded with 16 2,000lb GBU-31 joint direct attack munitions (JDAMs), took off from Whiteman AFB and headed westwards over the Pacific and Indian Oceans, carrying out refuelling five times from McDonnell Douglas KC-10 Extender and Boeing KC-135 Stratotanker. The first refuelling bracket was just off the Californian coast, with the others over Hawaii, Guam and the Strait of Malacca before a final pre-strike top-up near Diego Garcia. After delivering 16 JDAMs each onto targets in Afghanistan, the B-2 crews landed to refuel at Diego Garcia after a 44-hour flight. With round-trip distances of 600 to 700 miles, the 25 sorties flown by F-14B Tomcats and F/A-18C Hornets from the carriers were also long by their standards, lasting over 4½hrs with two AAR brackets. Equipped with the LANTIRN targeting system (LTS) pod, the Tomcats dropped laser guided bombs (LGBs) while the Hornets each fired a single AGM-84 SLAM-ER (standoff land attack missile-extended range) or an AGM-154A joint standoff weapon (JSOW). The Tomcats of VF-14, launching from USS *Enterprise*, carried out the opening attacks, striking the Kabul early warning radar facility. The USN fighter-bombers were supported by Lockheed S-3 Viking tankers and Grumman EA-6B Prowlers from the carriers, while RAF VC-10 and TriStar tankers also provided AAR support. The B-52s dropped 500lb Mk84 bombs onto terrorist training camps in eastern Afghanistan.

Additionally, in a 'hearts and minds' operation to complement the missile and air strikes, two C-17 Globemaster III of the 437th Airlift Wing from Ramstein AFB in Germany dropped packets of food and medical supplies over areas in southeastern Afghanistan which had been identified by the US Agency for International Development as locations where they might be needed. During the 13-hour mission, the aircraft transited across Ukraine and refuelled from KC-135s over the Black Sea. The ration packs, including barley stew, rice, shortbread cookies and peanut butter, were dropped in large cardboard boxes, which broke open in the air flow, scattering the individual packs over a three-square mile area. C-17s also landed at Karshi-Khanabad Air Base in Uzbekistan to deliver several HH-60G Pave Hawk helicopters in case they were needed for combat search and rescue (CSAR) missions.

Meanwhile, two B-2s had already taken off for the airstrikes scheduled for the second night. As one of the pilots, Col Tony Cihak, explained: 'We took off for the second night's mission before the war was on ... before the first night had even happened.'

ABOVE A Rockwell B-1B Lancer bomber from the 28th Air Expeditionary Wing, taking off for a combat mission over Afghanistan on 12 November 2001. In the first month of Operation *Enduring Freedom*, B-1B bombers flew 120 sorties. (NARA)

RIGHT A Northrop Grumman B-2 Spirit stealth bomber refuels from a Boeing KC-135 Stratotanker air-to-air refuelling (AAR) tanker. During the opening days of Operation *Enduring Freedom*, a B-2 flew the longest ever manned operational bombing sortie. (USAF)

In the second B-2, named 'Spirit of America', Maj Melvin G. Deaile and Capt Brian Neal were to set another record for the longest ever bombing mission. Deaile[13] recalled:

About four hours into the mission, we approached the California coast for our first air refuelling. The sun was just starting to rise on the east coast as we approached the KC-135 refuelling aircraft. We topped off our tanks and settled in for the next leg of our mission, which was the four-hour flight to Hawaii for our next air refuelling. While the B-2 is a two-person aircraft, operating rules say two people only have to be in the seats during critical phases of flight: take-off, air refuelling, landing and, of course, bombing. Between refuellings, Brian and I took turns trying to get a few hours of rest in the modified 'cot' behind the two ejection seats.

The pattern of meeting a much-needed gas station in the air happened at least three more times en route to Afghanistan. Our formation met tankers over Guam, through the Straits of Malacca and in the Indian Ocean, close to Diego Garcia. The voyage across the Pacific Ocean took more than 24 hours. Since the sun was coming up in the east as we started our voyage west, we travelled in daylight throughout our trek across the Pacific. The air refuelling over the Indian Ocean was the last before we reached Afghanistan. We turned north and headed up the coast of India to our destination.

By the time we approached the Pakistani coast, two things happened. First, the sunlight that had accompanied us the entire journey slowly went away. In order to fight off the release of melatonin that comes at that moment, the flight doctor had given each crew member an approved 'pick me up pill' to make sure everyone was alert going into combat. Second, 70 per cent of the targets we stepped out the door with back in Missouri had changed. This meant reprogramming the targets for a majority of the 16 JDAMs that filled the two bomb bays on the B-2. That night, we conducted bombing runs on multiple targets throughout Afghanistan with the primary mission being to secure air superiority for air forces that would conduct subsequent attacks. During some bomb runs, we used the B-2's onboard synthetic aperture radar to put eyes on target in order to refine target coordinates before releasing our JDAMs. After spending about two hours over enemy territory, we exited the country and headed for the last tanker that would give us the gas for our last leg of the journey. A radio call came over secure communications that the air operations center wanted to know if we would be willing to head back into country since we had four JDAMs remaining. We accepted the mission.

With gas running low, we orbited in the Arabian Sea waiting for a tanker that would give us the fuel necessary for another trip into Afghanistan. While Brian got the fuel, I programmed the mission. With fuel onboard and a mission loaded, we commenced another journey into Afghanistan to strike the identified target. After 90 minutes, we exited Afghanistan a second time to find a waiting tanker to provide the fuel we needed to reach Diego Garcia, our final destination.

Deaile and Neal finally landed after 44hr 20min airborne.

The second night also saw TLAM strikes. This time 13 missiles were fired, and a smaller number of aircraft, five land-based and ten carrier-based aircraft, attacked 13 targets. The F/A-18 Hornets carried out strikes near Kabul, Kandahar, Herat and Mazar-e-Sharif. Once again two Globemaster transports delivered food packs over southeastern Afghanistan.

The 12 carrier-based aircraft operating over Afghanistan on 9 October included a pair of Tomcats from VF-14 carrying out a restrike against Mazar-e-Sharif garrison. During this 1,700-mile round trip the aircraft were supported by RAF tankers and were re-tasked from a defensive counter-air mission. They succeeded in destroying three MiG-21s and two transport aircraft on the ground. Other carrier-borne strikes were carried out against Herat and Kandahar airfields. This was the last night that a pair of B-2s participated in missions over Afghanistan and the first that the 5,000lb GPS-guided GBU-37 weapon was used against tunnels and

ABOVE An RAF Vickers VC-10C1K tanker from 10 Sqn at Seeb in Oman. The RAF deployed a mixed force of ten VC-10 and Lockheed TriStar tankers to Oman to support US strike aircraft during Operation *Enduring Freedom*. (Crown Copyright/MoD)

underground bunkers in Al Qaeda training camps. The aircraft carriers had now split their operation so that USS *Enterprise* flew night sorties and USS *Carl Vinson* mounted day sorties.

On each of the subsequent four nights, strike missions were flown by ten to 15 carrier-based aircraft and ten bombers operating from Diego Garcia. On 11 October the B-52s and B-1Bs used the 5,000lb GBU-28 against mountain cave complexes which were being used by Al Qaeda personnel. TLAM attacks were also carried out on 10 October and 13 October. The humanitarian aid drops also continued each night, switching to northern Afghanistan on 9 October and expanding on 11 October to four C-17s. USN carrier operations continued to be supported by the RAF VC-10 and TriStar tankers operating from Oman.

On 15 October, 90 carrier-based aircraft carried out missions over Afghanistan. There were also five TLAM strikes. This date also saw the first employment of the Lockheed AC-130H Spectre gunship: two aircraft operating from Al Jaber Air Base in Kuwait engaged targets near Kandahar that night. The first land-based fighter-bombers, McDonnell Douglas F-15E Strike Eagles from the 366th Wing, which had also deployed to Al Jaber, flew their first mission in Afghanistan on 17 October. They were also joined by General Dynamics F-16 Fighting Falcons equipped with the Litening II targeting pod.

Al Udeid in Qatar on 7 November 2001: A USAF McDonnell Douglas F-15E Strike Eagle, from the 332nd Air Expeditionary Group, being readied for a strike mission over Afghanistan. The aircraft is armed with a GBU-15 electro-optically guided bomb and a GBU-12 Paveway II LGB. (NARA)

By the second week of operations, most of the fixed targets had already been struck and tasking was increasingly against targets of opportunity such as Taliban troops and vehicles, and Taliban and Al Qaeda leadership. The Boeing RC-135 Rivet Joints and EA-6B Prowlers played a pivotal role in this part of the campaign by listening in on and locating the handheld radios that were being used by the Taliban to co-ordinate their forces. Thanks to the poor

A McDonnell Douglas AV-8B Harrier of the Italian Navy (Nautica Militare) refuels from an RAF VC-10 tanker over Afghanistan during a combat mission in November 2001. The Italian aircraft were accompanied by US Navy F-14 Tomcats during the mission. (Roxburgh)

communications infrastructure in the country, VHF radios and mobile phones had become a vital part of the Taliban command and control routine and one which in the past had given them a significant advantage over their less well-equipped opposition. Now, this reliance on radios had become a fatal weakness that was fully exploited by US electronic warfare assets. After mobile targets had been located, strikes were directed by airborne forward air controllers (AFAC) in F-14s or F-16s. Much of the effort was also directed against the cave and tunnel complexes in the Zhawar Kili mountains near Khost, where Al Qaeda had established its stronghold. SOF helicopters used thermal cameras to locate caves which were occupied and directed fighter-bombers onto these targets.

The aircraft carriers USS *Theodore Roosevelt* (CVN-71) and *Kitty Hawk* (CV-63) had now arrived on station in the Arabian Sea approximately 100 miles south of the Pakistan coast. USS *Kitty Hawk* had only a small complement of aircraft, comprising only eight F/A-18 Hornets, three S-3 Vikings, two Grumman C-2A Greyhounds and two Sikorsky SH-60B Seahawk helicopters, as most of the deck space was taken up by 20 Boeing MH-47 Chinooks and Sikorsky MH-60 Black Hawks of the US Army 160th Special Operations Aviation Regiment (SOAR). However, USS *Theodore Roosevelt* had a full air wing, CVW-1, aboard and it replaced the USS *Enterprise* on station.

Working in conjunction with aircraft from the USS *Carl Vinson*, CVW-1 flew its first operational mission on 17 October. Lt Cdr Michael Vizcarra, an F-14 radar intercept officer (RIO) from VF-102 aboard the USS *Theodore Roosevelt*, took part in a mission over Afghanistan the following day:

I was scheduled for the second CVW-1 strike launched into Afghanistan from the USS *Roosevelt*. This would be the first and only mission throughout this entire combat cruise that I would actually have a target file to brief for the flight. Our target was a military complex which included a support building and numerous tanks in the open yard. VF-102 led the brief of two Tomcats, each loaded with two GBU-16s and four Hornets, each carrying two GBU-12s, to attack this military complex near the capital city of Kabul, the largest city in Afghanistan. The Hornets were tasked with targeting the building as it would be easier to acquire the larger target with the lower resolution F-18 Nighthawk Pod. The Tomcats were assigned to target the numerous tanks in the yard ... As we neared the target area, the Hornets dropped their bombs on their target [the building] as briefed. As smoke and dust now filled the air, the Tomcats attacked as the Hornets cleared the area. We attempted to designate our targets on the FLIR pod without success as we flew over the target. We quickly made the decision to circle and try again, realizing that historically, most shoot downs occur on the subsequent passes over the same target, but we went for a second time [third if you count the Hornets' pass]. This time

Two US Navy McDonnell Douglas F/A-18 Hornets flying a combat mission over Afghanistan in November 2001. Both are carrying external fuel tanks and are armed with GBU-16 1,000lb LGBs and AIM-9 Sidewinder AAMs. Carrier-based naval aircraft flew the majority of strike sorties in the early days of Operation *Enduring Freedom*. (NARA)

we designated the target and dropped. However, we didn't see the expected subsequent explosions and as we pulled up off target, our wingman informed us we had a 'hung bomb' [a bomb that has failed to release].

With the 'hung bomb' the aircraft could not recover to the carrier, so the crew decided to divert to Shahbaz Air Base, near Jacobabad in Pakistan.

Part of the 160th SOAR had deployed to Karshi-Khanabad Air Base in Uzbekistan on 5 October, and on 19 October two MH-47E Chinooks, escorted by MH-60L Black Hawk direct action penetrators (DAPs) inserted two SOF teams into Afghanistan. Operational detachment Alpha (ODA) -555 was inserted into the Panjshir Valley and ODA-595 into Dari-a-Souf, just to the south of Mazar-e-Sharif.

A B-52H Stratofortress from the 28th Air Expeditionary Wing over the Indian Ocean as it returns to its base on Diego Garcia after a bombing mission over Afghanistan on 30 October 2001. (NARA)

These teams linked up with Northern Alliance forces and the FACs were able to call in air support for Northern Alliance troops. Two more teams, ODA-585 and ODA-553, were inserted later in the month to join other Northern Alliance factions, and eight more teams were inserted the following month. On 21 October, four Lockheed MC-130H Combat Talons of 16th Special Operations Wing (SOW) dropped a force of 200 US Army Ranger paratroopers onto a desert airstrip codenamed Objective *Rhino*. Located approximately 40km south of Kandahar, *Rhino* had originally been built as a hunting camp for aristocrats from the United Arab Emirates (UAE) and boasted a 6,400ft runway. The mission of the paratroopers was to secure the airstrip and set up a forward arming and refuelling point (FARP) for helicopters of the 160th SOAR flying from the USS *Kitty Hawk*. Before the parachute assault, the defences in the area were suppressed by B-2s and AC-130s. Once the airborne forces had taken control of the objective, a flight of four MH-47s supported by MH-60 DAPs refuelled before pressing on to insert a team of 91 Delta Force soldiers into a compound on the outskirts of Kandahar that was being used by Mullah Omar as a command site. Before the SOF troops arrived, two B-1Bs dropped 36 GBU-31 LGBs with airburst fuses onto the Taliban defensive positions, while F/A-18 dropped LGBs on anti-aircraft artillery (AAA) emplacements. The helicopter landings were also supported by the AC-130s. The aim was to capture Omar if he was present and to gather any intelligence material. This part of the operation lasted an hour, before the helicopters returned to *Rhino*. Once the mission was complete, the helicopters returned to USS *Kitty Hawk* and the Rangers were airlifted out of Objective *Rhino* by the MC-130s.

At the same time, another four MH-60s landed at the small airfield at Dalbandin in Pakistan to start setting up another FOB. However, one of the helicopters crashed when the pilots became disorientated in 'brown out' conditions while landing in the dust. Conscious of the adverse publicity that would be generated if the loss of the helicopter became public, a pair of Sikorsky CH-53E Super Stallion helicopters attempted to recover the wreckage the next day. The salvage helicopters were led by Capt Jay M. Holtermann from the 15th Marine Expeditionary Unit (MEU). Flying from the USS

Peleliu (LHA-5), they refuelled at Shamsi in Pakistan before continuing to Dalbandin. After lifting the MH-60 hulk, the CH-53s flew 209km south to Panjgur to refuel; however, as they refuelled, they came under fire from gunmen and had to withdraw, abandoning the MH-60. Another recovery mission was mounted on 24 October, this time with three CH-53Es, escorted by four Bell AH-1W Super Cobra attack helicopters and a flight of USMC AV-8B Harriers. This time they were successful and had delivered the MH-60 to USS *Kitty Hawk* by 06:30hrs.

Tasking each day, during the third week of operations between 22 and 28 October, typically saw 65 to 85 strike aircraft flying from the carriers, five long-range bombers from Diego Garcia and six to ten land-based tactical aircraft, including the AC-130s. Many of these missions were flown in support of Northern Alliance offensives and directed by the ODA team FACs. The humanitarian drops by C-17s also continued each night, and operations were carried out by Lockheed EC-130 Commando Solo psychological operations aircraft of the 193rd SOW, which broadcast directly onto Afghan radio and television channels. In addition, two French Air Force Dassault Mirage IVP reconnaissance aircraft from Escadre 1/91 *Gasogne* began operating from Al Dafra in the UAE, flying their first mission on 23 October. They were supported by two dedicated French C-135FR

ABOVE LEFT Operating from USS *Enterprise* (CVN-65), an F-14D Tomcat aircraft from VF-41 waits to refuel from a USAF KC-10 Extender from the 763rd Expeditionary Air Refueling Squadron (EARS), during a combat mission flown in support of Operation *Enduring Freedom* on 5 October 2001. (NARA)

ABOVE RIGHT Many of the early strike sorties over Afghanistan were flown during the hours of darkness. Here an F-15E Strike Eagle refuels from a KC-135R Stratotanker of the 319th Air Expeditionary Group (AEG) in the night skies over Afghanistan during November 2001. (NARA)

tankers. Another important reconnaissance asset over Afghanistan was the Northrop Grumman RQ-4A Global Hawk RPAS. With the ability to loiter on task for 24 hours and to operate at 65,000ft, Global Hawk collected data via an array of electro-optical, infra-red, and synthetic-aperture-radar sensors. Three of these aircraft were employed over Afghanistan between November 2001 and September 2002, collecting some 17,000 images during 60 combat missions.

Four US Marine Corps (USMC) AV-8Bs operating from USS *Peleliu* made their first sorties over Afghanistan on 3 November, striking a Taliban and Al Qaeda training camp near Garmabak. As fighting between the Northern Alliance and Taliban raged around Mazar-e-Sharif, two 15,000lb BLU-82 bombs were dropped by MC-130s onto Taliban positions on 4 November. Five days later Mazar-e-Sharif fell to the Northern Alliance. Air support for Northern Alliance forces continued both in terms of offensive missions, but also supply drops by C-17s, which included horse feed since many of the Northern Alliance troops travelled on horseback. Meanwhile the battles continued around Herat and Bagram. At Bagram, the intervention of a B-52 Stratofortress on 12 November was decisive.

The wreckage of Soviet-era aircraft, including an An-12, at Kandahar airport. The few remaining aircraft that had once been in service with the DRAAF were targeted by US aircraft in the opening days of Operation *Enduring Freedom*, to deny their use to the Taliban. (NARA)

The aircraft carrier USS *Enterprise* prepares to launch three Grumman F-14 Tomcats for the last time. on 9 November 2001. The type would be withdrawn from service on the carrier at the end of its cruise in support of Operation *Enduring Freedom* and replaced by the Boeing F/A-18E/F Super Hornet. (NARA)

The aircraft was called in by a SOF forward air controller, Master Sgt William C. Markham, to drop its load of 45 500lb Mk82 free-fall bombs onto the airfield where a large Taliban force was massing to attack. The weapons decimated the Taliban troops while emboldening those of the Northern Alliance, who immediately went onto the offensive and took possession of the airfield. Herat was also taken by Northern Alliance troops on 13 November and Kabul was captured the following day. Kunduz fell on 26 November.

Many captured Taliban fighters were imprisoned in the Qala-e-Jangi fortress near Mazar-e-Sharif, but they were neither searched nor properly restrained by the Northern Alliance troops. As a result, when Taliban prisoners revolted on 25 November, they were able to overpower their captors and take control of much of the fortress. The battle to recapture the fortress and suppress the rebellion took place over the next five days and was heavily supported by aircraft, including AC-130s, and F/A-18s which dropped LGBs.

With the main cities under the control, at least nominally, of the Northern Alliance, arrangements were made to station aircraft closer to their operating areas. On 20 November two MC-130s dropped a US Navy SEAL team near Objective *Rhino* to establish a FOB. This was deep in enemy territory, since at that time the province of Kandahar was still very much under the control of the Taliban. On 25 November a force of four AH-1W Super Cobras and three Bell UH-1N Iroquois from HMM-163, and three CH-53 Super Stallions from HMM-365, supported by eight USMC AV-8Bs and a Lockheed KC-130 Hercules tanker from VMGR-352 (operating from Jacobabad) carried the main assault force to secure Objective *Rhino*. Once the airfield was completely under US control, the KC-130s were used to shuttle some 1,500 troops

BELOW LEFT Seen through night vision goggles (NVG), a USMC KC-130 Hercules from VMGR-252 being unloaded in darkness at forward operating base (FOB) Rhino on 3 December 2001. (NARA)

BELOW RIGHT Supporting special operations forces (SOF) during a night mission, this Sikorsky MH-53J Pave Low helicopter is from the USAF 6th Special Operations Wing (SOW). Note the AAR probe. (NARA)

of the 15th Marine Expeditionary Unit to the FOB over the next few days. On the night of 26 November, a convoy of Taliban vehicles including two BRDM-2 armoured personnel carriers was detected about 80km to the northwest of *Rhino*. Two F-14Bs from VF-102 (USS *Carl Vinson*) attacked with a GBU-12 LGB after which two Super Cobras then destroyed the military vehicles and Taliban fighters. Once the runway was assessed as being suitable for C-17 operations, two Globemasters were tasked into FOB *Rhino* each day to bring in supplies, equipment and personnel. These included Seabees of the Naval Mobile Construction Battalion 133, who repaired and extended the runway.

Similar maintenance and construction work was going on elsewhere from late October. At Jacobabad in Pakistan, USAF engineers set up a water treatment facility and built up the dispersal that was being used by CSAR helicopters and USMC KC-130 tankers. At Karshi-Khanabad in Uzbekistan a 'tent city' had to be built to accommodate a population of some 3,500 personnel from the 16th SOW, US Army SOF units and various other units that were deploying to Uzbekistan for operations. Whereas the work at Jacobabad and Karshi-Khanabad were started after the US forces had already deployed there, a tent city was already in place at Manas Air Base in Kyrgyzstan by the time that the 376th Air Expeditionary Wing (AEW) deployed there on 16 December 2001. At Manas, the limiting factor to the number of aircraft that could be supported was the size of the parking areas. The eventual complement there would be six USMC F/A-18 Hornets, six French Dassault Mirage 2000Ds, two Boeing C-135FR tankers from France and two Boeing (K)B-707 tankers from No.33 Sqn RAAF, as well as five C-130 Hercules from Norway, the Netherlands and Denmark.

An unfortunate error on 5 December nearly derailed the Coalition plans for the future government of Afghanistan when a SOF team called for an air strike against Taliban positions 10km north of Kandahar. The FAC inadvertently gave his own position rather than that of the enemy to a B-52, which responded to the request with a 2,000lb JDAM. The weapon struck friendly forces, killing eight and wounding 38 of the joint US-Afghan force. Hamid Karzai, the leading contender to govern post-Taliban Afghanistan, was lucky to

ABOVE A B-1B Lancer of the 28th Bomb Wing, assigned to the 405th Air Expeditionary Wing (AEW), departs Thumrait in Oman for a mission over Afghanistan in January 2002. With its long range and the ability to carry multiple weapons, the B-1B proved to be an ideal CAS aircraft in Afghanistan. (NARA)

RIGHT An F/A-18C Hornet from VFA-22 prepares to launch off catapult one on the deck of the USS *Carl Vinson* (CVN 70) for a mission over Afghanistan on 17 November 2001. (NARA)

escape being killed himself in the incident. The Taliban withdrew from Kandahar on 7 December and US Marines seized Kandahar airport on 14 December. The month of December had seen some ultra-long missions by F-15E Strike Eagles operating from Al Jaber Air Base in Kuwait and on the night of 14/15 December a pair of F-15Es from the 391st FS flew a 15hr 50min sortie over Kabul; this sortie involved 12 AAR brackets.

Phase one of Operation *Enduring Freedom* was considered to have ended on 18 December 2001 and by the end of the year, Afghanistan was being governed by the Afghan Interim Authority led by Hamid Karzai. The next phase would be to mop up the few remaining pockets of resistance and to establish an International Security Assistance Force (ISAF) in the country to support the new government. Offensive air operations to support troops on the ground, though still ongoing, had been scaled back considerably. In the north of the Arabian Sea the USS *Enterprise* had left in late October, and the USS *Carl Vinson* followed it in mid-December, being replaced by the USS *John C. Stennis* (CVN-74) with CVW-9 embarked. The new carrier joined USS *Theodore Roosevelt*, which would be replaced in turn at the beginning of March 2002 by the USS *John F. Kennedy*. In a reshuffle of long-range assets, the eight B-1Bs that had been flying from Diego Garcia were redeployed to Thumrait in Oman in order to reduce the sortie lengths and relieve some of the congestion on the island.

During December, the US forces received more support from their European partners. The Italian carrier *Giuseppe Garibaldi* (CVS-551) had deployed to the area with eight AV-8B Harriers on 22 November and its pilots were working up with US Navy crews in readiness for combat operations. Meanwhile, the French aircraft carrier *Charles de Gaulle* (CVN-91) arrived in the Arabian Sea on

A C-17A Globemaster III departs from Bagram Air Base in May 2002. The type formed the backbone of the air bridge since everything, from ammunition to rations, as well as personnel, had to be flown into Afghanistan. (NARA)

19 December bringing the 16 Dassault Super Étendards of 17F as well as two Dassault Rafales and a Grumman E-2C Hawkeye early warning aircraft. The Super Étendards commenced offensive support operations over Afghanistan on 19 December, while the first missions by Italian AV-8Bs were flown in mixed formations with F-14Bs on 4 January. During their 87 days at sea, the AV-8B pilots from *Giuseppe Garibaldi* flew 328 operational sorties over Afghanistan.

As Kandahar fell under the control of the Afghan Interim Authority, the focus of operations in Afghanistan shifted to the mountainous area of the Tora Bora, close to the Khyber Pass between Afghanistan and Pakistan. It was believed that Osama bin Laden had taken refuge in the many natural caves there and a campaign to clear the caves of Al Qaeda fighters took place between 6 December and 17 December. During a sustained effort, B-52s delivered a 3,000lb AGM-142 Have Nap missile into the entrance of one cave that was in use by Al Qaeda fighters, and an MC-130 Combat Talon delivered a 15,000lb BLU-82 in order to close off another cave. In addition, JDAMs were dropped by B-1s, B-52s and F-16s to cause landslides, burying equipment, including in one case a tank, under tons of rock. One B-1B Lancer was lost during this operation on 12 December after it suffered multiple systems failures, which were not caused by

Another critical element of the air bridge was the ubiquitous C-130 Hercules, which was used to distribute supplies across the country. In the foreground, a USMC KC-130/R from VMGR-352 waits at a forward operating base in Afghanistan in February 2002, while in the background another KC-130/R Hercules from VMGR-252 departs for Kandahar Air Base. (NARA)

enemy activity. The crew ejected successfully into the Arabian Sea. In January 2002, the focus shifted once more, this time to a complex of Al Qaeda and Taliban training camps in the Zhawar Kili area to the south of Khost, close to the border with Pakistan. The complex, which comprised a system of interlinked tunnels and caves, was subjected to 118 FAC-directed airstrikes between 4 and 7 January by B-1Bs, B-52s, F/A-18s and an AC-130.

More international support arrived in February in the shape of six French Air Force Mirage 2000D from Esc 1/3 *Navarre* which deployed to Manas Air Base on 27 February, supported by C-135FR tankers. These aircraft flew their first operational mission on 2 March and carried out strikes with LGBs two days later. Meanwhile, intelligence sources reported that Al Qaeda fugitives were beginning to regroup in the Shah-i-Kot Valley, 130km south of Kabul. An operation to neutralize this threat commenced on 28 February. Code-named Operation *Anaconda*, it was conceived as a swift affair to clear a small number of insurgents from the area. Unfortunately, the planning was flawed, firstly in that it underestimated the enemy strength, and secondly that the requirements for air support were not properly co-ordinated at the planning stage. Thus, when the combined force, comprising US mountain troops, Marines and SOF teams from the US, Australia and the UK, supported by Afghan army units, advanced into the area on 2 March, they were surprised to be fighting a well-trained and well-disciplined enemy fighting from well-prepared positions. The terrain, comprising 10,000ft mountains, also favoured the defenders. On the night prior to the air assault, the LZs had been checked by AC-130 gunships, which reported them to be clear of enemy activity. Landings were preceded by airstrikes by F-15Es, including dropping JDAMS and a BLU-118 thermobaric bomb onto cave areas along the sides of the valley. The Coalition troops were then inserted onto the LZs. Initially CAS was provided by seven Boeing AH-64 Apaches of the US Army 3rd Battalion 101st Aviation Regiment, but all of the AH-64s were hit and damaged by enemy fire, which included rocket propelled grenades (RPG). As the Coalition troops came under more pressure, B-52s, B-1Bs and F-15Es were called in to support them and the aircraft were in action throughout the day. One B-1B dropped 19 JDAMs onto ten different

A US Army CH-47 Chinook inserts Canadian soldiers onto a landing zone (LZ) 7,500ft above sea level in the Tora Bora region of Afghanistan during Operation *Torii* in May 2002. The 400 troops taking part in the operation to investigate four underground sites, as part of the search for Osama bin Laden, also included US and Afghan soldiers. (NARA)

targets over a two-hour period. However, there was congestion in the airspace above the small area of the fighting, which measured just 13km by 13km: a B-1B had to abort its weapon delivery after being advised that there was an AC-130 operating directly below it.

The fighting continued through the next day and in the early hours of 3 March two MH-47s attempted to insert an SOF team onto the top of the Takur Ghar ridge, an 11,000ft summit on the southeastern extremity of the area. The first helicopter was hit by small arms fire which damaged the hydraulic systems. During a second attempt by two more helicopters a few hours later, another MH-47 was shot down by an RPG, while the remaining one landed at the foot of a 3,000ft sheer cliff face. One of the survivors of the downed MH-47 was Staff Sgt Gabe Brown, who, although not a qualified FAC, managed to contact the crew of a Predator RPAS that was on station overhead. With a good radio link and a 'god's eye view' of the battlefield below, thanks to the systems on board the Predator, the RPAS operator, USAF Capt Stephen Jones, then attempted to co-ordinate the flow of F-15Es and F-16CGs into the area, so that

Brown could direct the aircraft to carry out multiple bombing and strafing runs on enemy positions. Jones[14] recalled:

> Gabe was doing a phenomenal job being a controller on the ground calling in close air support, but it was a lot of work. There were a ton of Coalition aircraft coming in and out and some of them didn't have much play time, meaning they had to get in, develop an understanding of what was going on, receive a nine-line and then drop bombs or shoot their missiles.

The Predator crew also tried to use their laser to illuminate targets so that the fighter-bomber crews could locate them more easily. However, the actions of the RPAS crew did not meet universal approval, and USMC F/A-18 pilot Capt Jonathan R. Ohman commented[15] that: 'It was an extremely frustrating experience, and there was some confusion over what authority the [unmanned aerial vehicle operator] had, particularly when the guy on the ground was not a trained [joint tactical air controller].' However, the Predator did destroy one enemy bunker that had proved difficult to hit, using a Hellfire missile. The

A Dassault Mirage 2000D of the French Air Force (FAF) aircraft during a mission over Afghanistan on 27 June 2002. The French deployed six of the type and two supporting Boeing C-135FR AAR tankers to Manas Air Base in Kyrgyzstan, in support of Operation *Enduring Freedom*. (NARA)

A typical scene at Manas Air Base in Kyrgyzstan during the summer of 2002. As well as four AAR tankers and five C-130 Hercules from different nations, there are six USMC F/A-18D Hornets and six FAF Dassault Mirage 2000D. (NARA)

Predator remained over the battlefield for 14 hours. Although the fighter-bombers carried out successful missions, one B-52 crew suffered extreme frustration as they attempted to carry out theirs.

During a 15-hour mission, they were tasked against multiple targets but in every case their clearance to drop weapons was cancelled because of deconfliction problems, and they returned to Diego Garcia without having dropped any of their weapons. During the pre-dawn morning of 3 March, Cpt Edward J. Lengel of the 66th Rescue Squadron carried out a remarkable casualty evacuation in his HH-60G Pave Hawk. Flying at ultra low level above the terrain he landed under fire on an 8,500ft ridge to pick up seriously wounded casualties, simultaneously co-ordinating covering fire from an AC-130. At high altitude and with his helicopter now at its maximum take-off weight, he had to fly downhill along a dry streambed until he had gained enough airspeed to climb away.

By the following day, 4 March, the system for organizing CAS had been altered and the situation began to improve. On this day the supporting aircraft included pairs of Fairchild Republic A-10 Thunderbolts, which flew the five-hour transit from Al Jaber Air Base in Kuwait. These aircraft, which were specifically intended for the CAS mission, were particularly effective. However, the airspace above the battlefield remained crowded and disorganized. Capt Scott Campbell, the leader of a pair of A-10s which was tasked into the area on the third night, later reported that there was no Air Support Operations Centre (ASOC) to pass on details of the ground battle and give the pilots priorities. Furthermore, because the airspace was not being actively managed, his A-10 flight also experienced several near misses with a C-130, a pair of F/A-18s and an RPAS, as well as seeing a bomb dropped through their level from an aircraft above them. Campbell had therefore decided that he and his wingman should adopt the role of an AFACs to deconflict the airspace themselves. For the remainder of the operation, the A-10 pilots took on this role whenever they were tasked into the airspace over the battlefield.

At night-time the task was taken by AC-130s, but over the next ten days A-10s, B-1Bs, B-52s, F-15Es, F-16s, F/A-18s, Super Étendards, and Mirage 2000Ds all flew missions into the valley. In addition, Predator RPAS and P-3 Orions were also flying in the airspace above the battle area. In response to a plea for more attack helicopter support to supplement the efforts of the AH-64s, five AH-1W Super Cobras from HMLA-369 deployed to Bagram and flew their first mission on 5 March, over the Sha-i-Kot valley.

A wide range of aircraft types were involved in operations over Afghanistan, including the USAF Lockheed U-2R Dragon Lady aircraft from the 99th Expeditionary Reconnaissance Squadron (ERS). The type was used for reconnaissance and also as a radio relay and is seen here after landing from an Operation *Enduring Freedom* sortie on 1 July 2002. (NARA)

The same day saw AV-8Bs of HMM-165 flying from USS *Bonnehomme Richard* join the AV-8Bs of the 13th MEU which were already in theatre. CAS operations were limited on 7 March when the cloud base dropped below the mountain tops, but even though laser-guided weapons could not be used, GPS-guided JDAMs could still be employed. Meanwhile, five A-10s were redeployed to Jacobabad to put them closer to the operating area. These aircraft were used for night sorties, working in conjunction with the AC-130s, but would have to leave Pakistan on completion of the operation. An ingenious FARP was also established 10km west of the Shah-i-Kot Valley so that the AH-1Ws could be maximized: two CH-53s were used as fuel tankers for the attack helicopters and once they had given up their spare fuel, they departed and refuelled from a KC-130 before returning to the FARP to repeat the process.

As Operation *Anaconda* approached a successful conclusion, Operation *Harpoon* was launched to support the mopping up operation. Led by Canadian forces, with support from the US Marines, this involved a battalion air assault to clear the ridge along the west of the valley, known as 'the whale.' The air landings took place on 13 March, with a force of ten USMC helicopters consisting of four AH-1Ws, four CH-47s and two CH-53s. Operation *Anaconda* was officially declared to have ended on 18 March; however, a

A US Army Boeing AH-64 Apache attack helicopter landing at Camp Harriman, a forward arming and refuelling point (FARP) near Orgun-e, in August 2002. Located at 7,000ft above sea level and close to the border with Pakistan, Orgun-e was in an area which strongly supported the Taliban insurgency. (NARA)

British-led mop-up operation in the mountains to the southeast of the Shah-i-Kot Valley, codenamed Operation *Jacana*, continued between 17 April and 2 July. This was supported by RAF CH-47 Chinooks and by USMC F/A-18s and French Mirage 2000Ds flying from Manas. When operating from Manas, the direct route to Afghanistan ran over the 25,000ft peaks of the Pamir mountains; but lacking any suitable helicopters for SAR support in case of an ejection amongst the high ground, the Mirages initially had to make an extended diversion around the mountains via the Vakhsh Valley in order to stay clear of Uzbek airspace. This in turn extended sortie lengths, impacting on the time that the Mirages could stay on task as well as affecting crew fatigue. In May the French Air Force set up a multi-national effort CSAR system specifically optimized for high altitude operations, which enabled the Mirage crews to take the direct route across the mountain range. A French C-130 based in Dushanbe co-ordinated with Spanish Aerospatiale SA330 Puma and Kyrgyz Mi-8 helicopters carrying a platoon of French high mountain *gendarmerie* from Chamonix. Both the Danish and Netherlands air forces also deployed C-130s to Manas Air Base and they began to plan the detachment of F-16s from the European Partner Air Force (EPAF) group for operations over Afghanistan later in the year. In the meantime, a Royal Netherlands Air Force (RNLAF) McDonnell Douglas KDC-10 tanker was seconded to the USAF 379th EAW at Al Udeid Air Base in Qatar from April to June 2002. This was in addition to the Royal Netherlands Navy P-3C Orion, which operated from Al Minhad Air Base between December 2002 and June 2003, and six Dutch Army AH-64D Apaches that were sent to Afghanistan in April. At this point, the B-1B Lancers returned to the USA and the US Naval contribution was reduced to just one aircraft carrier. The contribution of carrier-borne fighter-bombers during the first phase of Operation *Enduring Freedom* should not be underestimated: three-quarters of the strike sorties were carried out by US Navy and USMC aircraft. Air operations over Afghanistan were now much reduced and had switched to a policing role rather than active combat operations. F-15E Strike Eagles and F-16 Fighting Falcons patrolled Afghanistan from their bases in Kuwait and Qatar, flying sorties which typically lasted up to ten hours. AC-130 gunships also undertook long night

A US Army CH-47 Chinook helicopter over the mountainous terrain near Jegdalek, approximately halfway between Kabul and Jalalabad, in September 2002. Able to lift heavy loads of cargo or troops, the Chinook was the workhorse of the ground forces in Afghanistan. (NARA)

missions. There were two unfortunate incidents in April and July 2002 when US aircrews attacked ground activity under the mistaken impression that they had been fired on themselves. The incidents caused significant damage to US prestige in the country because of the heavy-handed approach. The first occurred on 17 April when two F-16s from the Illinois Air National Guard (ANG) mistook a night live firing exercise by Canadian troops at the Carnak Farm facility to the south of Kandahar for hostile fire. Maj Harry Schmidt dropped a bomb onto the source of the shooting and killed four Canadian soldiers. The second incident happened on 1 July when an AC-130 crew fired on ground activity after they saw small arms fire being directed upwards. In fact, it was an Afghan wedding party, where it had become traditional to fire weapons into the air as part of the

celebrations. The resulting death of 48 people and wounding of 117 more resulted in the Afghan provisional governors demanding more control over US air operations.

The in-country air assets were increased when six A-10 Thunderbolts from the 74th Expeditionary Fighter Squadron (EFS) deployed from Al Jaber Air Base to Bagram on 23 March 2002. The 74th EFS was relieved shortly afterwards by the 706th EFS and the detachment of A-10s became a permanent fixture at Bagram, manned by personnel from different units which each took responsibility for the detachment for a 90-day period. The 706th EFS was a 'rainbow team' consisting of a mixture of regular and reservist personnel, and this format continued through the subsequent units which served at Bagram. A further improvement to the air support capability took place in October 2002 when six USMC AV-8B Harriers from VMF-513 deployed to Bagram. Concentrating on the night CAS role, the squadron brought only the AV-8B(NA) night attack variant, rather than the heavier and more complex radar-equipped AV-8B+. The choice proved a wise one in the austere conditions at Bagram and the night attack AV-8s maintained a high degree of serviceability

The Fairchild A-10A Thunderbolt II CAS aircraft were permanently deployed to Bagram Air Base from the summer of 2002. The aircraft, photographed in December 2002, is from the US Air Force Reserve Command (AFRC) 926th Fighter Wing, which was normally based in New Orleans. Both the AFRC and ANG deployed aircraft or pilots to Afghanistan in support of Operation *Enduring Freedom*. (NARA)

thanks largely to their simpler avionics. Equipped with the Litening II targeting pod, the AV-8Bs took over the night CAS role from the A-10s, which retained responsibility for daytime CAS missions. Because of the shortage of Litening II pods the A-10 would not receive them until the following year, and the AV-8Bs were also limited to just one pod in each pair; they operated as hunter-killer teams, with the leader configured with the Litening and a 1,000lb GBU-16 LGB, while the wingman carried two 500lb GBU-12 LGBs, or one bomb and one pod of Zuni 5-inch rockets.

Also in October 2002, 18 F-16AM Fighting Falcons from the EPAF deployed to Manas Air Base, replacing the contingent of French Air Force Mirages and the F/A-18s of VFMA(AW)-121 which returned home. Denmark, the Netherlands and Norway each provided six aircraft which were to remain at Manas for six months. Over the year of the EPAF deployment, there was a continuous presence of at least one pair of F-16s over Afghanistan every day, unless the weather conditions at Manas precluded flying. The Danish and Dutch F-16s were equipped with the LANTIRN targeting pod, but the Norwegians were not, so the pods were pooled to enable all of the aircraft to be LANTIRN-equipped and armed with LGBs. The Royal Norwegian Air Force (RNoAF) F-16s dropped their first live weapons on 27 January 2003, when aircraft were tasked to drop four LGBs onto a bunker near the town of Spin Boldak near the Pakistan border to the southeast of Kandahar; the first weapons drop by Royal Danish Air Force (RDAF) F-16s was on 4 February 2003, when aircraft were tasked to drop four LGBs onto a cave complex in southeast Afghanistan. The RNLAF F-16s dropped on a similar target the next day. On the night of 9 February, a pair of RNLAF F-16s was providing overwatch for a US convoy moving through the Lejay in the Baghran Valley some 160km north of Kandahar when the ground troops were ambushed by Taliban insurgents. The F-16s dropped a GBU-12 onto a suspicious vehicle, which enabled the convoy to continue, but all three EPAF F-16 contingents saw action in the same area over the next two days.

Although the three nations operated as a single detachment, each air force had to work within a different set of national Rules of Engagement (ROE). 'We always fly in national pairs – aircraft and

ABOVE A USAF C-130 Hercules is marshalled over rough ground at a forward operating base during December 2002. The aircraft was carrying supplies to Bagram Air Base. (USAF)

LEFT Grumman E-2C Hawkeye airborne early warning (AEW) aircraft were used to co-ordinate the airspace corridors through Pakistan into Afghanistan. This aircraft photographed in December 2002 is from VAW-121, part of CVW 7 embarked on USS *John F. Kennedy* (CV-67). (NARA)

With a backdrop of mountains, a USAF A-10 Thunderbolt from the 455th Air Expeditionary Wing (AEW), Bagram Air Base, takes off on a mission in support of Operation *Enduring Freedom*, January 2003. (NARA)

pilots of the same air force,' explained the detachment commander, Lt Col Jack Goense RNLAF. 'It's not that we operate in such different ways – on the contrary I would say – but it has to do with legal aspects in relation to the use of weapons.' With a transit between Manas and the operating area of between 1 ½ and 1 ¾ hours, sortie lengths were typically around six hours, but might last as long as ten hours. For these sorties the aircraft were armed with two 500lb GBU-12 LGBs. One RNoAF F-16 was written off on 19 December 2002 when it overran the runway at Bagram after diverting there because of the weather at Manas. The Bagram runway had a very poor braking surface, particularly if wet, and when it became apparent that aircraft would not stop in time the pilot ejected; the aircraft came to rest in the middle of a minefield. The remaining RNoAF F-16s returned to Norway as planned in April after six months, but the Dutch and Danish aircraft were extended until October 2003. However, in June the EPAF was informed that it could reduce its presence at Manas from 12 to eight aircraft, and each nation returned two of its F-16s home.

Because of differing ROE between the two partners, the RNLAF took responsibility for night missions, while the RDAF flew the day missions. This split of responsibilities became significant during Operation *Haven Denial* and Operation *Warrior Sweep* by ground forces in August 2003, when the demand for air support increased. The Danes were unable to participate in these missions, so the tasking was flown entirely by the RNLAF pilots. On 20 August, F-16s were called to support a convoy which had been ambushed to the east of Urgun, near the border with Pakistan about 190km south of Kabul. One F-16 fired 120 rounds during a strafing pass on the insurgents. Nine days later, responding to a troops in contact (TIC) event to the northeast of Kandahar, two F-16s dropped three GBU-12s on insurgent sniper positions, following up with strafing passes in which 400 rounds were fired. On the following day, 30 August, a pair of F-16s were again called to carry out three strafing passes.

Coalition air operations over Afghanistan were run under the auspices of the USAF Central Command Air Forces (USCENTAF), initially from the Combined Air Operations Center (CAOC) at Prince Sultan Air Base at Al Kharj Air Base in Saudi Arabia and then from the beginning of March 2003 from the newly built CAOC at Al Udeid Air Base in Qatar. The transfer to the new CAOC also marked the change of title of the command to USAFCENT. The CAOC was responsible for coordinating and tasking all air operations over both Afghanistan and Iraq, issuing a daily air task order (ATO) which gave specific instructions to each unit. Tactical management in-country was conducted by the Air Support Operations Center (ASOC), which had been established at Kandahar in the aftermath of Operation *Anaconda*. The ASOC co-ordinated the requests of the FACs, who were now termed 'Joint Terminal Attack Controllers' (JTACs).

A USAF Air Mobility Command (AMC) KC-135R Stratotanker from the 319th Air Refueling Wing, lands at 'a forward deployed location' in support of Operation *Enduring Freedom* in March 2003. AAR was another critical function during air operations over Afghanistan. (NARA)

There were two major events during 2003 which impacted directly on affairs in Afghanistan. Firstly, in March a US-led Coalition invaded Iraq, defeating the Iraqi forces and toppling the Ba'ath leadership. Thus started a long-running insurgency in Iraq

RIGHT The Combined Air Operations Center (CAOC) at Al Udeid Air Base in Qatar. The air campaigns over both Afghanistan and Iraq were controlled and co-ordinated here. (USAF)

BELOW A B-1B Lancer taking off for a mission over Afghanistan, February 2003. (NARA)

that would also call on Coalition air resources at the same time as they were required to support the ISAF operation in Afghanistan. Secondly, on 11 August NATO took over the lead of the ISAF mission in Afghanistan from the USA, but the US continued to run counter-terrorist operations in Afghanistan under Operation *Enduring Freedom*. Thus, there were, in effect, two parallel operations ongoing in the country. Initially the ISAF concentrated on establishing control of security in the area around Kabul, but it later expanded its operations over the next few years to include the rest of the country. Nevertheless, through most of 2003 and 2004, the situation in Afghanistan seemed to be relatively calm.

When he arrived at Bagram in June 2003 Col Bill Busby[16], commanding the 455th Expeditionary Operations Group, had said:

A Royal Danish Air Force (RDAF) F-16CM Fighting Falcon, operating from Ganci Air Base in Kyrgyzstan, refuels from a KC-10A Extender of the 380th Air Expeditionary Wing over Afghanistan in August 2003. The F-16 was part of the detachment of aircraft from the European Participating Air Forces (EPAF) operating from Ganci that delivered CAS for Coalition ground forces. (USAF)

our mission at Bagram is to kill, capture and deny sanctuary to al-Qaida and Taliban and provide humanitarian assistance to the Afghan people. I am confident that the 81st Expeditionary Fighter Squadron will help us take the fight to these terrorists and in so doing, significantly reduce the terrorist threat back home and around the world.

In the event, there was little call for the 81st EFS to use its weapons in anger, for it seemed that the Taliban and Al Qaeda had been defeated: although security incidents continued to occur, there was little sign of any sustained or co-ordinated resistance to ISAF policing. Aircraft routinely provided overwatch for convoys and ground patrols and if trouble was encountered a low-level 'show of force' flyby was frequently enough to deter any further activity by insurgents. However, so-called 'kinetic events' where weapons were employed did still occur occasionally. On 11 August, two A-10 Thunderbolt pilots from the 81st EFS, who had deployed from Spangdahlem Air Base in Germany just two days previously were called in to support ISAF troops involved in a TIC. The pair was led by Lt. Col. Pat Malackowski, commanding the 81st EFS, with newly combat-ready First Lt Erik Axt[17] on his wing. 'Afterward, I realized how much this combat sortie mirrored the training I received. We train like we fight,' commented Axt.

In October 2003 the A-10 detachment at Bagram began to receive the Litening II targeting pod, which gave the pilots a vastly improved capability over Afghanistan where target identification and the use of precision guided munitions both depended on the visual acquisition of the target. This was particularly crucial in responding to TIC incidents where insurgents might be in very close proximity to friendly forces. As Capt Matt McGarry[18], the weapons officer of the 355th EAS, explained:

Litening is another sensor to help us find targets, friendly forces and other points of interest – for example, a potential ambush site in front of a convoy. The pod gives us information we may not be able to see with the naked eye, binoculars or night-vision goggles ... With my eyes, I can see a vehicle. With binoculars, I can tell if it

is a car or a truck. With Litening, I can tell if the vehicle has been driven recently and how many people are standing next to it.

Also based at Bagram was the 41st Expeditionary Electronic Combat Squadron (EECS) equipped with the Lockheed EC-130H Compass Call electronic warfare aircraft, a derivative of the C-130 transport. The role of Compass Call was to support the ground operations and to deny the enemy the use of the radio frequencies.

Col Chris Kirschman[19], commander of the 41st EECS, described how:

When you transmit on a radio, Compass Call can see and hear what you're doing and very accurately locate where you are. Sometimes we tracked signals to help special forces find people that they couldn't see at night with drones or other aircraft. The system can jump from

Armed with AIM-120A advanced medium range air-to-air missiles (AMRAAM) on each wing tip and two GBU-12 500lb bombs, this USAF F-16C Fighting Falcon also carries an AN/AAQ-28(V) Litening targeting pod under the air intake. The aircraft is from 174th Fighter Wing, a New York ANG unit normally based in Syracuse, New York State, and seen here in flight over Afghanistan in November 2003. (NARA)

one frequency to another and jam many more frequencies simultaneously. When you begin talking on a walkie-talkie, Compass Call jams it. You would say what you're trying to say, but nobody would respond because nobody heard you. That delays the enemy's communications so people can get in and out before the adversary reacts. Our linguists listened to what enemies were trying to do and passed that to the ground forces. We knew where our infiltration and exfiltration points would be and would hear the adversary talk about going to the exfil. We told ground forces to use an alternate site to avoid getting ambushed. That happened nightly.

Another Compass Call operator, Col Don Bacon, added:

When special forces went after a high-value target, Compass Call would fly in the vicinity and take down all the early-warning systems in order to bomb the target. We would disable remote-controlled improvised explosive devices, blocking their ability to turn on or turning them on when we wanted.

By late 2004, B-1B Lancers were flying missions over Afghanistan once again, having redeployed to Thumrait and Diego Garcia in support of Operation *Enduring Freedom* and Operation *Iraqi Freedom* in August. After the transit to the operating area, B-1Bs might spend between

A USMC AV-8B Harrier from VMA-513 on the ramp at Bagram Air Base in August 2003. At one stage, the AV-8Bs were the only CAS aircraft based in the country. (NARA)

ABOVE A USMC AV-8B Harrier from VMA-513 takes off from Bagram Air Base for a combat sortie over Afghanistan. (NARA)

RIGHT This General Atomics MQ-1 Predator remotely piloted air system (RPAS), seen on approach to Kandahar, appears to have fired one of its AGM-114 Hellfire air-to-ground missiles. During the campaign in Afghanistan, RPAS took on an increasing share of reconnaissance and strike missions. (Stradling)

seven and 16 hours on task. With this long loiter capability and armed with up to 24 JDAMs, the B-1B was one of the most important air support assets over Afghanistan. In May 2004 one aircraft flew a 23-hour sortie after a storm hit Thumrait as it was about to land there, and the crew was forced to divert to Diego Garcia.

In the autumn of 2004, ISAF was reinforced to ensure the integrity of the Afghan presidential elections which were scheduled for 9 October 2004. The British contribution of six BAe Harrier GR7As from No.3 Sqn RAF deployed to Kandahar on 24 September, for what was intended to be a nine-month detachment. The Harriers would eventually leave Afghanistan five years later. The Dutch also dispatched six RNLAF F-16sAM to operate from Manas over the period from 10 September to 19 November. Meanwhile, the French were still concerned by the transit time from Manas Air Base to the operating area over Afghanistan and decided to move their operation

Between 2001 and 2006, USAF F-15E Strike Eagles continued to fly missions in support of Operation *Enduring Freedom*, operating around the clock from bases in the Persian Gulf. This aircraft taking off for a combat sortie over Afghanistan was photographed in late 2001. (NARA)

22 June 2005: A UH-60 Black Hawk helicopter flying over Kandahar province, carrying soldiers who were escorting former Afghan detainees back to their villages. (NARA)

to Dushanbe, Tajikistan, in October 2004. Three Dassault Mirage F1-CR reconnaissance aircraft began a 20-day reconnaissance and surveillance operation from there on 20 October.

As well as support helicopters, air transport and offensive support aircraft, electronic warfare aircraft were also deployed to Afghanistan. From November 2004, the EC-130H Compass Call based at Bagram were augmented by US Navy and Marine Corps EA-6B Prowlers, which were also based at Bagram, with individual units taking their turn for a six-month tour in the country. Originally intended to jam enemy radar signals, the role of the EA-6B in Afghanistan was to jam signals for systems such as mobile phones and garage door openers, which were being used by the Taliban to trigger IED. Additionally, the aircraft could serve as airborne radio relay stations where direct communication between agencies was not possible and could also monitor Taliban radio and telephone transmissions. Just as the Soviets had found in the 1980s, the lack of a port and the poor state of the transport infrastructure meant that everything from military hardware to rations had to be air freighted into the country. Like the AAR tanker support that had been such a vital part of the long-range operations at the start of Operation *Enduring Freedom*, air transport now took on an increased importance. Using C-17 Globemasters, an air bridge was established between Spangdahlem Air Base in Germany and Kabul and Bagram in Afghanistan. C-130 Hercules from the USAF and from other Coalition countries (including Australia, Belgium, Canada, Denmark, France, Greece, Japan, Italy, the Netherlands, New Zealand and Spain) also helped to bring supplies into the country and to distribute them to the smaller airfields that could not be served by the larger jet transports. Because of the shortage of fuel on the ground in Afghanistan, aircraft had to land with enough fuel to take off and either fly to an airfield in the Persian Gulf or refuel from an AAR tanker. The 28 CH-47 Chinooks on the US Army strength in Afghanistan were also used to resupply detachments of ground troops in remote areas.

A Lockheed EC-130H Compass Call electronic warfare aircraft belonging to the 41st Expeditionary Electronic Combat Squadron starting up at Bagram Air Base for a mission over Afghanistan on 22 January 2005. The aircraft deployed to Bagram in November 2004. (USAF)

An A-10 Thunderbolt II takes off on a combat mission from Bagram Air Base in December 2005, as maintenance crews prepare other aircraft for their next sortie. During the preceding three months, the A-10s at Bagram flew more than 1,700 combat sorties. (USAF)

During 2005 ISAF began to expand its mandate into western Afghanistan, but this move was met by a reinvigorated Taliban which had infiltrated Kandahar and Helmand provinces. The Taliban began an insurgency against the transitional government and its ISAF support. Guerrilla-style attacks and IED incidents against government officials, aid workers and security forces became more common. At the same time, the country began to gear up for elections to the National Assembly which would take place on 18 September 2005. With concerns about the security situation in Afghanistan, ISAF was strengthened by an extra 2,000 troops and its air support was increased. In February, the Dutch government approved the deployment of four RNLAF F-16s to Kabul to support ISAF, the Provincial Reconstruction Teams and the Afghan National Army (ANA). These aircraft arrived in theatre on 28 March and flew their first missions on 1 April. The Belgian government followed suit in the summer and four Belgian Air Force (BAF) F-16s arrived to join the Dutch element in Kabul on 12 July. A French force of three Mirage 2000Ds and Mirage F1-CRs was deployed to Dunshabe on 6 August 2005.

The 354th EFS from Davis Montham AFB, Arizona, took responsibility for the A-10 detachment at Bagram from 15 September 2005, in time to play their part in the security arrangements for the national elections, which took place three days later. As the squadron commander, Lt Col Martha McSally[20], reported a few months later:

Our A-10s have provided non-stop presence and lethal firepower since we arrived. From ensuring the success of Afghanistan's first-ever provincial elections on September 18 to the first seating of an Afghan national parliament in history on December 19, we are continuing to make a footprint on the world around us.

However, an indication of the worsening of the situation in Afghanistan was that in the 1,700 combat missions flown in the three months of its detachment, the 354th EFS had fired more than 20,000 rounds of 30mm cannon shells.

Another indication of a resurgent Taliban was the shooting down, to the northeast of Kandahar, of a US Army CH-47D on 24 September with the loss of all five crewmembers. Then, on 14 October two RAF Harrier GR7s were damaged during a mortar attack on Kandahar airfield and, in two separate incidents on 5 December to the north and northeast of Kandahar, two US Army CH-47s were also brought down by hostile fire.

Medical personnel from the German Army attached to the Kabul Multi-national Brigade Hospital receive familiarization training from the crew of US Army Sikorsky HH-60 Pave Hawk medical evacuation (medevac) helicopter, January 2003. (NARA)

The RAF British Aerospace (BAe) Harrier GR7s that had deployed to Kandahar in September 2004 were tasked with supporting Operation *Mountain Lion* during April 2006. This aircraft is armed with two pods of BAe Canadian Rocket Vehicle (CRV)-7 70mm rockets. (Townsend)

CHAPTER 4

TALIBAN INSURGENCY 2006–2008

As for the United States' future in Afghanistan, it will be fire and hell and total defeat, God willing, as it was for their predecessors – the Soviets and, before them, the British

Mohammed Omar

The increased Taliban insurgent activity in Afghanistan in late 2005 continued to gather momentum into the following year. Taliban leaders returning from Pakistan took advantage of inter-faction rivalry as well as the xenophobic tendencies of Afghans to foment discord across the country, especially in the green zones of Kandahar and Helmand. On 7 February, the Taliban incited a riot in the city of Maymana in response to the cartoons depicting the Prophet Mohammad that had been published in in the Danish newspaper *Jyllands-Posten* in the previous September. Situated in the northwest of the country, Maymana lies approximately halfway between Mazar-e-Sharif and Herat and at the time the Provincial Reconstruction Team (PRT) in the city was under the protection of Norwegian troops. The mob attacked the PRT headquarters in the centre of the city with rocks, Molotov cocktails and RPGs. Air support was called in by the resident JTAC and in response two RNLAF F-16 Fighting Falcons were launched from ground alert. The F-16s were soon overhead, but the CAOC would not authorize the aircraft to release weapons, despite repeated requests from the JTAC to do so, it since the situation did not comply with the Dutch ROE. Nor did it seem sensible to drop relatively large bombs onto a civilian crowd in a city centre, especially when the rest of the area was still relatively calm. In the end, the F-16s made low-level 'shows of force' and the Norwegian team was eventually relieved by British troops.

At the time, the EPAF F-16 detachment at Kabul comprised only the four RNLAF aircraft, as the Belgian participants in the detachment had departed from Afghanistan on 15 January. However, in a pre-planned rotation they were replaced on 15 February by four RNoAF aircraft. The Norwegian F-16s would remain at Kabul until 12 May, when they would be replaced in turn by four more Dutch aircraft, so from that date the strength of eight F-16s would be made up entirely of RNLAF aircraft.

Meanwhile, following decisions made the previous year, British and Canadian forces prepared to move into Helmand province to establish ISAF control over this former Taliban stronghold. With expansion into the north and west of the country, a total of nine PRTs would be operating in these regions. A FOB was established at Camp Bastion, some 30km northwest of Lashkar Gah. This large encampment would include a fully equipped hospital and an airstrip capable of taking large transport aircraft. As part of the initial deployment, four RAF C-130 Hercules were dispatched to Kandahar

A F-15E Strike Eagle from the 336th Expeditionary Fighter Squadron (EFS) on patrol over Afghanistan on 11 April 2006. The aircraft was detached from the 4th Fighter Wing based at Seymour Johnson AFB, North Carolina. (USAF)

in April. They were followed in May by the rest of 16 Air Assault Brigade, which included eight AgustaWestland AH-64D Apache AH1 attack helicopters and four AgustaWestland Lynx light utility helicopters from 9 Regiment Army Air Corps (AAC) supported by six CH-47 Chinooks from No.27 Sqn RAF. Based initially at Kandahar, some of these aircraft were then deployed forward to Camp Bastion once hangarage had been completed there. In a separate national deployment, the Australian Army sent two CH-47 Chinooks from the 5th Aviation Regiment to Kandahar to provide heavy troop airlift and medical evacuation support to the Australian SOF already operating in the country.

An F-15E Strike Eagle from the 336th EFS over the mountains and high desert of Afghanistan during a mission in support of Operation *Mountain Lion* on 12 April 2006. (USAF)

As insurgent activity ramped up, so, too, did the importance of intelligence, surveillance, target acquisition and reconnaissance (ISTAR). In 2006, Coalition ISTAR assets operating over Afghanistan included a USN Orion, as well as an RAAF AP-3 Orion based at Minhad Air Base in the UAE: these aircraft flew reconnaissance and counter-IED missions. Another maritime patrol aircraft (MPA), the RAF Nimrod MR2, was also employed in the ISTAR role, as well as providing more direct support to army units. Using the Wescam MX-15 electro-optic/IR sensor, the crew could pass on detailed descriptions to troops on the ground about any threats in their area: for example, telling them what was on the other side of the high walls of *kishlaks*, or around the corner of a street. With the capability to remain on task over the operational areas for extended periods, long-range MPAs were well-suited to intelligence gathering and surveillance.

RPAS were also now playing a larger part in ISTAR missions, and their endurance of 24 hours made them especially suited to the task of monitoring activity over a long period. Previously flown from Uzbekistan and Jacobabad,

During Operation *Mountain Lion* in the Kunar Valley, US Army AH-64D Apache attack helicopters provided CAS for the ground forces. (Crown Copyright/MoD)

MQ-1 Predator RPAS operations were transferred to Bagram and Kandahar from 2003. This coincided with the capability for 'remote split operations' using satellite communications to control the aircraft completely remotely, with the operating crew located at Creech AFB near Las Vegas, while a launch and recovery team at the deployed base flew the aircraft during the take-off and landing phases. From 2004, the CIA also carried out armed Predator operations from Shamsi in Pakistan, hunting for Taliban and Al Qaeda bases in the Federally Administered Tribal Areas along the border between Pakistan and Afghanistan. The same year saw introduction of the remotely operated video enhanced receiver (ROVER), a laptop-sized device which enabled the JTAC to see a direct video feed from the RPAS or an aircraft targeting pod. This made it much easier for the JTAC to talk the pilot

RIGHT Attached to the 455th Air Expeditionary Wing at Bagram Air Base, this A-10 Thunderbolt II is flying over Afghanistan during a combat mission in May 2006. (USAF)

BELOW During Operation *Mountain Lion*, USAF Boeing B-52 Stratofortress bombers, flying from Diego Garcia in the Indian Ocean, provided CAS for the ground forces. This B-52 is taking off for a combat mission over Afghanistan on 13 April 2006. (USAF)

onto the target, especially during a TIC when the enemy might be very close to friendly forces. It also enabled the JTAC to see for himself a 'god's eye view' of the battle area.

As the British and Canadian forces replaced those of the US in the southwest, the US Army was able to concentrate on the area around Jalalabad. Operation *Mountain Lion* was launched on the night of 11 April to extend the sovereignty of the Afghan government into this volatile region. The participating forces in Combined Joint Task Force 76 (CJTF-76) included the US Army 10th Mountain Division, USMC and ANA. Learning the lessons of Operation *Anaconda*, the planners of Operation *Mountain Lion* had liaised closely with the CAOC to ensure that air support was resourced, co-ordinated and tasked in advance. USAF A-10s, F-15Es and B-52s, as well as RAF Harrier GR7s, were all to fly missions in support of the ground forces. The troops were airlifted into the first objective in the Kunar Valley by helicopter, including CH-47s and Afghan Mi-17s escorted by US Army AH-64 and Afghan Mi-35 gunships. Air support continued throughout the operation, as did insertion by helicopters. On 5 May, the crew of a CH-47 Chinook carrying Lt Col Joseph M. Fenty, commander of 3rd Squadron, 71st Cavalry Regiment, was attempting to unload on a rocky outcrop, when a rotor blade struck a tree and the helicopter plunged 300m down the mountainside, killing all aboard.

During May 2006 air support was not limited to Operation *Mountain Lion* but covered ground activities across the country and day-on-day the number of offensive sorties began to increase. For example, on 14 May Coalition aircraft flew 16 CAS missions, including one by A-10s which responded to a TIC incident near Orgun-e, which lies close to the border with Pakistan some 180km to the south of Kabul. The next day, in which 24 CAS missions were flown, A-10s and a Predator RPAS struck a band of insurgents near Oruzgun, approximately 135km north of Kandahar, who had been responsible for numerous attacks in the area. In two separate attacks the aircraft engaged the group with Hellfire missiles, Paveway II LGBs and 30mm cannon, killing a number of them. A-10s and a B-1B also supported troops in another TIC event near Orgun. In addition, on the same day French Mirages commenced daily reconnaissance missions, using their electro-optical targeting pods as reconnaissance sensors. Twenty-four CAS missions were also flown on 16 May, this time including an AC-130 gunship and four A-10s, which were called in to support Coalition troops in contact with insurgents near Bagram and Kandahar. By 17 May, the number of CAS missions flown had risen to 30. A-10s provided CAS for Coalition troops in TIC incidents near Asmar in the Kunar Valley, Jalalabad and Orgun. Four A-10s working with a B-1B also supported Canadian troops as well as ANA forces and Afghan police during their operations against Taliban groups. The aircraft performed two separate attacks, killing 18 insurgents and enabling the ground forces to capture another 26.

In addition to these tasks each day, ISTAR aircraft flew intelligence gathering sorties over the country and USAF and RAF tanker aircraft supported both tactical strike and transport aircraft in theatre, with a daily transfer of a staggering one million kilogrammes of fuel. There were 160 air transport flights into both Afghanistan and Iraq on each of those days, delivering some 400 tonnes of supplies and 3,000 passengers each day. In addition, as part of the 'hearts and minds' aspect of Operation *Mountain Lion*, air transport aircraft dropped humanitarian aid packs into the areas from which the Taliban rebels had been cleared. On 16 May this amounted to some 3,000kg, as well as another 8,000kg of stores that were para-dropped to resupply troops in the field. Air transport flights were not without risk: on 26 May, an RAF Hercules was destroyed as it landed on the tactical

Aircraft drawn from the US AFRC and ANG were involved in the tactical air transport network across Afghanistan. Here a C-130 from the Texas ANG taxies on the ramp at Bagram Air Base on 31 May 2006. (USAF)

In the glow of the setting sun, a pair of General Dynamic F-16 Fighting Falcons taxi past a line of Lockheed AC-130 gunships at Kandahar Air Base. (Stradling)

landing zone at Lashkar Gah after detonating an anti-tank mine that had been buried under the airstrip.

The B-1B Lancers of the 9th EBS had been redeployed to Diego Garcia on 6 May and forward-based some of the aircraft from Thumrait. Since their last appearance over Afghanistan, two years previously, the aircraft had been substantially upgraded in the Block E modification programme and, in the words of B-1B pilot Maj Jonathan M. Creer[21]:

> the Block E modifications represented a quantum leap in computing capability, information management, and weapons innovations for the B-1 weapon system ... For many experienced B-1 commanders, the combined weapons, avionics, communications, and situational awareness upgrades on the aircraft by 2006 made it seem like an entirely new strike platform than it had been in 1998.

The modification package included the replacement of six 1970s-vintage computers with four Pentium high speed devices as well as giving compatibility with new precision-guided munitions, including the 500lb JDAM. This weapon had been introduced specifically for occasions when it was important to minimize collateral damage, for example when engaging enemy forces that were close either to friendly troops or to civilian bystanders.

Starting on 10 June, Operation *Mountain Thrust* was intended to clear Taliban strongholds from Kandahar, Zabul, Uruzgan, and Helmand. Here US, Afghan, British and Canadian forces carried out a

The 2,000th air transport movement into Bagram Air Base since May 2006 was flown on 2 September by a C-17 Globemaster III from the 62nd Airlift Wing. During that summer, there was an average of 17 such movements each day. The aircraft is being guided to its parking spot by a 'Follow Me' truck. (USAF)

series of search and destroy missions each targeted on a Taliban stronghold. Troops were supported by ISTAR assets and CAS aircraft. The activity on 13 July gives a good idea of the intensity of the action: there were airstrikes in support of ISAF ground troops at Musa Qala (on the river valley running north from Sangin), Tarin Kowt (also written Tarinkot) 110km due north of Kandahar, and Gereshk, on the Helmand River halfway between Sangin and Lashkar Gah. A-10s and a B-1B intervened when Coalition forces came under attack from small arms fire and RPGs near Musa Qala. The enemy fire ceased after the B-1B dropped a GBU-31 onto the Taliban position. RAF Harriers also took part in CAS missions in this area. At Tarin Kowt, once again, A-10s and a B-1B broke up a TIC: the B-1B dropped GBU-13s and GBU-38s onto a bunker being used by the insurgents as well as a Taliban mortar position and insurgents hiding in a treeline. Shortly afterwards, A-10s were called in by another ISAF unit involved in a firefight with insurgents in the same area, strafing enemy positions and dropping 500lb bombs and a GBU-12 onto them. A-10s were also in action near Gereshk, strafing and bombing a compound that was being used as a fire base by insurgents from which to engage ISAF forces. RAF Harriers also flew CAS missions in this area.

At the beginning of June, a joint detachment of 14 A-10s from the 81st FS and 303rd FS deployed to Bagram. The detachment was known as the 384th EFS (achieved by adding 81 and 303 together). At first there was little action, but the pilots soon found themselves responding to TICs on almost every sortie. In the early hours of 27 June, Capt Matthew Robins led a pair of A-10s for a complex CAS mission in which he and wingman Lt Jay Pease supported an ANA convoy and a SOF foot patrol that had become separated from it near Sangin. Because of the terrain the patrol, convoy and nearby FOB were unable to communicate with each other, but Robins could speak with and see all the groups, so was able to co-ordinate support fire. During the 6½hr sortie, the A-10s strafed Taliban machine gun posts that were engaging both the convoy and the patrol, enabling the foot patrol to regain the convoy and for the friendly forces to disengage themselves safely.

On 4 June 2006, a force of British Army paratroops and Gurkhas accompanied by ANA troops set out on Operation *Mutay*, to secure a Taliban compound near Now Zad. The paratroopers were inserted by two RAF CH-47 Chinooks, which came under fire as soon as they landed. The Gurkhas and ANA, who were based in the Now Zad platoon house, were transported in vehicles. Air support for the troops was provided by A-10s and British AAC AH-64D Apaches, which suppressed the insurgent fire sufficiently for the paratroops to secure and search the compound. Meanwhile, the Gurkha and ANA convoy was ambushed, and the troops were forced to take cover behind a mud wall. After an hour-long sustained firefight, the Gurkha JTAC was able to retrieve his radio and called in Apache gunships which made three strafing runs. Although the Taliban still held on to their positions, the Gurkhas and ANA were able to withdraw safely.

Operation *Augustus* was a British-led search and cordon operation near Sangin, which opened in the early hours of 15 July. Troops from

The organic CAS assets used by the USMC included the Bell AH-1W Super Cobra. This aircraft from HMLA-169 was photographed departing from FOB Dwyer, near Garmsir, Helmand province in 2010. (USMC)

ABOVE An AV-8B Harrier from VMM-365 lands on USS *Iwo Jima* (LHD-7) on 9 September 2006 after a mission over in Afghanistan. The Harriers were part of the Aviation Combat Element of the 24th Marine Expeditionary Unit (MEU). (USMC)

RIGHT In the background, a Canadian Armed Forces Lockheed C-130 Hercules on the approach to Kandahar Air Base as two McDonnell Douglas AV-8B Harriers from the 24th MEU are re-armed. (USMC)

the 3rd Battalion Parachute Regiment were inserted by CH-47 Chinooks in darkness, supported by AH-64 Apaches. The next day was another busy one for offensive support aircraft across Afghanistan, with 30 CAS missions flown, as well as ISTAR and reconnaissance missions. A B-1B dropped GBU-38s onto Taliban-held buildings near Musa Qala, while A-10s and Harriers responded to a TIC

incident near Oruzgan where a SOF team was involved in a fierce firefight with insurgents. Noticing that the two sides were too closely engaged to allow CAS intervention, Capt Scott Markle flying the lead A-10 made a low pass dropping flares and succeeded in generating some space between the sides. Markle and Lt David Kikendall then strafed three insurgent machine gun positions and bombed them with 500lb Mk 82 airburst fused bombs. This action enabled the SOF team to withdraw safely. Then in another engagement, A-10s, a B-1B and Harriers provided CAS near Tarin Kowt, and once again the B-1B shut down Taliban fire with GBU-31s and -38s.

Having driven off Taliban forces, the British Army was faced with the dilemma of having to control a large region with a relatively small number of troops. It adopted the policy of covering the area of

Kandahar Air Base: An MH-47E Chinook, from the 160th Special Operations Aviation Regiment, which has been optimized for use by SOF. (Stradling)

responsibility by placing small units in 'platoon houses' across the region. However, this proved to be a flawed strategy, since the Taliban had left only temporarily and soon drifted back, recruiting large bands of local rebels that outnumbered the troops: individual platoon houses were frequently attacked and almost overrun by insurgent bands, who then laid siege to them. With the road access cut off, the only method of resupply was by helicopter, adding to the workload of the CH-47 Chinook crews and their AH-64 Apache and Lynx escorts. The helicopters often came under fire while landing to drop off supplies or pick up casualties. CAS aircraft were also frequently called on to intervene when the platoon houses came under sustained attack.

Between 1 July and 22 July, the platoon house in Now Zad was the subject of 28 separate attacks by Taliban insurgents, some lasting as long as six hours. The main attack occurred on 12 July, when the building was heavily fired on from multiple well-prepared positions, some of which were located along a treeline and in a building to the north of the platoon house. These were strafed by A-10s and AH-64s, but in response the insurgents simply withdrew until the aircraft had departed and then resumed their assault. Further airstrikes eventually drove off the Taliban, but they reattacked the following night. On this occasion, the contact was broken by an airstrike of A-10s. Then on 16 July another insurgent attack was driven off by an AH-64 Apache, although the Taliban attempted unsuccessfully to shoot down the helicopter with a AAA gun.

Such overwhelming attacks were not restricted to British positions. Fire Base Chalekor (Shal Kalay) on the Arghandab River some 130km to the northeast of Kandahar and manned by US Infantry from the 10th Mountain Division had repelled an attack by a band of ten insurgents on 5 June. After a three-hour firefight, a B-1B bombed enemy positions, causing them to break contact and flee. On 19 July the fire base was attacked again, this time from at least eight directions by approximately 150 guerrillas. These were mainly local men, led and co-ordinated by Taliban insurgents. The US troops called for air support, which arrived almost immediately in the form of a B-1B. Over a three-hour period, the bomber dropped more than 26 bombs on enemy positions, eventually driving off the insurgents.

The British Army platoon positioned in the centre of Musa Qala was also effectively besieged by the Taliban for most of July. On 21 July, a column set off from Camp Bastion to relieve the small garrison of paratroopers, but it took five days to reach Musa Qala and the

OPPOSITE As an illustration of the scale of the AAR task in support of operations over Afghanistan, on 15 September 2006 Coalition AAR tankers flew 46 sorties and transferred approximately one million kilogrammes of fuel to 210 receiving aircraft. Photographed on that day is a US Navy McDonnel Douglas F/A-18 Hornet refuelling from a USAF McDonnel Douglas KC-10. (US DofD)

BELOW A Fairchild A-10 Thunderbolt II from the 455th AEW takes off from Bagram Air Base on the first day of operations from the new runway on 20 December 2006. (USAF)

intervention of a B-1B was needed to extract the relief column from a Taliban ambush on the outskirts of the town. The column was unable to break through the Taliban positions to the platoon house, and was forced to withdraw. Then on 1 August, the paratroopers attempted to break out of the garrison and link up with another combined Danish and Irish force that was due to replace them. More B-1B strikes onto known Taliban strongholds were needed before the relief force could link up with the paratroopers.

The pace of operations picked up during August and September, with almost daily 'kinetic' events when live weapons were expended. The areas around Musa Qala and Kandahar were particular trouble spots, as ISAF and ANA troops took the battle to Taliban strongholds. The 25 CAS missions flown on 15 August included three separate engagements near Musa Qala: Harrier GR7s firing rockets and dropping Paveway II LGBs in response to a TIC incident near Musa Qala, A-10s providing CAS to troops near Musa Qala and a B-1B supporting ISAF troops near Musa Qala and again near Kandahar. Two days later RAF Harriers used CRV-7 rockets and also bombs near Musa Qala and again near Kandahar, and a USAF B-1B dropped a GBU-31 onto a mortar position near Musa Qala. Also on this day, A-10s strafed a group of insurgents near Moqor (halfway between Kabul and Kandahar), and French Mirage 2000s and A-10s were in action over Asadabad. B-1Bs, A-10s and Harriers were involved in two separate incidents near Musa Qala and one near Kandahar again

OPPOSITE A USAF F-15E Strike Eagle, from the 336th EFS, armed with AIM-120 AMRAAM, 500lb GBU-12 bombs and GBU-31 JDAM, flying a CAS mission during Operation *Mountain Lion*. In contrast to Operation *Anaconda*, four years earlier, air support was properly planned and resourced. (NARA)

BELOW A B-1B Lancer takes off from Thumrait Air Base in Oman for a mission over Afghanistan on 5 March 2007. (USAF)

on 26 August, one near Kandahar and another near Musa Qala on 27 August and yet another near Musa Qala on 28 August. During these days A-10s continued to engage insurgents near Asadabad in the east of the country and CAS aircraft employed weapons near Tarin Kowt and Now Zad, both in the mountains to the north of Kandahar.

An RNLAF F-16 crashed near Ghazni, 130km southwest of Kabul, on 31 August. The pilot, Capt Michael Donkervoort, had been flying at high level when he put out a distress call, but did not eject and was killed. The accident was not considered to have been caused by enemy action. A search and recovery mission was launched immediately, involving an RC-135 Rivet Joint, Predator RPAS and A-10s, as well as HH-60G Pave Hawk helicopters. The Pave Hawks were used for MEDEVAC missions, known colloquially as 'Dustoff' missions, and typically the crews mounted three medevac operations each day, recovering troops who had been wounded in action. CAS airstrikes near Musa Qala continued on 31 August, with two being carried out by USAF B-1Bs and one by RAF Harriers; the latter also fired rockets on Taliban mortar positions near Now Zad.

OPPOSITE The General Dynamics GAU-12/U Equalizer 25mm rotary cannon mounted on the port side of a Lockheed AC-130U Spooky gunship, based at Kandahar Air Base. The majority of missions flown by the type were during the hours of darkness. (Stradling)

BELOW A Strike Eagle takes off from Bagram Air Base to support ISAF ground operations on 21 May 2007. On that day, Coalition offensive support aircraft flew 66 CAS missions in support of ISAF. (USAF)

ABOVE A RNLAF F-16AM Fighting Falcon over Kandahar in 2007. From the summer of 2006, the EPAF contingent in Afghanistan was made up entirely by RNLAF aircraft. (Netherlands MoD)

RIGHT A C-130H Hercules, from the Minnesota ANG, takes off from Bagram Air Base on 27 March 2007. (USAF)

A second fatal accident occurred just two days later on 2 September when an RAF Nimrod MR2 exploded in mid-air after refuelling from a tanker aircraft near Kandahar. Fuel had leaked into a wing section that was heated by engine exhaust gas which ignited it, causing an explosion that destroyed the aircraft and killed all on board. Once again, a search and recovery mission was initiated with Predators and Pave Hawks. Meanwhile, Operation *Medusa*, a Canadian-led offensive to clear the Taliban from Panjwai in the green belt along Arghandab River immediately to the west of Kandahar, had already commenced. In two incidents near Kandahar on the same day USAF B-1Bs and A-10s, RAF Harriers and French Mirage 2000s employed weapons against Taliban forces and the Harriers and A-10s were in action again over Musa Qala.

Air support for Operation *Medusa* continued over the next two weeks, including missions flown from USS *Enterprise*, which took up station in the Arabian Sea at the beginning of the month with CVW-1 embarked. F/A-18C Hornets of VFA-86 flew the first missions over Afghanistan on 3 September, dropping a GBU-38 onto insurgents engaging ISAF troops near Qalat (120km northeast of Kandahar). On the same day, there were three separate TIC incidents in the Operation *Medusa* area near Kandahar, involving USAF B-1Bs, A-10s and RAF Harriers, as well as two further engagements near Now Zad and two more near Musa Qala. The F/A-18Cs flew further missions the next day, 4 September, joining A-10s in the Kandahar/ Operation *Medusa* area, RAF Harriers near Musa Qala and a B-1B at a TIC incident near Tarin Kowt. Unfortunately, during one airstrike near Pamjwai (30km due west of Kandahar Air Base), an A-10 mistakenly strafed a Canadian position, killing one soldier and wounding 30 others. Meanwhile, a US SOF team had seized the summit of Sperwan Ghar, a 3,000ft hill some 5km southwest of Panjwai which overlooked the whole area and gave a clear field of view for the JTAC team. That night an AC-130 gunship was called in to engage a group of 200 insurgents who were gathering to the north of the Arghandab River for a counter-attack, and neutralized all of them.

The next day the Taliban launched a concerted attack to regain Sperwan Ghar, but they were driven off in a five-hour firefight with almost continuous CAS support. The F/A-18E Super Hornets of

Electronic Warfare (EW) played a surprisingly significant role in the Afghan campaign, both in intercepting Taliban radio and telephone traffic and in jamming the frequencies used to trigger IEDs. Here a USMC Grumman EA-6B Prowler operating from Bagram Air Base is conducting EW operations over eastern Afghanistan. (USAF)

VFA-211 flying from USS *Enterprise* saw action dropping 500lb GBU-12s onto Taliban positions in the area. By 9 September, over 40 CAS missions were being flown each day and 9 September itself was a day of heavy activity. There were four separate TIC incidents in the Kandahar/Medusa area, the first of which involved A-10s, a B-1B, a Predator, F/A-18s and RAF Harriers. Attacking various insurgent positions, the A-10s used cannon fire and GBU-12s, while the B-1B dropped GBU-31 and GBU-38 and the Predator fired Hellfire missiles. The F/A-18s dropped GBU-31 and GBU-38 and RAF Harriers fired rockets and dropped a 540lb bomb. In the other three separate incidents, A-10s and Harriers responded to the call for support with cannon, bombs and rockets. F/A-18s also responded to two separate TICs near Musa Qala and one near Gereshk, driving off the insurgents with cannon fire. A B-1B provided CAS for troops near Oruzgun and in the east of the country, and A-10s supported ISAF troops in the Kunar Valley.

Over the next six days, Coalition aircraft, including the AV-8B Harrier IIs of the 24th MEU operating from the USS *Iwo Jima* (LHD 7) as well as French Mirage 2000s, delivered CAS to ISAF forces at Lashkar Gah, Musa Qala, Sangin and Gereshk in the Kandahar/Helmand area, at Oruzgun and Now Zad to the north and at Shkin (on the border 40km south of Urgun), Asadabad and Khost in the

east. In addition, the AV-8Bs responded to a TIC near Shindand in the west of the country.

On 16 September, Operation *Mountain Fury* was launched in the east of the country, aiming, over a six-week period, to clear Taliban influence from the provinces of Paktika, Paktya, Khost, Ghazni and Logar (known colloquially as 'P2KGL') near the Pakistan border. This offensive involved around 7,000 US Army and ANA troops, many of whom were inserted to the operational area by helicopters from the 10th Combat Aviation Brigade (CAB), which included a fleet of CH-47 Chinooks, UH-60 Black Hawks and AH-64 Apache attack helicopters. A-10s supported troops in contact with insurgents near Orgun and Jalalabad on 17 September, a day on which Coalition aircraft flew 54 CAS missions. Despite the new offensive in the east, there was still a requirement to support troops in Kandahar and Helmand, for although Operation *Medusa* ended on 17 September, the Taliban had far from given up their insurrection in those provinces. US Navy F/A-18s flew CAS missions over Musa Qala while USAF A-10s and USMC AV-8Bs supported ISAF forces near Deh Rawood. Offensive support missions against Taliban forces near Musa Qala, Lashkar Gah, Garmsir and Gereshk continued with A-10s, B-1Bs, F/A-18C and Fs, and RAF Harriers employed live weapons on most days

AAF Mi-17 helicopters take off for a formation practice in preparation for the flypast at the 2007 Afghan National Day in Kabul. The rugged Mi-17 was the most numerous aircraft type in the AAF inventory. (USAF)

throughout the rest of September. By 21 September, the USMC Harriers of the 24th MEU had flown 136 combat missions over Afghanistan and had dropped 17 LGBs.

There had been a rapid increase the number of munitions delivered by US aircraft in 2006: in 2004 weapons were used on only 86 CAS sorties but in 2006 they were employed on 1,770 sorties. The RAF Harrier GR7 detachment dropped fewer than 20 LGBs in 2005, but in 2006 the figure was nearly 80; if the expenditure of free-fall bombs and CRV-7 rockets is included, the total number of weapon releases by RAF Harriers increased from 58 in 2005 to 326 in 2006. The activities of offensive support aircraft took place against the background of routine air transport flights carrying cargo and passengers into the country by strategic transports such as the C-17 (which flew by far the largest majority of flights), RAF TriStars, Luftwaffe Airbus A310s and CAF Airbus CC-150 Polaris, as well as chartered civilian Russian types such as Il-76s, An-12s and An-124s. In 2006 there were nearly 58,000 US airlift flights serving operations in both Iraq and Afghanistan. These fed into a distribution network of smaller aircraft, such as the ubiquitous C-130 Hercules, and also helicopters, including the CH-47 Chinook, CH-53 Super Stallions

and even Mi-17s to move reinforcements and supplies to the dispersed FOB airstrips. Where no suitable airfield existed, supplies were dropped to ground forces and in 2006, this amounted to 1,600 tonnes. With GPS guided joint precision airdrop system (JPADS), which was first employed on 31 August, supplies could be air dropped from high altitude onto the DZ with great accuracy. In addition to the airlift, there were over 12,000 AAR support sorties by US tankers (again serving both Iraq and Afghanistan) in 2006.

Helicopters played a critical role in the air support to ground forces. AH-64 Apaches flown by the US, Dutch and British armies as well as USMC AH-1W Super Cobra gunships provided fire support to ground operations, complementing the CAS missions flown by fast-jet aircraft. Transport helicopters such as the CH-46 and CH-47 played a crucial role inserting troops into position for ground operations, as well as flying vital supplies to troops in dispersed locations. A vital role played by the RAF CH-47 Chinook force from 2006 was the medical emergency response team (MERT). The MERT was based at Camp Bastion and comprised a single Chinook which carried a medical team comprising a doctor, an emergency nurse and two paramedics; in addition, four RAF Regiment gunners could

A US Navy P-3C Orion MPA from VP-16 on a flight in support of forces deployed for Operation *Enduring Freedom* during 2002. Fitted with sophisticated communications, detection, monitoring and reconnaissance sensors, the P-3C was an ideal platform for the ISTAR role over Afghanistan. (NARA)

ABOVE The F-15E Strike Eagle continued to be one of the most important offensive support aircraft in the Coalition inventory. Here a pair of F-15Es patrol over Afghanistan on 13 June 2007. (USAF)

RIGHT After the improvements made to the runway at Bagram Air Base in the previous December, a Lockheed C-5A Galaxy landed at the base for the first time on 22 September 2007. Previously, loads had been flown in by C-17 Globemaster III and C-130 transports. (USAF)

engage enemy forces if required to allow the paramedic to recover the casualties. The MERT was kept on immediate alert at Camp Bastion 24 hours a day, 365 days of the year. In contrast to the single ad hoc MERT helicopter, USAF and US Army 'Dustoff' medevac teams were drawn from dedicated combat search and rescue (CSAR) units, flying the HH-60G Pave Hawk. The Dustoff helicopters did not carry the same medical equipment and personnel as those carried on a MERT Chinook, but their crews included two pararescue jumpers (PJ) who were qualified as both paramedics and parachutists. Both MERT and Dustoff helicopters aimed to evacuate casualties to proper medical facilities within the so-called 'golden hour' – for if the casualty could be treated within 60min of being injured, their chances of survival were greatly increased.

A French Navy Dassault Super Étendard performs a touch and go landing on the USS *John Stennis* (CVN-74) in the North Arabian Sea on 12 April 2007. Super Étendards and Dassault Rafales were flying combat missions over Afghanistan from the French carrier *Charles de Gaulle* (R-91).(USN)

The new $68 million runway at Bagram was opened on 20 December 2006, significantly improving the operational capabilities of the base. The old runway was showing considerable signs of wear and tear after decades of use and a new one was badly needed. The new runway was much stronger than the previous one, as well as being some 2,000ft longer, enabling it to support aircraft such as the Lockheed C-5 Galaxy. The improved facilities at Bagram enabled the deployment in early January 2007 of USAF F-15E Strike Eagles of the 391st EFS, replacing the detachment of A-10s which had been there for the previous five years. With its radar and other sensors, the F-15E was a more robust CAS platform in the winter months. Meanwhile, the runway at Kandahar was not standing up well to heavy use either.

RAF Harrier pilot Sqn Ldr Ian Townsend recalled:

After each take off, the runway would disintegrate due to the poor Soviet design [one inch tarmac and then simply a layer of gravel]. This meant that our first jet would take off from the threshold almost certainly damaging the runway at the 'STO point' [where the nozzles were rotated to launch airborne]. The second jet would then enter the runway at a point after the damage and do what Harrier did so well i.e. short take offs. Once airborne, any available Sqn personnel would be stood next to the runway with brushes ready to sweep the gravel back into the hole, remove any massive chunks of runway [of which there were plenty] and, once complete, a tarmac lorry would appear, fill the hole, flatten the surface and wait for the jets to arrive 2 hours later at which point the runway was good enough to use again.

On 15 January 2007, British troops from 45 Commando Royal Marines (RM) mounted Operation *Glacier 2* to drive Taliban forces from the Jugroom Fort complex, near Garmsir. The Marines were supported by two Apaches from 656 Sqn Army Air Corps (AAC) flown by Capt Tom O'Mally and WO Ed Macy as well as a B-1B. During a ferocious firefight, four Marines were wounded, and the team was forced to withdraw. However, on regrouping it was discovered that one of the wounded soldiers, L/Cpl Matthew Ford, was missing. He was located by an Apache crew, apparently disabled, close to the position that the Marines had just been forced to leave. The only means of reaching him was by helicopter, and a plan was hastily conceived whereby two commandos lashed themselves onto

After flying from Manas Air Base in Kyrgyzstan to pick up their cargo on 11 October 2007, two Boeing C-17 Globemaster III from the 817th Expeditionary Airlift Squadron completed one of the largest single airdrops in Afghanistan since Operation *Enduring Freedom* began. This image shows the second aircraft releasing its load of bundles above the first during the combat cargo drop in Paktika province. (US Army)

A Boeing C-17 Globemaster III takes off from an airfield in Afghanistan on 2 November 2007, while another similar aircraft waits to cross the runway. (USAF)

the stub wings of each of the Apaches and were flown into position to make the rescue. Despite heavy fire from the Taliban, the Apaches landed close to Ford and he was successfully recovered. Unfortunately, despite the successful rescue, Ford subsequently died during the transfer to Camp Bastion in the MERT helicopter.

Between 30 January and 4 February 2007, 42 Commando RM carried out Operation *Volcano* to clear the village of Barikju near the Kajaki Dam. The village was a complex of 26 compounds which were being used as a strongpoint by Taliban forces. During the operation Wg Cdr Andy Lewis, commanding No.1 Sqn RAF, scrambled from ground alert CAS (GCAS) after the Marines became pinned down by heavy fire from a compound. After Lewis dropped an EPW II into one compound, the No.2 Harrier fired CRV-7 rockets into three more compounds that were being used by enemy firing parties. Shortly afterwards, the Apache helicopters arrived on the scene, but they could not identify their target; however, Lewis was able to mark the aiming point using the thermal imaging airborne laser designation (TIALD) pod, enabling the helicopters to attack with Hellfire laser-guided missiles. By now the Harriers were running short of fuel, but before they recovered to Kandahar, Lewis dropped another EPW II into a compound which was being used as the Taliban headquarters.

Operation *Volcano* was followed by Operation *Kryptonite* on 10 to 12 February to clear the Kajaki Dam from insurgents. Both operations were precursors to Operation *Achilles* by ISAF and ANA troops from early March to the end of May to clear the Taliban from Helmand province. During a surveillance and overwatch mission in support the ground operation near Qurya on 4 March, the Harrier pilots and the JTAC all noticed suspicious personnel climbing onto the roof of a nearby building. The JTAC believed them to be Taliban insurgents preparing an ambush and this was confirmed when he came under small arms fire. At this point the Harriers carried out a show of force, releasing nine flares as they flew past the insurgent position. This manoeuvre had the desired effect and the JTAC reported enemy fire had ceased and that ISAF forces had moved into cover. The next day, the Harriers provided surveillance of an enemy compound and known enemy firing positions near Sangin. Two weeks later, on 21 March, a pair of Harriers responded to a call from ISAF troops who were pinned down by heavy enemy fire coming from a hillside. They dropped 540lb bombs and an EPW II on the enemy position and fired CRV-7s onto the hillside, successfully silencing the enemy fire. On the same day, the Taliban were also active near the Kajaki Dam and a building that was being used by insurgents was destroyed by an EPW II dropped by a Harrier. Then on 29 March, Harriers were called in by a JTAC to fire CRV-7 and drop an airburst 540lb bomb on Taliban firing positions near the dam. After these weapons were employed, the JTAC confirmed that the enemy fire had ceased.

Armed with AGM-114 Hellfire missiles and 500lb GBU-12 LGBs, a General Atomics MQ-9 Reaper RPAS approaches to land after a mission over Afghanistan in November 2007. (USAF)

The Dassault Rafale made its operational debut over Afghanistan in March 2007. Three French Air Force Rafales deployed to Dushanbe on 12 March and General Stephane Abrial[22] described how:

> at the operational level, the aircraft's multi-role capability permits a leap forward. Link 16 will make it possible to work in a network with all the other actors in the theatre. With its air-to-air capability, the aircraft has the means to defend itself, and radar equipment is useful in an area with no airspace control ... In its air-to-ground capability, [Rafale] can carry six bombs, as against the Mirage 2000's two.

The Rafales operated with the Mirage 2000Ds which provided co-operative laser designation for the LGBs carried by the Rafales. Three more French Navy Rafales, which had joined the carrier Charles de Gaulle earlier in the month, began flying over Afghanistan on 15 March. Cdr Patrick Zimmermann[23], commanding the embarked squadron, explained:

After receiving fuel over Afghanistan, a B-1B Lancer from the 9th Expeditionary Bomb Squadron pulls away from a KC-135 Stratotanker of the 22nd Expeditionary Air Refueling Squadron in January 2008. (USAF)

Despite the deployment of the General Atomics MQ-9 Reaper, the MQ-1 Predator RPAS remained an important part of the air campaign over Afghanistan. This Predator has recently landed back at Bagram Air Base after a combat mission. (USAF)

There is a whole range of missions. Photographic reconnaissance, pre-emption with the opening up of routes for convoys on the ground in order to identify possible ambushes; deterrence using a 'show of force'; rapid low altitude passes over hostile groups. And of course, strikes, if absolutely necessary.

In the case of naval Rafales, the laser designation was provided by Super Étendards.

In the last week of March, B-1B Lancers were in action over Sangin almost daily. Two shows of force were also flown on 21 March: one over a police station in Jalalabad that was surrounded by and taking fire from insurgents; the other was at Worzhanah Kalay (near the Pakistan border, 160km south of Kabul) where a Coalition convoy was negotiating a known ambush point. An aggressive low pass by the bomber, releasing multiple flares as it flew over, was enough to dissuade insurgents from engaging the convoy. Exactly a week later, B-1Bs dropped 2,000lb GBU-31s on four buildings being used by insurgents in Sangin. On the same day, F-15Es dropped bombs on enemy-occupied buildings and strafed insurgent firing positions hidden in the nearby green zone. On 4 April, Operation *Silver* mounted by US, British, Canadian, Danish and Estonian troops, supported by the ANA, recaptured Sangin. There was little opposition since the Taliban had withdrawn so that the poppy crop would not be damaged by extensive fighting.

The reconnaissance assets available to NATO ground forces were increased with the arrival at Mazar-e-Sharif on 5 April of six Luftwaffe Panavia Tornados from Aufklärungsgeschwader 51 '*Immelmann*'. These aircraft began flying operational sorties over Afghanistan on 15 April. Twelve USAF A-10 Thunderbolts also returned to Bagram in April 2007, when the 354th EFS arrived on 17 April to complement the F-15E Strike Eagle squadron, which remained in theatre.

The last day of April saw another phase of Operation *Achilles* with the advance by 1,000 ISAF troops and ANA forces into the Sangin Valley. The advance pushed northwards, driving Taliban insurgents from Gereshk and the surrounding settlements. The operation continued

A USAF F-15E Strike Eagle over Afghanistan on 28 May 2008 after refuelling from a KC-135R Stratotanker of the 22nd Expeditionary Air Refueling Squadron. (USAF)

through May. Heavy fighting continued through the summer of 2007 and Coalition troops faced not just Taliban forces, but also a mixture of militias loyal to various tribal warlords taking the opportunity to settle old scores, as well as criminal gangs. In response to the insurgency, ISAF troop numbers were increased and by June 2007 there were some 36,750 troops under ISAF command in Afghanistan, plus another 20,000 US troops engaged in Operation *Enduring Freedom*. The ISAF troops were drawn from 37 countries, with the largest contingent from the USA, which had deployed 15,000 troops, followed by the UK, with 7,700 troops. These figures would rise further over the next two years. Approximately half of the ISAF contingent was in Regional Command – South (RC–S) which was responsible for Helmand and Kandahar provinces. The Dutch contingent had responsibility for the Chora area near Tarin Kowt and between 16 and 19 June the Dutch army, with support from the Australian Special Air Service Regiment (SAS), mounted a battalion-sized operation to clear Taliban influence this

A British Army AgustaWestland Apache Longbow AH-64D attack helicopter fires a salvo of CRV-7 rockets at insurgents during a patrol in June 2008. (Crown Copyright/MoD)

region. The successful operation was supported by RNLAF F-16 Fighting Falcons.

In 2007 Coalition aircraft mounted on average 40 CAS sorties each day in support of ISAF troops. One of the most important CAS assets over Afghanistan was the B-1B Lancer. In July, the B-1B equipped 9th EBS began to replace the 34th EBS at Al Udeid and crews were soon in the fray. Recalling one incident in late July in which Taliban fighters were engaging Coalition forces at close range from two directions, B-1B weapons system operator (WSO) Capt Matt Steele[24] described how:

> we heard the JTAC say 'I need a show of force NOW!' and you could hear AK-47s in the background, I was punching out flares with my left hand and writing down his nine-line with my right, it happened that quickly. Normally you'll get a response with some [bomb damage assessment] fairly quickly, but after a long period of silence, all we heard was 'Stand by for next nine-line.'

The show of force was enough to make the insurgents pull back from close quarters and seek cover in a tree-line, enabling the B-1B crew to strike them with bombs. After refuelling, the B-1B returned to the scene, where the insurgents were now attempting to capture two vehicles that had been abandoned by the Coalition troops. The bomber destroyed both vehicles to deny their valuable contents to the Taliban.

The air actions on 8 August give a good idea of the intensity of CAS operations over Afghanistan during the summer months of 2007: an A-10 flew a show of force near Bagram and also dropped a GBU-12 onto an insurgent group, and in a separate incident in the same area another show of force was flown and a GBU-12 dropped, this time by a Mirage 2000D. At Garmsir an A-10 delivered a GBU-12 to destroy a bunker that was being used by a Taliban mortar team and a B-1B carried out a show of force and also destroyed enemy-held buildings with GBU-38s. Near Kandahar an F-15E carried out a show of force in support of ISAF forces, while an A-10 dropped a 500lb bomb on insurgents near Shkin. Another A-10 deterred an insurgent band from counter-attacking Coalition troops by flying a

NEXT PAGES An F-16AM Fighting Falcon of the RNLAF photographed over Afghanistan from a USAF KC-135R Stratotanker during a combat mission on 28 May 2008. (USAF)

OPPOSITE A MH-47E Chinook helicopter passes over a temporary aircraft shelter housing a BAe Harrier GR7 of 4 Sqn RAF at Kandahar Air Base in December 2008. (Crown Copyright/MoD)

show of force near Bermal, 15km south of Urgun. An F-15E flew show of force near Musa Qala, while RAF Harriers flew a show of force to deter an insurgent mortar team from engaging troops near Gereshk, and another over a Taliban position near Uruzgan. Such was the CAS task on a 'typical day' in Afghanistan.

By the autumn, the infrastructure at Kandahar had been improved, and on 26 September, the French Air Force detachment of three Mirage 2000Ds was redeployed there from Dushanbe. Three weeks later, the three Mirage F1-CRs were also moved to Kandahar. Thereafter, the French maintained a force of six fighters in theatre, made up from a mix of Mirage 2000, Mirage F1 and Rafale, by rotating squadrons through Kandahar.

There were also improvements at Bagram, which allowed the arrival of the C-5 Galaxy without interrupting all other flying at the air base. Until September 2007, C-5s had used Bagram only occasionally

RIGHT An A-10 Thunderbolt II returns to the fight after receiving fuel from a KC-135 Stratotanker during a combat mission over Afghanistan on 29 May 2008. (USAF)

because the size of the aircraft meant that they could not taxi off the runway, thus blocking its use to all other aircraft. From 22 September the aircraft could taxi onto an apron to be unloaded, paving the way for regular Galaxy flights into Bagram. The ability to use the huge payload of this aircraft to support operations was an enormous bonus, since it could deliver as many as 36 cargo pallets, as against only six to eight in a C-130 load. Meanwhile, the C-17 continued to play its vital role in the delivery of air supplies. On 11 October, two C-17s from the 817th Expeditionary Airlift Squadron (EAS) dropped 62 bundles of supplies, weighing in total some 37,500kgs, to troops of the US Army 1-503 Infantry Regiment deployed in the mountainous region close to the Pakistan border. The US troops needed winter equipment in order to continue their pursuit of Taliban forces in the mountains, but resupply by land was almost impossible; using the JPADS the C-17s delivered their equipment to them within the space of a few minutes. The use of C-17s for this mission meant that the C-130 operation in-country was not affected, since it would have taken at least four C-130s to deliver the supplies.

A pair of Thunderbolts of the 354th EFS responded to a call for emergency CAS to assist Coalition troops who had been caught in a large-scale ambush on 14 October.

Cpt Dennis Hargis[25] recounted how:

We got on station and realized the situation was dire. A ten-vehicle convoy had come under ambush from two sides by heavy machine gun and mortar fire and multiple RPGs. It was a four-mile kill zone of constant ambush. An orchard near the convoy was just alive with muzzle flashes. The ground commander was calling up to us, saying 'We need your help!' I told my wingman we were going in and told the ground commander that because of his proximity to the enemy the bullets would come close. He gave us the go-ahead ... The guys on the ground did an extremely good job of telling me where the enemy fire was coming from and at what distance ... The whole mission was one of the most intense and memorable experiences of my life. It's the toughest part of the job, but for A-10 pilots, this is what we train for every day. Taking care of the guys on the ground is our first and foremost mission.

ABOVE An A-10 Thunderbolt II supporting Coalition ground forces in Afghanistan in November 2008. (USAF)

LEFT The Belgian Air Force deployed six F-16AM Fighting Falcons to Kandahar in September 2008. Here two aircraft are on patrol over Afghanistan two months later. (USAF)

In the space of ten minutes, the A-10 pilots flew six passes, successfully driving off the insurgents. The A-10s were withdrawn from Afghanistan once again in late October 2007, but their absence was only brief. On 3 November, nine A-10C Thunderbolts from the 104th EFS were transferred to Bagram from Iraq after a flying accident in the USA had temporarily grounded the F-15E Strike Eagle fleet.

Towards the end of October, there was a resurgence of anti-Coalition activity around Tarin Kowt. On 28 October targets around Tarin Kowt were engaged by RAF Harriers, which fired CRV-7 rockets to suppress enemy fire from a ridgeline, and a Mirage 2000, which bombed an enemy compound with GBU-12s. An F-15E also dropped GBU-38s on mortar positions near Tarin Kowt and performed a show of force over another Taliban position. The F-15Es were in action over Tarin Kowt again on 1 November, striking an enemy bunker with GBU-38s and the following day they flew a show of force in the same place. A Mirage 2000D also strafed insurgents near Tarin Kowt before bombing them with a GBU-12.

On the last day of October, the RAF flew its first operational General Atomics MQ-9A Reaper RPAS sortie over Afghanistan. The Reaper had been introduced into the USAF inventory during 2007 as a replacement for the Predator, although the latter type continued to be used for some time. Reaper had an improved performance over its predecessor and could fly both higher and faster; it also had a better weapon-carrying capacity. RPAS operations over Afghanistan were overseen by the USAF 432nd Wing from Creech AFB near Las Vegas. The RAF component comprised three Reapers which were also controlled from Creech. Reapers could be armed with up to four Hellfire missiles and two 500lb LGBs, and a USAF Reaper was in action over Tarin Kowt on 22 November, engaging insurgents with a GBU-12 and a Hellfire.

Having been seized by the Taliban in February 2007, Musa Qala was relieved by a combined force of British, US and ANA troops, after a five-day campaign, on 12 December. However, despite this success, and at the end of a year during which air dropped munition usage increased from the 1,770 of the previous year to 3,572, there

was no sign of the insurgency ending. Daily air tasking over Afghanistan typically comprised 40 fast jet CAS missions and 10 dedicated ISTAR missions; in early 2008 the CAS providers over Afghanistan included USAF B-1B, A-10, F-15E, USN F/A-18, RAF Harrier GR7, French Air Force Mirage 2000D and Dutch F-16. RAF Nimrod and USN P-3C Orion MPAs were also flying in the ISTAR role, as well as the Northrop Grumman E-8 (Joint Surveillance Target Attack Radar System – Joint STARS). In addition to the CAS and ISTAR tasks, there were numerous air transport and AAR flights mounted each day. Ground forces relied heavily on helicopters for day-to-day operations, including the UH-60, CH-46, CH-47, CH-53 and Mi-17 for troop insertion, resupply and casualty evacuation, as well as helicopter gunship support from the AH-64

An F-15E Strike Eagle on patrol over Afghanistan in November 20008. (USAF)

A General Atomics MQ-1 Predator RPAS armed with GBU-12 Paveway II LGBs and AGM-114 Hellfire missiles, on a combat mission over southern Afghanistan in November 2008. (USAF)

Apache, AH-1W Super Cobra and the Italian Army AgustaWestland A129C Mangusta. Large-scale patrols and convoys were invariably supported by helicopter gunships.

Although the insurgency covered most of the country, the main focus, which was reflected in the target areas for aircraft, was in Helmand and Kandahar provinces in the southwest and Paktia and Nangahar provinces along the border with Pakistan in the east. During early 2008, CAS aircraft frequently engaged targets at Sangin, Deh Rawood, Kandahar and Now Zad and at Orgun-e, Nangalam, Asadabad and Bermal. At Deh Rawood in January for example, an F-15E used GBU-31 and a GBU-38 to destroy buildings being used by insurgent RPG teams, a Harrier GR7 used a 1,000lb Enhanced

Paveway LGB to neutralize a mortar team and a B-1B used a GBU-38 to destroy an enemy-held compound. RPAS strikes became more common, too: on 24 February an MQ-1 Predator, working with an F-15E, fired a Hellfire missile at a weapons cache and on the same day an MQ-9 Reaper attacked motorcycles transporting weapons, destroying them with a GBU-12. By the beginning of May 2008, Reapers flown by the USAF 42nd EAS and No.39 Sqn RAF had completed 320 missions over Afghanistan.

Throughout much of 2008, Coalition troops mounted various battalion-sized operations to clear the Taliban from contested areas. However, despite successfully driving Taliban out of each area in the short term, these initiatives were not long-term successes, since there were insufficient troops to hold the areas and the Taliban, who in many cases had quietly withdrawn, simply returned once it was safe for them to do so. From an airpower perspective, these sweeps involved short but intensive helicopter operations to insert troops, keep them resupplied and to evacuate casualties and a similarly short but intensive CAS phase flown by fixed wing aircraft and helicopter gunships.

The Kunar Valley, which had caused so much trouble to the Soviets in the 1980s, continued to be a thorn in the side for the US and ISAF. The US Army had established combat outposts in the area, including the Pech Valley and Waygal Valley that connected into the Kunar Valley. The local population was hostile to Coalition troops, the area was known to be heavily infiltrated by insurgents, and ambushes were

A B-1B Lancer from the 34th Expeditionary Bomb Squadron during a combat mission over Afghanistan in December 2008. (USAF)

frequent. On 12 July, a platoon of US paratroopers from the 173rd Airborne Brigade Combat Team (BCT) established a combat outpost at the village of Wanat, in the Waygal Valley. At dawn the next day, the unit was subjected to a heavy and sustained assault by a large force of professional and experienced fighters, armed with small arms, heavy machine guns and RPGs. After an hour of intensive fighting, the US troops were on the verge of being overrun. At this point, two AH-64 Apaches from the 2nd Sqn 17th Cavalry Regt arrived on the scene. The gunships immediately engaged insurgents closest to the outpost with cannon fire and then employed Hellfire missiles against nearby buildings that were being used as firing points. The contact continued for another hour, during which the Apaches played a vital part in defeating the attack. Meanwhile, four MH-60 Dustoff helicopters from 6th Battalion 101st Aviation Regiment evacuated casualties from the outpost, landing under fire and in difficult conditions with smoke obscuring much of the LZ. Later that day there were sporadic contacts around the area, and on a day when 60 CAS missions were flown, a B-1B dropped GBU-31 and GBU-38, an A-10 strafed and dropped 500lb bombs and a GBU-12, a Predator fired Hellfire missiles and an F-15E carried out a show of force over the area. That night an AC-130 continued to engage insurgent groups in the vicinity. Over the next two days, insurgent activity continued in the wider area around Nangalam while at the same time the daily CAS tasking over Afghanistan reached over 70 missions.

In late August, a long-awaited third turbine for the Kajaki Dam hydro-electric powerplant was delivered to Kandahar airport. It then had to be transported through some 160km of contested territory in order to be installed at the dam. Between 28 August and 2 September, the 100-vehicle British-led convoy made its way, avoiding main roads, to Kajaki while a Danish-led dummy convoy followed the main highway route to distract the Taliban insurgents. The convoy was escorted by helicopter gunships while fixed wing aircraft maintained an overwatch, poised to strike any attempted ambush. The air assets included included A-10s, B-1Bs, F-15Es, F/A-18s, Mirage 2000Ds, Harrier GR7s, AC-130s and both MQ-1 Predator and MQ-9 Reaper RPAS. The offensive support aircraft were supported by KC-10s and KC-135s which flew 86 sorties, offloading 2.5 million kilogrammes of fuel. In addition, the convoy was resupplied by transport aircraft which made six tactical air drops delivering food, water, ammunition and fuel as well as tools, medical supplies and vehicle spare parts. The two convoys were subjected to numerous attacks by Taliban groups and in response, CAS aircraft were called in on 55 occasions to carry out airstrikes.

'Kinetic events', in which live ordnance was expended, continued to be daily occurrences During the seven years of Coalition military operations in the country, the role of offensive support aircraft had evolved, as had the role of the JTAC, who formed the link between aircraft and ground troops. In contrast to early missions where the tactical aircraft would take off with a well-defined plan and detailed knowledge of their target, pilots would now get airborne with just a grid reference, a radio frequency and would then rely on the JTAC to give them all the target details. The tactical situation was often unclear, with small groups of enemy fighters, or perhaps even individuals who were often within close contact of friendly forces. The ability of the JTAC to describe the locations of friendly and enemy forces and to explain their exact needs was a critical skill. Laser pointers or the ROVER equipment often made that task easier, but on other occasions JTAC and aircrew might have to rely simply on radio calls.

Capt Jeff Sliwoski[26], an A-10 pilot with the 190th EAS, explained:

The air force JTAC is absolutely our go-to guy on the ground to start any mission. The JTAC provides a [briefing] with all the essential information we need to employ ordnance. His other big piece of the puzzle is making sure we understand the situation on the ground – any threats, where the targets are, deconfliction of artillery ... Emergency CAS is very rare, but we are prepared for the situation. We train for it in our pre-deployment spin-up. We are very familiar with the steps we need to take to employ weapons around friendlies who are not qualified JTACs. You have to find out what you have to do to help the guys on the ground. There is a lot of talking to the guy on the ground and understanding his situation – the friendly situation in general – and find out exactly what they need. If the people on the ground are not currently taking contact then you can afford to take more time to develop a plan for the AO; if they are taking contact then it ratchets it up another notch to employ weapons quickly, efficiently and above

all, safely. Normally, a JTAC will assume some responsibility – he identifies what you are bringing and how you can use it. In emergency CAS, the pilot is assuming all the responsibility and risk in weapons deployment.

Six Belgian F-16AMs were despatched to Kandahar in September 2008, joining the RNLAF F-16 detachment that had remained in Afghanistan. By the end of 2008, Coalition troop numbers were rising steadily and at that stage there were some 55,000 Coalition troops based in the country. However, some 20,000 of the US troops were not part of ISAF but remained under direct US control as part of Operation *Enduring Freedom*. Thus, there continued to be two separate military structures operating in Afghanistan, each using different rules of engagement. These differences became apparent, for example, in the 35 airstrikes carried out during the year by US-operated RPAS against targets in Pakistan.

During 2008 the number of CAS sorties flown by Coalition aircraft had risen by over a third in comparison to 2007, to over 19,000, but the number of weapons employed remained roughly the same as the previous year at just over 5,000.

The Italian Air Force deployed four Panavia Tornado IDS from 6° Stormo to Mazar-e-Sharif in November 2008 to fulfil the tactical reconnaissance role using the Rafael RecceLite reconnaissance pod. This aircraft is carrying out a combat mission over Afghanistan in December 2008. (USAF)

An A-10 Thunderbolt II from the 74th Expeditionary Fighter Squadron on patrol in the skies of Afghanistan on 8 May 2011. (USAF)

CHAPTER 5

ISAF TAKES BACK CONTROL 2009–2014

The struggle in Afghanistan cannot be won by force of arms alone. We must also help the Afghan government strengthen democratic institutions, provide essential services, create jobs and opportunity, and show its people that freedom can lead to a better life. But for this to happen, Afghanistan needs security – and that is what NATO is helping to provide

George W. Bush, 2008

By the beginning of 2009, Coalition forces were beginning to gain the upper hand against the Taliban insurgency. This was due both to the increasing numbers of Coalition troops in theatre and to the improved intelligence gathering that enabled those troops to focus their efforts effectively. In such a large and remote country where extreme terrain shielded the movement of insurgents and where informant networks might not be reliable, aerial reconnaissance assumed a special importance. The sheer size of the task meant that that the data needed to monitor activity over the whole of Afghanistan could not be captured by a single platform, but that numerous pieces of information gathered by many diverse sensors would have to be fused together in a mosaic that built a complete picture of day-to-day

ABOVE An RAF BAe Harrier GR9 on the approach to land at Kandahar after one of the last combat sorties flown by the Harrier over Afghanistan before it was replaced by the Panavia Tornado GR4 in 2009. RAF Harriers had been supporting ISAF ground forces from Kandahar since 2004. (Stradling)

RIGHT A USAF General Atomics MQ-9 Reaper RPAS, armed with GBU-12 Paveway II LGBs and AGM-114 Hellfire missiles, on a combat mission over southern Afghanistan in January 2009. (USAF)

life in the country. By understanding the normal patterns of life, intelligence staff could then detect the abnormalities that indicated insurgent activity. Strategic reconnaissance over Afghanistan was provided by Lockheed U-2S Dragon Lady aircraft and RQ-4 Global Hawk RPAS. High resolution imagery from these aircraft was particularly useful in detecting IEDs and other details such as the paths and routes used by Taliban groups. They also carried out electronic eavesdropping, capturing mobile phone and radio transmissions that would otherwise have been hidden from prying sensors by high mountains.

RPAS began to take an increasing share in air operations over Afghanistan. The USAF had also commenced operations with the Lockheed Martin RQ-170 Sentinel RPAS, which was particularly used for intelligence gathering over the Pashtun areas of Pakistan. At the tactical level, US and Italian MQ-1 Predator along with US and British MQ-9 Reaper RPAS monitored individual points of interest, sometimes 'staking out' buildings suspected of housing important Taliban personnel. A Canadian detachment, Task Force *Erebus*, was established at Kandahar in December 2008 to operate the Israel Aerospace Industries (IAI) Heron RPAS (known in Canadian service as the CU-170), flying its first mission on 1 January 2009. The following month, the French Air Force deployed three European Aeronautic Defence and Space (EADS) Harfang RPAS were to Bagram. The Harfang was a variant of the Heron and both types were used together with the MQ-1 and MQ-9 RPAS in the tactical reconnaissance role. In August 2009, the RAAF also sent Heron crews to Kandahar to gain experience with the Canadian detachment before their own aircraft arrived there at the end of the year.

Not to be confused with the RPAS of the same name, the RAF also deployed the Raytheon Sentinel R1 reconnaissance aircraft to Kandahar in February 2009. The initial deployment was for just two months, but it later became a permanent detachment. Equipped with a synthetic-aperture moving target indicator radar, it complemented the capabilities of the E-8C JSTARS which was already operating over Afghanistan. These two systems fed Coalition commanders with detailed battlefield information on ground forces. Electronic information was also collected by the RC-135 Rivet Joint. Along with role-specific assets like the E-8C, maritime patrol aircraft continued to be deployed for intelligence gathering over Afghanistan. These aircraft included the USN Orion, operating from Al Minhad Air Base in the UAE, and the RAF Nimrod MR2, based at Seeb in Oman. The efforts of the USN and RAF aircraft were reinforced in July 2009 when two RAAF Orions, also based at Al Minhad and previously used for operations over Iraq, were transferred to the Afghan theatre when combat operations over Iraq ceased. In addition, two CAF CP-140 Aurora MPAs were deployed to Afghanistan by the Canadian government in May for a two-month mission to produce accurate high-resolution mapping of some of the remote areas the country.

Responding to the increased demand for tactical air reconnaissance over Afghanistan, the Italian Air Force dispatched four Panavia Tornado interdictor strike (IDS) from the 6° Stormo to Mazar-e-Sharif in late November 2008. Like the German Tornados which were already based at Mazar-e-Sharif, the aircraft were equipped with

TOP A French Air Force EADS-built *Harfang* (Owl) RPAS seen at Bagram Air Base on 11 July 2009. The type was based on the Israeli Aircraft Industries (IAI) Heron RPAS, which was itself used for surveillance operations over Afghanistan by the Canadian and Australian air forces. (USAF)

RIGHT A Raytheon Sentinel R1 of 5 Sqn RAF on the apron at Kandahar. Based on the Bombardier Global Express business jet, the Sentinel was equipped with a dual-mode synthetic-aperture radar/moving target indication (SAR/MTI radar for battlefield surveillance. (4 Sqn Association)

the Rafael RecceLite reconnaissance pod. Tactical photoreconnaissance was also carried out from Kandahar by the French Mirage F1-CR detachment and the RAF Harrier GR7/GR9 detachment which flew missions with the British digital joint reconnaissance rod (DJRP). Other offensive aircraft carried out non-traditional intelligence surveillance and reconnaissance (NTISR), using their targeting pods to feed data into the overall intelligence picture.

Further enhancements to the Coalition ISTAR capabilities came at the end of 2009, with the introduction into service of variants of the Beechcraft B-300 and B-350. The US Army Task Force *Odin* (observe detect identify neutralize) operated the medium altitude reconnaissance surveillance system (MARSS) variant of the B-300, while the USAF operated the MQ-12 Liberty version of the B-350 from Bagram. Both of these types were fitted with sophisticated radio intercept equipment, high-resolution cameras and Wescam MX-15 video cameras. Datalink enabled the aircraft to provide battlefield commanders with real-time full-motion video and signals information. In late 2009, the RAF also fielded a B-350 variant, the Raytheon Shadow R1. Flying from Kandahar, and equipped with surveillance and radio intercept equipment, the Shadow was used in direct support of ground force patrols.

A major limitation on communications in Afghanistan was the way in which high mountain ranges blocked the line-of-sight radio signals, thus preventing ground forces operating in the valleys, or aircraft flying below the peaks, from contacting other units. The later variants of the

Operating from Al Udeid Air Base in Qatar, a Boeing RC-135 Rivet Joint from the 763rd Expeditionary Reconnaissance Squadron flies over Afghanistan on 19 June 2011. The RC-135 Rivet Joint electronic surveillance aircraft had the capability to detect, identify and locate the source of signals throughout the electromagnetic spectrum. (USAF)

Soviet-era helicopters flown by civilian contractors, like this Vertical-T operated Mi-26T, were used extensively to move supplies and equipment around Afghanistan. (Stradling)

RQ-4 Global Hawk had the capability to act as relay stations for radio and datalink. In addition, the USAF E-11A battlefield airborne communications node (BACN), a variant of the Bombardier Global 6000, had also been specifically procured for the task, after the communications problems that were encountered during military operations in Kunar province in 2005. The E-11A, a type unique to the Afghan theatre, was flown from Kandahar by the 430th Expeditionary Electronic Combat Squadron (EECS). Another solution to the problems of communication was found in the fitting of the roll on beyond-line-of-sight enhancement (ROBE) system to KC-135 tankers operating from Manas Air Base. ROBE acted as a repeater station for voice and datalink communication networks. The value of the new system was illustrated two weeks later, as described by Col Chris Bence[27], commander of the 376th AEW:

> During the fourth mission with a ROBE refueller on July 27, our aircrew overheard radio chatter between an F-15 pilot and a Joint Terminal Air Controller on the ground. A forward operating base deep in a valley was under attack and in danger of being overrun. We could tell the F-15 pilot was struggling to identify and strike the targets without causing collateral damage or friendly casualties. We turned on ROBE and within minutes, we knew the system was a success by a comment made by the F-15 pilot. The fighter pilot said, 'I don't know where the picture [target imagery] is coming from, but I got it [the target] now. Thanks.'

In mid-June Gen Stanley A. McChrystal assumed command of ISAF and US Forces Afghanistan (USFOR-A). McChrystal brought a new direction to the way aircraft operated over Afghanistan, commenting that: 'Airpower contains the seeds of our own destruction if we do not use it responsibly. We can lose this fight.' His concern was that the unrestricted use of large (1,000lb or heavier) weapons to break TICs was causing civilian casualties and unnecessary collateral damage, which was alienating the local population and hardening their support for the Taliban. The emphasis was now on using minimum force commensurate with achieving the aim and being willing to hold fire rather than cause needless civilian casualties. The 500lb LGB (GBU-12 or British Paveway IV) became the new weapon of choice.

June 2009 also saw the replacement of the RAF Harrier GR7/GR9 detachment at Kandahar with eight Tornado GR4s from No.12 Sqn RAF. These aircraft were armed with Paveway IV LGB and also the MBDA Brimstone dual mode seeker (DMS) missile, a focussed weapon which caused virtually no collateral damage. Tornado also brought with it the reconnaissance airborne pod for Tornado (RAPTOR) sensor, which was capable of providing real-time high-resolution imagery. The first RAF Tornado mission over Afghanistan was flown on 24 June. In the following month, the 421st EFS, equipped with the F-16, deployed to Bagram Air Base, marking the first F-16 deployment to the country by the USAF. In July, US naval wing CVW-14 from USS *Ronald Reagan* (CVN-76) took over responsibility for naval air support over Afghanistan from CVW-7 which had been operating from USS *Dwight D Eisenhower* (CVN-69). The first mission over Afghanistan by the F/A-18 Super Hornets and EA-6B Prowlers from USS *Ronald Reagan* was flown on 6 July.

A USMC F/A-18C Hornet of VMFA-122 armed with 500lb GBU-12 LGBs taxies at Kandahar in December 2010. After Gen Stanley A. McChrystal assumed command of US and Coalition Forces in Afghanistan, in 2009 there was a greater emphasis on using smaller weapons to minimize collateral damage and civilian casualties. (Stradling)

ABOVE In 2010, Canadian Armed Forces leased four Mi-17-V5 helicopters to supplement the six CH-47 Chinooks already in Afghanistan. In Canadian service the aircraft were known as the CH-178. (Stradling)

RIGHT A typical Kandahar scene in December 2010. A Beechcraft MC-12W Liberty surveillance aircraft taxies past a civilian Il-76. As well as military transport aircraft, the air bridge which supported US and ISAF forces in Afghanistan also included numerous aircraft chartered from civilian operators. (Stradling)

A British-led offensive, Operation *Panchai Palang* (panther's claw) commenced in the early hours of 20 June with an air landing by ten CH-47 Chinooks (four RAF and six US Army) to insert troops near Babaji, north of Lashkar Gah in Helmand province. The airlift helicopters were supported by AH-64 Apaches and an AC-130 gunship as well as RAF Harriers on one of their last missions in-country. The troops made good progress in clearing insurgents from the area but later in the day, a B-1B was called in to drop an LGB onto a sniper who had pinned down the advance.

Taking advantage of the extra 10,000 US troops, and especially those of the 24th MEU which had deployed to Afghanistan earlier in the year, Operation *Khanjar* commenced on 2 July with the objective of clearing the Taliban from the Garmsir district in southern Helmand. In the early morning darkness, the Marines were airlifted to the start point near Nawa-l-Barakzayi, to the south of Lashkar Gah, by a fleet of CH-47 Chinook and CH-53 Super Stallion helicopters. As the Coalition troops advanced, Taliban fighters engaged them with RPGs and automatic fire, but the insurgents were soon neutralized by A-10s which strafed their firing positions. Other Coalition aircraft, including USMC AV-8B Harriers, also provided offensive support and shows of force.

Although the main thrust was taking place in Helmand, insurgents were active elsewhere. Often a mixed force of RPAS and manned aircraft carried out a co-ordinated response to TICs. On 3 July an MQ-9A Reaper was working with A-10s in the Soltani region, some 100km west of Khost, where an ANA unit had come under fire from gunmen armed with automatic weapons and RPGs. The Reaper engaged two groups with GBU-12s, while the A-10s attacked two other enemy groups, one in a building and the other in a field. In a similar incident the following day, an MQ-1 Predator neutralized an enemy sniper with a Hellfire missile.

The main operational focus in July and August was to ensure that provincial elections could take place on 20 August and efforts were made to sweep the Taliban from the various regions. Offensive air patrols were stepped up, with around 90 missions each day, culminating in the election day itself when 101 CAS and 34 ISTAR

An RAF Panavia Tornado GR4 on patrol over southern Afghanistan in June 2009. The aircraft is armed with 500lb Enhanced Paveway (EPW) IV LGBs and Matra-BAe Dynamics-Alenia (MBDA) Brimstone missile as well as a 27mm cannon. (Stradling)

ABOVE 6 November 2009: Bell Boeing MV-22B Ospreys of the 22nd Marine Expeditionary Unit (MEU) prepare to take off from the flight deck of the amphibious assault ship USS *Bataan* (LHD 5) for a flight to Camp Bastion, where they were transferred to VMM-261. This was the first time the type had been used in Afghanistan. (USMC)

ABOVE RIGHT Both the French Navy and French Air Force operated the Dassault Rafale over Afghanistan. The type was operated in formation respectively with the Dassault Super Étendard and Mirage 2000D, as laser target designators. (Stradling)

tasks were flown. On that day aircraft provided armed overwatch for Coalition forces who were ensuring the security of the election process. F-16CJ Fighting Falcons and F-15E Strike Eagles were on station over Asmar in the Kunar Valley to protect the convoys transporting ballot papers from the polling stations to counting houses. Taliban snipers who engaged the convoys with RPGs and automatic fire were strafed by the aircraft, which also dropped LGBs on other firing positions along the route and ended with a show of force. The intervention was successful, and the ballot papers were safely delivered to the intended site. Aircraft of the USAF and USN continued to provided assistance either with weapons or with shows of force across the country.

Flt Lt Chris Stradling, the navigator of an RAF Tornado, recalled how:

20 August 2009 was election day and one of the busiest sorties I have ever flown in a Tornado. We were sent to a number of different tasks as TICs developed and closed with amazing speed. The last event of the sortie was to support a TIC near Sangin, where the Brits had taken casualties earlier in the day and they were again taking incoming fire from an unknown position. We did two high angle [about 30 degrees] strafe attacks against small wooded areas close to a friendly patrol base. Our number 2 also did three attacks against similar positions, in the hope of flushing them out, although nothing was seen. We were extremely low on fuel when we eventually handed over to a pair of A-10s.

British helicopter reinforcements during 2009 included the introduction of the Royal Navy Westland Sea King ASaC7 airborne surveillance and control helicopters. Operating in the ISTAR role, these aircraft were based at Camp Bastion from May. Royal Navy support to operations in Afghanistan also included Westland Sea King HC4 'Commando' troop carrying helicopters from No.845 Naval Air Squadron (NAS) and No.846 NAS, which had first deployed in 2007 and would remain in the country until 2011. In November 2009, the

A Grumman EA-6B Prowler from VMAQ-1 based at Bagram Air Base on an operational sortie over eastern Afghanistan on 26 November 2009. (USAF)

RAF deployed the AgustaWestland Merlin HC3 transport helicopter from No.28 Sqn RAF to Camp *Bastion* to supplement the Chinooks. The AgustaWestland Lynx Mk9A was also deployed by the British Army Air Corps in early summer, while the Italian Army also added five NH Industries NH90 TTH helicopters to join their force of ten AW-129 Mangusta gunships and six CH-47C transports.

The French Army also brought in reinforcements in the shape of the Eurocopter EC665 Tiger *hélicoptère d'appui protection* (HAP – attack and support helicopter). Three Tigers joined a helicopter battalion of 12 aircraft in Kabul on 26 July and commenced operational flying on 10 August. The battalion also included three Eurocopter EC725 Caracal, three Eurocopter AS532 Cougar and three Aerospatiale SA341/342 Gazelle helicopters. The Tigers were regularly used in the CAS role, mainly in the Regional Command – East (RC–E) area of responsibility, but they also took part in escort, intelligence, and reconnaissance sorties, often operating as a pair with Gazelles armed with the HOT missile. Like Apache crews, the Tiger crews adopted the tactic of remaining 1,500m away from their target so that they could fly in to make a rocket or gun attack. Some 25 percent of the Tiger sorties were flown at night.

'All the different systems are very complementary,' explained Lt Col Francois D'Argaignon[28]. 'The Tiger has the 30mm gun and the [68mm] flechette rockets while the Gazelle provides us the capacity to destroy a hard target.'

Another Tiger pilot recalled that:

> in Afghanistan we were embedded with a [US Army] Apache patrol, where we might fly the first two hours and they would relieve us and then we would come back, so it was quite simple for us to judge the performance of the two helicopters. At the beginning of each mission, we had to check in with the JTAC on the ground and we had to state our payload and playtime [mission endurance] in the area – and we couldn't lie, because it was operational task data. We heard the Apache pilots giving all this information too and it was exactly the same as ours – exactly the same payload, exactly the same playtime – so we were not inferior to the Apache patrol, we provided exactly the same service to the troops on the ground.

OPPOSITE TOP A chartered Il-76 departs from Kandahar Air Base as a USAF C-130 Hercules taxies out for take-off. (Stradling)

OPPOSITE BOTTOM A pair of F-15E Strike Eagles from the 335th Expeditionary Fighter Squadron flying from Bagram Air Base drop 2,000lb JDAM on a cave and tunnel complex in eastern Afghanistan on 26 November 2009. (USAF)

A pair of Tigers and two Gazelles were kept on permanent alert at Kabul.

On the evening 3 September, two civilian fuel tankers carrying fuel for ISAF were hijacked by Taliban insurgents on the main highway between Kunduz and the Tajikistan border. The tankers were captured after they had become stuck while trying to ford a shallow river. A B-1B Lancer supporting another task in the area noticed and reported the presence of the tankers. Based on that report, the German Army commander responsible for ISAF forces in the area declared the tankers to be a threat and requested air support. At 02:00 hrs, two F-15E Strike Eagles arrived overhead, by which time an Afghan informant had indicated that the numerous people surrounding the vehicles were Taliban. In fact, they were local people who were taking advantage of the stranded tankers to help themselves to fuel for their own domestic purposes. At the request of the ground commander, one F-15E dropped two 500lb GBU-38 LGBs on the tankers to deny their use to the Taliban. As a result, there was a massive explosion which resulted in the deaths of at least 125 people, only a small proportion of whom were armed; after this unfortunate incident relations between the ISAF and the local Afghans deteriorated significantly.

As the size of the RPAS operation over Afghanistan increased, so, too, did the risk of mishaps involving drones. On 13 September 2009, the operational crew of an armed MQ-9 Reaper lost the datalink contact with their aircraft, leaving them unable to control the machine. The Reaper continued on its course and was heading towards Tajikistan when it was intercepted by an F-15E which had been instructed to destroy it. The F-15 fired on the Reaper, disabling the engine, at which point the operational crew regained control, and steered the drone to crash in a remote area of Afghanistan.

In December, the Italian Air Force Tornado detachment at Mazar-e-Sharif was replaced by a detachment of AMX A-11 *Ghibli* (desert wind). Like the Tornados, the aircraft were also configured with the IAI RecceLite reconnaissance pod for their prime role. Although they were primarily tasked with reconnaissance missions, the *Ghiblis* were also capable of offensive action if required. The statistics for CAS missions flown by US and Coalition aircraft during 2007 and 2009 make an interesting comparison, for although the number of sorties

OPPOSITE TOP A Mi-35M attack helicopter of the ANA Air Corps (which became the Afghan Air Force in the following month) over Afghanistan on 11 May 2010. The aircraft was being flown by Hungarian Air Force Maj Bela Lazar, commander of the Hungarian Operational Mentoring Liaison Team, and ANA Capt Gholar Mohaiudin. (USAF)

OPPOSITE BOTTOM The Italian Air Force deployed the AMX A-11 *Ghibli* (desert wind) light attack aircraft to Afghanistan during 2009. This aircraft has completed refuelling from a KC-10A Extender from the 908th Expeditionary Air Refueling Squadron over Afghanistan on 7 December 2009. (USAF)

The longest dirt runway in Afghanistan was at the multi-national base at Tarin Kowt, some 115 km due north of Kandahar. This view of a USAF Lockheed C-130 Hercules taxiing in after landing at Tarin Kowt on 6 July 2010 gives an idea of the harsh conditions with which tactical transport aircraft had to cope. (USAF)

A British Army Air Corps AgustaWestland Lynx AH9 on patrol over a green zone in Helmand province during July 2010. (Crown Copyright/MoD)

increased markedly, the number of weapon events decreased slightly. In 2007, US aircraft flew 13,962 CAS sorties and expended 5,198 weapons, whereas two years later the sortie rate had almost doubled to 26,474, but only 4,184 weapons had been expended. The RAF recorded a similar experience, flying 5,593 hours in 2007 with 298 weapons events and 10,633 hours (including almost half by MQ-9 Reaper) in 2009 with just 140 weapons events. Another reflection on the changing emphasis in air operations over Afghanistan is that in 2009 US aircraft flew 18,898 ISTAR sorties – a threefold increase since 2006. The statistics seem to indicate firstly that the combats of 2006 to 2009 had taken their toll of Taliban fighters but also that the surge in both troop numbers and air sorties was having a positive impact on the security situation in the country. Perhaps, too, the increased ISTAR commitment was also helping to shape the situation on the ground.

The next major ground offensive in Afghanistan was Operation *Moshtarak* which commenced in February 2010. US, British and other SOFs carried out shaping operations around Marjah (15km west of Lashkar Gah) from 6 February before the main assault on 13 February. Massed pre-dawn helicopter landings inserted a British and Canadian force around Nad Ali, to the north of Marjah, while the main force, which included elements of Marine Aircraft Group 40 and Task Force *Pegasus* from the US Army 82nd Airborne Division, attacked Marjah. The combined helicopter force of some 50 aircraft included three Canadian CH-147 Chinook and four Bell CH-146 Griffon helicopters, as well as British Chinooks, Merlins and Sea Kings along with US Army CH-47, CH-53 and UH-60s.

RAF Chinook pilot Flt Lt Chris Hasler[29] described how:

we struck out at low level under the moonless night towards our objective which was the insurgent-held town of Showal. En route to target the ambient light levels were so poor that even our NVGs [night vision goggles] struggled to provide much more than a dark green nothingness. However, with only a few short miles to go, the goggles erupted in a bright and clear picture provided by infra-red flares, invisible to the naked eye, dropped from a circling C-130 Hercules from overhead. On short finals to the target, the formation of Chinooks tightened spacing and pitched noses up hard to decelerate quickly. The back wheels dug into the soft ground of the muddy field, and we disgorged our complement of Royal Welsh and ANA [Afghan National Army] troops. Seconds later we were

Maj Skyler Hester, a USAF pilot, flying on an exchange tour with the French Air Force, taxies for a combat mission in a Mirage 2000D accompanied by Capt Mathieu Boireau at Kandahar Air Base on 11 November 2010. (USAF)

A line up of Mil Mi-17 helicopters of the AAF. Ideally suited to operations in Afghanistan, the rugged Mi-17 formed the backbone of the AAF. (Stradling)

wheels up and racing back to Bastion airfield to pick up our next chalk of soldiers. In just over two hours our packet of four RAF Chinooks had delivered approximately 650 soldiers to the heart of the insurgency. An insurgency who after being forewarned of our attack wisely kept their heads down or fled the scene.

Air Cdre Stuart Atha, the British Air Officer Commanding No.83 Expeditionary Air Group, commented that using A-10s and Tornado GR4s[30]:

for every single helicopter landing site we had a fast jet with a targeting pod examining the site before the troops arrived and watching as the troops were unloaded, looking for enemy activity or threat, and providing that attack overwatch to protect the troops unloading.

Operation *Moshtarak* was also supported by an RC-135 Rivet Joint, and, as Lt Col Richard Linehan[31], commander of the 763rd Expeditionary Reconnaissance Squadron (ERS) explained, the crew detected indications that insurgents were setting up an ambush against US helicopters:

the crew was able to tip forces of imminent danger. The helicopters then positively identified enemy forces preparing mortars for attack, concurrent with the RC-135's information. The helos assumed a defensive posture and an attack helicopter was called in to eliminate the enemy threat … what sets the Rivet Joint apart from other reconnaissance aircraft – is that we're picking up real-time information on the enemy and getting that information directly to our customers on the ground real-time. It can be intel about an attack or intel to aid in operations where they're going to take out high-value targets.

ISAF ground operations also continued in the north of the country and on 2 April, the medical evacuation service for the whole of northern Afghanistan was being provided by two UH-60A Dustoff helicopters of the 5th Battalion 158th Aviation Regt based at Kunduz. In the early afternoon, one Dustoff crew flown by Chief Warrant Officer (CWO)3 Jason LaCrosse and CWO2 Jason Brown was scrambled in response to a call from a German Army unit that had been ambushed near Isa Khel, some 10km southwest of Kunduz. Accompanied by an armed UH-60L Black Hawk, flown by CWO2 Sean Johnson and CWO2 Eric Wells, LaCrosse and Brown reached the German unit to find it engaged in a fierce firefight. After several attempts in which heavy fire forced the crew to abort their approaches, the first Dustoff managed to land nearby to pick up the casualties. During the landing, the insurgents had switched from firing at the Germans and concentrated their attentions on the helicopter. However, in doing so they exposed themselves to fire from the German soldiers as well as the armed UH-60, which in turn forced the insurgents onto the defensive. Above the battlefield, F-15Es and F-16Cs also carried out shows of force in order to dissuade further intervention by the insurgents. After making two trips to Isa Khel to collect German wounded, the two Dustoff crews were then advised that yet more casualties had been caused by an IED blast in Isa Khel. Responding to this call, the two helicopter crews recovered four more casualties and had just shut down engines when they were scrambled for a third time after the blast from a second IED at Isa Khel caused four more casualties amongst ISAF troops.

In line with the policy for the Afghan government eventually to assume full responsibility for security in the country, the US began to rebuild the AAF in 2006. The aim was for an air force with fixed-wing attack capability from 2012. By 2010, the inventory included 18 Mi-17 transport and three Mi-35 gunship helicopters, two An-26 and six An-32 transports. There were also two Aero L-39 Albatros trainer aircraft, which had been used only for ceremonial flypasts. A pilot training school was to be opened at Shindand, but the bulk of the air force was based at Kabul where it included a number of pilots with experience from Soviet days who had previously flown the MiG-21 and Su-7. In November 2006, an order had also been hastily placed by the US, on behalf of the AAF, for 20 refurbished Italian-built Alenia G222 (C-27A) transport aircraft, at a cost of US$549 million. The aircraft were to be flown initially

A Dassault Mirage F1CR carrying the markings of ER 2/33 *Savoie* taxiing out at Kandahar Air Base for a combat mission over Afghanistan. The aircraft is loaded with a single GBU-12 LGB on the centre-line pylon. (Stradling)

A sunset parade of ISTAR aircraft at Kandahar. A US Army B300 KingAir MARSS is sandwiched between two USAF Beechcraft MC-12W Liberty surveillance aircraft. In the background in the far right of the image, the wing of a NASA-operated Martin WB-57 weather reconnaissance aircraft is visible. (Stradling)

by USAF pilots and then gradually transferred to Afghan service. The first of these was delivered in 2009 and the last of the 16 that were actually delivered to Afghanistan arrived in 2013. Unfortunately, the aircraft proved to be singularly unsuitable for operations in the country: their performance was poor in the hot and high conditions that they encountered in the country, and the type also proved to be very unreliable. The G222s were sold for scrap in 2014. Meanwhile, a contract for 20 Embraer A-29 Super Tucano light attack aircraft was signed in 2011. After an appeal by a rival manufacturer, the contract was cancelled in 2012, but then reinstated in 2013. These aircraft would eventually become combat ready two years later.

By late 2010, the nature of CAS operations had changed once more, reflecting better intelligence and the ability to track individual Taliban groups.

Late in the afternoon of 11 November 2010, RAF Tornados were scrambled from GCAS to support an SOF operation against: 'high value individuals' to the northwest of Kandahar.

One of the Tornado pilots involved describes the mission:

Airborne in less than 15 minutes we blast the 20 minutes to the target area Northwest of Kandahar. Jim [his navigator] and I are the lead with Matt and his WSO Emma as our wingman. The targets are mobile in a car and motorbike convoy, all others are considered guilty by association, they are driving along a dusty, undulating track miles away from any habitation. As a formation we put into action our well-practiced tactic for moving targets and ensure all aspects of the ROE are in place. A Reaper RPAS is also on station above us, and we know that their video feed is being watched live in the CAOC in Al Udeid, I can feel the lawyer's critical eyes watching us, a strange scenario. Jim and I get into position and are ready to strike the car with a DMS Brimstone, an outstanding weapon for hitting moving targets, critically our clearance to fire is delayed and we have to hand the first shot to our wingman. Matt and Emma to their credit are in the perfect position and shoot, their DMS Brimstone strikes the car just as it comes to a halt and the motorbike pulls alongside. Both are brought to a halt permanently. Incredibly, the back doors of the car open and three insurgents appear and start running in three different directions. As briefed the Reaper RPAS follows one, Matt and Emma another and us the third. The SOF JTAC ask us to strike the vehicle again to ensure all contents are destroyed. Jim and I do so with a DMS Brimstone whilst the Reaper RPAS maintains a track on our insurgent. Matt and Emma are tasked to neutralize the target they have been following and they do so with a further DMS Brimstone. Unfortunately, the Reaper has lost one of the two they were following and hand over the remaining target they have to us. The SOF JTAC requests that target be neutralized too. We oblige with DMS Brimstone. The pace is beginning to slow now so I send Matt and Emma to refuel [a KC-10 tanker has been tasked to head our way] so that we can maintain overwatch as efficiently as possible. Jim and I begin to help the Reaper look for the third and final target who escaped from the car. Amazingly Jim finds the needle in the haystack after about 20 mins searching the sandy wilderness and once again, we are tasked with neutralizing the final target. We have used both our DMS Brimstones, and we have two Paveway IV LGBs and 135 rounds of 27mm HE in the gun and the JTAC requests strafe. We do not have a lot of fuel and Matt and Emma are still at the tanker so we setup for a strafe attack. Jim has the target on the Litening III targeting pod, and I am able to see the area on the ground, but I cannot see the target itself. I tip into the dive and try and pick up the target around the cross in the Head Up Display provided by Jim but cannot see the target, so I put the pipper in the cross and shoot. I miss. The light is failing, and I am really struggling to see

A panorama of RAF types at Kandahar Air Base in 2010. In the foreground is a Raytheon Sentinel R1 surveillance aircraft and to the right a VC-10 tanker aircraft; in the background on the left, a British Aerospace Nimrod MR2 MPA. (14 Sqn Association)

an individual now lying down in a dried riverbed, the traditional clothing providing almost perfect camouflage. We have fuel for one more pass and then we have to go and refuel. I strafe once more, and the rounds appear to surround the target but neither of us can provide a positive BDA and we have no fuel left to do so. The Reaper takes over the situation and, frustrated, we make our way to the tanker providing a handover to Matt and Emma who are on their way back. We arrive at the tanker on fumes, and I have to put the frustration over the strafe passes to the back of my mind as I need to get in the basket and refuel on the first attempt! We return to the target area, but the op is complete. When Matt and Emma had arrived back the Reaper had been tasked with taking on our target and had done so with a Hellfire missile.

This was a very dynamic situation throughout and I was very proud of our performance as a team. The most interesting aspect of this experience which I still think of from time to time is how the targeting became so personal. Often fast jets, certainly the Tornado Force, are tasked with targets that don't have a human angle to them … a radar, a weapons storage facility, a HAS. Often faceless targets that may or may not have people in or around them, but you very rarely are exposed to that aspect. Suddenly we are striking

individuals. Up close and personal. The quality of the imagery from the Litening III ATP is such that from 10,000ft I can see the facial features of the target for example. After this sortie it really brought home how different some of these scenarios are from the traditional strike missions we had often spent hours training for. After the debrief I made sure we talked through it as a formation as I felt I had a pastoral responsibility to my team to ensure they were all comfortable with our mission. Even our Royal Marine who had experienced plenty in Iraq in 2003 expressed his surprise at the feeling of being able to strike individuals as we had done with such power and control. A very interesting life experience for all of us.

Continuing in their efforts to control the Pech Valley region, US forces carried out Operation *Bulldog* in November 2010, targeting insurgent training camps in the Watapur Valley. On 12 November, some 250 troops were inserted by helicopter. Two days later an HH-60G Pave Hawk responded to a call for a medical evacuation, but when the PJs abseiled down to the ground and joined a platoon of paratroopers, they were pinned down by heavy fire and unable to move. Over the coming hours, the Taliban fire was suppressed by Hellfire missiles from AH-64s, as well as a 2,000lb bomb dropped by a USN F/A-18. As darkness approached, the PJs were able to move and gather the casualties, and they were extracted that night, along with 47 wounded soldiers and five dead.

One of the most intense combat rescue missions of the Afghan conflict occurred on 23 April 2011. In the early hours, a US Army Bell OH-58 Kiowa helicopter was shot down by an RPG in the Alasay region, some 80km northeast of Kabul. Two HH-60G Pave Hawks were dispatched to rescue the Kiowa pilots, but after dropping off two PJs, one helicopter was damaged by heavy fire and was forced to withdraw. The remaining helicopter also came under sustained gunfire. Although two AH-64 Apaches were on scene, it was clear heavier firepower was required, and in response to an emergency call, an A-10C of the 303rd EFS flown by Maj Mike Hilkert was diverted from another task. Hilkert gathered two more A-10s and took charge as the on-scene commander, co-ordinating their efforts as well as those of the helicopter gunships and a support tanker aircraft. When two teams of US Army ground forces were inserted into the vicinity, Hilkert tracked one group with his binoculars and the other with his

A US Army Bell OH-58D Kiowa Warrior armed reconnaissance helicopter at Kandahar Air Base in December 2011. The machine is armed with a pod of Hydra 70 rockets and a .50-calibre heavy machine gun. (Crown Copyright/MoD)

targeting pod. He also carried out low flypasts over the insurgent positions to draw fire away from the rescue helicopters. Eventually the operation was completed, despite almost continuous heavy fire from the insurgents.

On 2 May, two MH-60K Black Hawk and three MH-47 Chinook helicopters from the 160th SOAR set off from Jalalabad and set up a FOB approximately two-thirds of the way between Jalalabad and Abbottabad in Pakistan. US Intelligence sources had tracked the Al Qaeda leader Osama bin Laden to a compound in the city and US Navy SEAL SOFs had been tasked with killing or capturing him. From the FOB, the two Black Hawks inserted the SOF teams into the compound. At this point of the mission, one MH-60 was lost when it entered a vortex ring while hovering over the compound, causing the helicopter to land heavily just outside, striking its tail on the high surrounding wall. The damaged helicopter was then destroyed by its crew to ensure that no classified information or equipment would be compromised. After the SEAL team had

US Marines extinguishing the fire caused when explosives were used to remove the wings from the Mirage 2000D, which had crashed in the Bakwa district, so that the fuselage could be recovered more easily. (USMC)

ABOVE The tail of an RAF TriStar tanker and transport aircraft from 216 Sqn is illuminated in this night-time scene on the apron at Kandahar Air Base in late 2010. A Raytheon Sentinel R1 is silhouetted in the background. (Stradling)

RIGHT The nose of an A-10 Thunderbolt II at Kandahar Air Base showing the 30mm GAU-8/A Avenger seven-barrel rotary cannon. The hydraulically powered weapon has a rate of fire of 3,900 rounds per minute. (Stradling)

accomplished their objective and bin Laden had been assassinated, one of the MH-47s was flown from the FOB to take the place of the damaged MH-60 and the SOF teams were extracted and recovered to Bagram.

Three weeks later, on 24 May, a French Air Force Mirage 2000D and a Mirage F1-CR were providing armed overwatch for a convoy that had been stopped after an IED explosion had destroyed one of the vehicles. With a smaller fuel load than its leader, the Mirage F1 departed the area to refuel, leaving the Mirage 2000D on station. Shortly afterwards this aircraft suffered a catastrophic engine mechanical failure. 'It was a purely mechanical breakdown,' recalled 'Noug', the pilot[32]. 'It was not our day. We tried to restart the engine, in vain. In one minute and forty – the time to activate the ejection seat and descend under canopy – we were on the ground.'

In response to the distress call, six A-10s arrived promptly on the scene and when rescue helicopters arrived some 20 minutes later, the pilots co-ordinated the recovery of the Mirage crew.

ISAF reached its peak strength during 2011, with some 132,000 troops deployed in Afghanistan, provided by 50 NATO and partner nations. The year also represented the peak of aerial operations, with 34,514 CAS missions, resulting in the expenditure of 5,411 weapons. There were also 57,000 airlift sorties, 38,000 ISTAR sorties and 19,500 AAR sorties mounted in support of operations over or within Afghanistan. RPAS also continued to gain in importance. The Luftwaffe replaced its Tornados at Mazar-e-Sharif with three IAI Heron RPAS in June 2010, while the hours flown by five RAF MQ-9 Reapers already outstripped the hours flown by its eight Tornado GR4s. In 2011, RAF Reaper RPAS flew some 12,000hrs, while the Tornados flew just 6,000hrs, and while Reapers released 111 weapons in the year, Tornado crews only released 73. European NATO partners moved the focal point of their operations over Afghanistan to Mazar-e-Sharif during 2011, with the deployment of two NATO-operated Boeing E-3 airborne early warning and control system (AWACS) aircraft in January 2011 and the re-deployment of the RNLAF F-16 Fighting Falcon detachment there. Like other offensive support assets, the RNLAF F-16s also flew reconnaissance missions using the RecceLite pod. The aircraft flew in pairs with one RecceLite aircraft

ABOVE Between 2007 and 2011, Fleet Air Arm (Royal Navy) operated its Westland Commando helicopters as tactical transports, until they were replaced in theatre by the AgustaWestland Merlin. Here a Commando, escorted by a Westland Lynx, releases infra-red decoy flares, during a October 2011sortie. (Crown Coyright/MoD)

RIGHT Winter brings cold conditions to central Afghanistan. A de-icing team at Bagram Air Base prepares a USAF Thunderbolt II for a mission during a snowstorm on 29 December 2013. (USAF)

and the other equipped with the Litening targeting pod, so that they could respond if called upon to support any TIC incidents.

Meanwhile, ISAF and US troops continued to hunt down Taliban leaders. On 6 August, intelligence revealed that Qari Tahir, the leader of the Taliban in the Tangi Valley region of Wardak province (to the west of Kabul), was in the village of Juy Zarin. Escorted by AH-64 Apaches and an AC-130 gunship, a SOF team was sent to neutralize Tahir. The initial assault went well, but Tahir was not caught and remained at large, while Taliban reinforcements were detected entering the area. As the US Immediate Reaction Force arrived by CH-47 Chinook, an insurgent fired an RPG which hit the rotor blades and put the machine catastrophically out of balance. The aircraft crashed almost immediately, killing all 38 on board: it was the greatest loss of life amongst the US SOF in a single incident. It also gave a good indication of the risks faced by helicopter pilots in Afghanistan. The RPG was not a particularly accurate weapon, but the weapon had successfully shot down an MH-47E Chinook in June 2005 and an AH-1W Super Cobra in July 2010. One means of reducing such risks was the use of RPAS helicopters such as the Kaman K-Max, which was used experimentally in Afghanistan for three years by the USMC to transport supplies. Two K-Max carried out autonomous supply deliveries to USMC outposts across Helmand with some success, although one aircraft crashed near Camp Leatherneck on 5 June 2013.

At the NATO conference in Chicago in May 2012 it was agreed that combat operations in Afghanistan would cease at the end of December 2014. A slow but steady reduction in ISAF forces followed this decision, although the French government had already decided to withdraw its combat forces by the end of December 2012. The French Air Force Mirage 2000D/F1-CR detachment left Kandahar in November 2012, but the French Army helicopter detachment at Kabul remained in the country until the following May.

The AV-8B Harriers of VMA-211 redeployed from Kandahar to Camp Leatherneck in July 2012, putting them at the same airfield as the USMC helicopter force. However, despite the declaration by NATO that combat operations would shortly end, the Taliban remained very much engaged in hostilities towards US and ISAF forces. At around 22:00hrs on 14 September, a force of 15 heavily armed Taliban insurgents, dressed in US Army uniforms, cut through the perimeter wire at Camp *Leatherneck* and destroyed six USMC AV-8Bs from VMA-211 and severely damaged another two, along with a C-130E. During the attack, Lt Col Chris Raible, the commanding officer of VMA-211, was killed by the attackers. In the chaos of the attack, an AH-1W flown by Maj Robert Weingart of VMLAH-469 took off, accompanied by two UH-1Y Venom Hueys, with the aim of providing CAS to the airfield defenders. Four intruders had been cornered in the cryogenics facility, but in the smoke of the battle, Weingart could not positively identify the enemy.

Lt Col Stephen Lightfoot, the commanding officer of HMLA-469, explained:

Usually, we respond to TICs for other units. However, everyone acted instinctively, got to the aircraft and got the alert aircraft launched despite taking fire on the flightline ... It was a very dark night. There was no moon. However, on the flightline there were multiple aircraft on fire and a couple other areas were on fire as well, so it was extremely bright. There were 50-to-100 feet-high flames and a lot of thick smoke ... We knew we had a lot of friendly [forces] on the ground. We wanted to make sure we did no harm to them or to their positions ... The pilots were danger-close to friendly positions but were able to use the information received to engage the enemy without endangering friendly forces; they used the information to engage the enemy from approximately 200 feet in the air and were able to eliminate the threat.

A typical scene at Kandahar Air Base: an RAF Panavia Tornado GR4 holds short of the runway, while a pair of F-16 Fighting Falcons takes off. (Stradling)

Weingart later recalled[33]:

I asked if [the Marines on the ground] could concentrate their automatic weapons' fire on the point of origin, so I could [identify] it and get manoeuvred to where we could engage it for them. They saw where the friendly vehicle was engaging at the [enemy], and then they started opening up with the [M-240 machine gun] from the vicinity of our compound. The combination of seeing the rounds from the vehicles and seeing our marines from the northeast gave us a pretty good pinpoint location of where the bad guys were.

Escorted by a Boeing AH-64 Apache gunship, an AgustaWestland Merlin of 1419 Flight RAF departs from Camp Bastion for a sortie on 7 January 2012. (Crown Copyright/MoD)

With support from the helicopters, the insurgents were tracked down and killed, but they had delivered a hard blow to the Marines.

The German Army became the second force after the French Army to deploy the Eurocopter Tiger attack helicopter to Afghanistan, sending four machines to Mazar-e-Sharif in December 2012. In March 2013, the Spanish Army also deployed Tiger gunships. These latter helicopters were transported to Herat in a civilian chartered Antonov An-124 for use by the 1st Attack Helicopter Battalion to support the withdrawal of Spanish forces later in the year.

Unfortunately, there were three fatal aircraft accidents in Afghanistan in early 2013. The first occurred on 23 April when an MC-12W Liberty crashed in Zabul province, killing all four crew members. The pilots had lost control while attempting to avoid a cumulonimbus cloud. Six days later a Boeing 747-400 freighter operated by National Air Cargo crashed immediately after take-off from Kabul. The load of five armoured vehicles had not been properly secured and when the aircraft rotated on take-off, they rolled backwards, damaging the hydraulic systems and the tailplane actuator thereby rendering the aircraft uncontrollable. The aircraft pitched up, stalled and crashed. Then on 3 May, a KC-135 crashed shortly after

A C-5A Galaxy vacates the runway at Kandahar Air Base after landing. (14 Sqn Association)

take-off from Manas Air Base, killing the three crew members. The tanker had suffered a control system malfunction and entered a divergent Dutch roll which quickly became so violent that the tail section of the aircraft separated from the fuselage.

Late on 23 July 2013, during a routine highway clearance patrol by a convoy of 12 ISAF vehicles, the lead vehicle ran off the road and overturned. The troops began to recover the vehicle at sunrise the following morning, but as they did so they came under attack by insurgents. Two A-10s were dispatched to support the ground troops, but the insurgents were well hidden, and their exact location was unknown. The lead A-10 pilot reported[34]:

An An-32 tactical transport aircraft of the AAF, at Kandahar Air Base. The type was withdrawn from the AAF inventory in 2011 and replaced by the ill-suited Italian-built Alenia G222 (C-27A). (14 Sqn Association)

I flew over to provide a show of force while my wingman was looking for gunfire below. Our goal with the show of force was to break the contact and let the enemy know we were there, but they didn't stop. I think that day the enemy knew they were going to die, so they pushed even harder and began moving closer to our ground forces ... Even with all our top-of-the-line tools today, we still rely on visual references. Once we received general location of the enemy's position, I rolled in as lead aircraft and fired two rockets to mark the area with smoke. Then my wingman rolled in to shoot the enemy with his 30mm rounds.

Two RAF CH-47 Chinook helicopters during an operational troop insertion near Lashkar Gar in January 2012. (Crown Copyright/MoD)

In previous recent incidents, the Taliban had disengaged after the second pass from aircraft, but on this day, they continued the engagement, moving closer to the ISAF troops in an attempt to close the distance such that the A-10 pilots could not fire on them for fear of hitting friendly troops. The second A-10 pilot continued the story:

We just kept putting down more 30mm rounds. The bad guys were closing in and according to the muzzle flashes there were a lot of them, but because people were shooting all over the place, the JTAC didn't feel safe bringing in helicopters in to evacuate the wounded personnel. We train for this, but shooting danger-close is uncomfortable, because now the friendlies are at risk. We came in for a low-angle strafe, 75 feet above the enemy's position and used the 30mm gun – 50 metres parallel to ground forces – ensuring our fire was accurate so we didn't hurt the friendlies.

The insurgents were eventually forced to withdraw after a two-hour firefight during which the A-10s carried out 15 strafing passes, firing almost 2,300 rounds of 30mm ammunition and dropping three 500lb bombs. Meanwhile, an MC-12W Liberty which had arrived on the scene carried out a search of the area to ensure that the Taliban would not return for a counter-attack and a HH-60G Pave Hawk Dustoff helicopter from the 83rd ERS recovered a wounded soldier. The transfer of responsibility from ISAF to the ANA began to gather pace during 2013, as ISAF forces began to withdraw and to switch to more of a mentoring role. ISAF ground facilities were also transferred to Afghan control. In one such transfer, which took place on 1 October, the FOB at Sharana, 160km south of Kabul, was handed over to the Afghan government. Under their control, the airfield that had been constructed there, which had been heavily used by C-130 Hercules delivering supplies to the ISAF forces garrison, became a civilian airport.

In December 2013, the AC-130H Spectre gunships of the 16th Special Operations Squadron were withdrawn from Afghanistan, having flown 400 missions in the year. The aircraft were replaced by the more capable AC-130U Spooky gunships. Meanwhile, the rundown of the US presence in Afghanistan was reflected in the disbandment of the 451st EAW at Kandahar on 1 January 2014. At its height of operations, the wing had comprised four groups responsible for operating a number of aircraft types including the F-16, C-130, HH-60 Pave Hawk, E-11A BACN, MQ-1B Predator and MQ-9 Reaper. With the withdrawal of some of those aircraft, the four groups were merged into a single group to continue operations;

A USMC Bell UH-1Y Venom Huey landing at Camp Bastion/Camp Leatherneck on 27 October 2014. The type augmented the firepower of the AH-1W Super Cobra gunship. (USMC)

a large USAF detachment also remained at Bagram. The Predator and Reaper RPAS of the 62nd ERS continued to fly from Kandahar, providing 600 hours of ISTAR daily. The switch in emphasis from manned systems to RPAS was reflected, once again, in the usage by the RAF during 2014 of the MQ-9 Reaper and the Tornado GR4: the Reapers flew 15,000hr and carried out 55 weapon releases, whereas the Tornados flew just over 5,200hr and released only 14 weapons. The Italian Air Force also replaced its MQ-1 Predator at Herat with the MQ-9 Reaper in January 2014.

The Italian Air Force AMX *Ghiblis* saw action on 19 May 2014, when they were tasked to neutralize a Taliban telecommunication and radio transmitter. The transmitter, which was positioned in the mountains in the Bakwa district approximately halfway between Kandahar and Herat, had been located by a Reaper RPAS. Two aircraft took off from Herat and dropped LGBs onto the transmitter, destroying it.

On the ground, Taliban insurgents continued to ambush and engage ISAF and ANA forces. Operating from Bagram, the A-10s of the 303rd EFS were also engaged in offensive action while supporting ISAF ground troops in the Kunar Valley.

A-10 pilot Lt Col John Marks[35] described afterwards how:

> a mission I flew on our most recent trip to Afghanistan, relieving a ground force pinned down by Taliban on three sides and in danger of being surrounded, using our own weapons while also coordinating strikes by an AC-130 gunship, two flights of F-16s, Apaches, and AH-6 Little Birds, stands out as a mission I'm proud of … I was able to use every skill I ever learned as an A-10 pilot to help extract [ISAF troops] from an intense troops-in-contact situation when they were nearly surrounded by Taliban.

The six Belgian F-16s that had deployed to Kandahar during 2008 operated over Afghanistan until they were withdrawn in October 2014. Meanwhile the final RNLAF F-16 mission was flown from Mazar-e-Sharif on 30 June 2014, after which the aircraft returned to the Netherlands. The British also withdrew their aircraft from Kandahar: the Tornado GR4s left Afghanistan on 11 November 2014.

By the end of 2014, it seemed that campaign carried out by ISAF and by US troops under Operation *Enduring Freedom* over the previous five years had been successful and the Taliban had been driven out of its former strongholds. However, the Taliban was by no means a spent force; insurgent attacks against ISAF and US troops continued, albeit at a lower frequency. Nevertheless, the Coalition would enter 2015 with a much-reduced force both on the ground and in the air.

On a damp day, 14 March 2016, USAF Capt Tim Six, from the 421st
Expeditionary Fighter Squadron, takes off from Bagram Air Base for a combat
sortie in an F-16 Fighting Falcon. The 421st EFS was the only dedicated
fighter squadron in Afghanistan at the time. The aircraft is armed with
AGM-65 Maverick missiles. (USAF)

CHAPTER 6

ENDGAME 2015–2021

I don't think the Taliban will ever come back to take Afghanistan, no

Hamid Karzai, 2012

On 1 January 2015, the US-led Operation *Enduring Freedom* was replaced by Operation *Freedom's Sentinel* (OFS) and the NATO-led ISAF mission was replaced by the Resolute Support Mission. OFS was subdivided into two separate but complementary parts: firstly, it involved continuing combat operations against Al Qaeda, ISIS-K, and their affiliates in Afghanistan, and secondly it involved the training, advising, and assisting of the Afghan National Defence and Security Forces (ANDSF) – including the ANA, police and various other security forces under government control through the NATO-led Resolute Support Mission. In turn, the aim of the mission was 'to provide further training, advice and assistance for the ANDSF and Afghan institutions.' Resolute Support had a defined timescale and NATO planned to withdraw its personnel by 1 May 2021, with formal termination of the mission in the September of that year. The drawdown of ISAF and US combat forces in Afghanistan from the end of 2014, and the passing of responsibility for internal security to the government, made the 'Afghanization' of the security forces critically important. Pilot training for Super Tucano pilots commenced

During early 2015, the parallel taxiway at Bagram Air Base was converted into a second runway and a mobile aircraft arresting system (MAAS) was installed. This F-16 Fighting Falcon is testing the functionality of the MAAS on 20 March 2015, prior to the runway being opened for use in April. (USAF)

at Moody AFB, near Valdosta, Georgia, USA, in January 2015. The pilots would graduate in December that year, almost exactly coincident with the end of service life for the Mi-35 attack helicopters which until then had provided CAS to the ANA. The intention was that eventually 30 A-29 pilots would be trained in the USA. However, the difficulty in finding suitable candidates with a good enough command of English meant that only 50 percent of the places on training courses were actually filled, and even then, there was a 26 percent wash-out rate of the remaining trainees. The training of helicopter pilots was also undertaken by various Coalition countries, including the UK, which trained pilots on the Mi-17.

Bagram continued to be the main base for Coalition air operations and April 2015 saw the completion of the project, started the previous autumn, to convert the parallel taxiway into a second runway. The taxiway had been strengthened in some areas and a Mobile Aircraft Arresting System (MAAS) was installed for fast jet operations. Having two useable runways at Bagram ensured that any incidents on the main runway would not affect the ability of the resident 455th AEW to meet its tasking from the CAOC. The number of CAS missions flown over Afghanistan in 2015 illustrated the change in emphasis in Coalition strategy in the country. Just 5,774 missions were flown in 2015 as compared to nearly 13,000 the previous year. The number of weapons releases was also significantly down with fewer than 1,000 releases in 2015 as against 2,365 in 2014.

Tactical transport operations also recorded the lowest number of sorties for over ten years, flying 6,900 sorties, or less than half the number that was flown in the previous year. As ever, though, flying in Afghanistan was relentlessly unforgiving: a fatal accident involving a C-130J Hercules from the 774th EAS at Jalalabad on 2 October resulted in the deaths of six aircrew and five passengers. During the turnaround at Jalalabad, one pilot jammed the control column in the full backwards position with a night vision goggles case to ensure that the elevators were not inadvertently moved while the aircraft was being loaded. Unfortunately, the case had not been removed when the aircraft took off for Bagram, and during the short 28-second flight the aircraft pitched up uncontrollably and then stalled into the ground.

A gunner aboard an AC-130 gunship loads rounds into a 40mm cannon ammunition, while supporting ground operations in the Parwan province to the north of Kabul. This photograph was taken on 3 March 2010. (US Army)

RIGHT A Lockheed AC-130U Spooky gunship from the 4th Special Operations Squadron during a local training sortie in Florida. The type was used extensively to support ground operations by US and Coalition Forces. (USAF)

Fast jet CAS was by now exclusively provided by the detachment of 12 USAF F-16 Fighting Falcons operating from Bagram, whereas previously the task had been shared between A-10 Thunderbolt and F-15E Strike Eagle detachments. On 28 October, the 421st EFS arrived to take its turn at Bagram. Like its predecessor units, it flew

RIGHT An AC-130U Spooky gunship at Kandahar: the setting sun highlights the barrels of its 105mm howitzer, a 40mm cannon and a 25mm rotary cannon armament. (Stradling)

the F-16CM, which had been modified in the common configuration complementation program (which included, inter alia, incorporation of a digital terrain-following capability and the joint helmet-mounted cueing system or JHMCS), giving the aircraft a full night-attack capability. The detachment flew round-the-clock patrols, with at least two aircraft airborne over Afghanistan 24 hours a day, with further fully-armed aircraft kept on strip alert, ready to respond to any call for support. After a relatively quiet start to 2015, with roughly 40 weapon releases a month, the need for 'kinetic' support increased in the summer months and peaked in October with 203 weapons released – a doubling of the monthly rate through the summer months. Capt Bryan Bouchard[36] of the 455th AEW at Bagram explained:

> For the Air Force, in many ways, the mission hasn't changed. We're still here to support the guys on the ground with whatever they need ... When Afghan forces request support, the request is vetted through the proper channels. Then we fly close-air support missions to keep Americans safe and, in limited circumstances, to prevent detrimental strategic effects to the [Afghan forces].

As well as kinetic events, the F-16s were also called upon regularly to fly low-level shows of force, which were often enough to persuade insurgents to withdraw from a fight.

Complementing the F-16s, MQ-1 Predator and MQ-9 Reaper RPAS were flown from Kandahar and Jalalabad and the US Army operated its organic CAS in the shape of AH-64 Apaches. In addition, AC-130U Spooky gunships of the 4th Special Operations Squadron operating from Bagram brought their considerable firepower to bear. On 25 July 2016, an AC-130 commanded by Capt Jonathan Rodgers was providing overwatch for US and Afghan SOF troops during a daylight armed infiltration operation in Nangahar province. After the Coalition forces had pushed deep into the valley, they were ambushed by approximately 50 insurgents, who surrounded them, making good use of high ground and fortified buildings to pin down the friendly forces. Despite a number of gun malfunctions, the AC-130 fired its 105mm howitzer at enemy fighters who were just 120m away from

ABOVE A McDonnell Douglas Helicopters MD 530F Cayuse Warrior of the AAF flies over Kabul, in early December 2014. The type was intended to replace the aging Mi-35 gunship as an offensive support aircraft. (USAF)

RIGHT USAF Capt Dakota Olsen of the 555th Expeditionary Fighter Squadron takes off from Bagram Air Base in an F-16 Fighting Falcon, on 17 June 2015, for an operational mission over Afghanistan. (USAF)

friendly positions. When the gunship needed to return to base to refuel, the crew had already alerted a replacement which joined them over the target area. At this point the insurgents renewed their attack and instead of leaving the area, the first AC-130 remained on task and both gunships flew a co-ordinated formation, firing on the insurgents with four heavy artillery guns. When the lead aircraft became critical on fuel and was forced to leave, a third gunship arrived and once again the two remaining AC-130s took up the fight. On landing, Rogers and his crew had flown a 12-hour sortie, in which 31 insurgents had been killed and there were no casualties amongst friendly forces.

The security situation in Afghanistan deteriorated significantly once US and NATO combat operations ceased. At this stage the ANDSF was incapable, through lack of resources, of providing security across the country without further international help. By September 2015, the Taliban had gained control once more of Kunduz as well as the Musa Qala district of Helmand. In another joint operation, between 30 September and 4 October, ANA and US SOF troops re-captured the city of Kunduz from the Taliban. Airstrikes, which played a critical role in supporting the friendly forces, were co-ordinated by a JTAC, Tech Sgt Brian Claughsey, who was embedded with the US SOF team. On the first day of the assault, the 50-vehicle convoy was ambushed, but an AC-130 suppressed the enemy fire and prevented Taliban forces from engaging the convoy from the rear. Over the four days of the battle, Claughsey controlled 17 strikes by AC-130s and F-16, many of them against insurgents within 140m of friendly positions. Thanks to air support, the

A Mi-17 of the AAF flies over Kandahar Air Base on 2 March 2016. AAF personnel worked closely with Train Advise Assist Command – Air (TAAC–Air), a US-controlled functional command intended to assist the Afghanis to develop a professional, capable and sustainable force. (USAF)

Coalition forces were able to clear the Taliban from the city, although the area remained volatile.

On the night of 2 November 2016, an AC-130U gunship, callsign Spooky 43 and commanded by Maj Alexander Hill, was called to support a joint US SOF and ANA force at the village of Boz-e-Qandahari, on the western outskirts of Kunduz. The troops had been inserted by two MH-47 Chinooks, on a mission to capture a Taliban leader named Qari Mutaqi, but they soon came under heavy fire from a group of insurgents. A pair of AH-64 Apaches supporting the SOF team killed these assailants with Hellfire missiles and gunfire, enabling the friendly forces to continue into the village. The troops reached the compound being used by Mutaqi, where once again they came under heavy defensive fire from the Taliban, causing casualties amongst the US and ANA soldiers. It was at that stage that the US troops realized that the entire village was being used as a depot by the Taliban. The JTAC, Staff Sgt Richard Hunter, called in the AC-130U, which fired

11 February 2016: Afghan aircrew and ground crew parade in front of representative types from the AAF inventory at the 'Rebirth of the Afghan Air Force' ceremony at Hamid Karzai International Airport, where they were addressed by President Ashraf Ghani. The aircraft are, from left to right: Mi-35, Embraer A-29 Super Tucano, C-130H Hercules, Mi-17 and MD 530F Cayuse Warrior. (USAF)

its 105mm howitzer as well as 40mm cannon. 'You end up shooting a lot out there in Afghanistan, right now in particular.' commented Maj Alexander Hill[37]. 'So that night started off not being really out of the ordinary.' Some of the targets were just 12m away from the friendly forces, who were protected by a low wall. Hill continued:

> I'm pretty sure we concussed [Sgt Hunter] a few times. There was an enemy element that was advancing very close to them ... and we pretty much told Sgt Hunter to put his head down, and we fired one round closer than we're pretty sure anyone has ever fired an air-burst round ... It took that for them to finally quiet down to their east.

As dawn approached, the US and Afghan soldiers managed to withdraw from the village, with continued fire support from the AC-130 and one remaining AH-64 (the other had departed after

expending its weapon load). The team was then evacuated by CH-47. Of the force of 50 friendly troops, two US and three Afghan soldiers were killed, and four US and 11 Afghans were wounded during the two-hour firefight; however, 32 civilians had been killed in the village, including 20 children and six women, plus another 36 people injured.

Four A-29 Super Tucano light attack aircraft destined for the AAF arrived at Kabul on 20 March 2017, bringing the total AAF A-29 force up to 12 aircraft. Two of the AAF Super Tucanos were detached to Mazar-e-Sharif from late 2016 to support ground operations around Kunduz. The AAF inventory also included 18 McDonnell Douglas Helicopters MD 530F Cayuse Warrior gunship helicopters, which were also based at Mazar-e-Sharif. All the MD 530s were armed with .50-calibre guns, and the later models to be delivered also had a rocket firing capability. 'Some Afghans were sceptical of the MD 530 when it first started operating, however, it has proven itself in combat,' commented Lt Col Bill Ashford[38], commander of the 438th Air Expeditionary Advisory Squadron. 'Now everyone wants MD 530 support. The pilots are doing great work flying daily combat missions supporting [ANA] troops on the ground and escorting AAF Mi-17s in the air.' The AAF still had 26 serviceable Mi-17s in service (plus another 22 unserviceable airframes) and it remained the hardest working

One of the eight Embraer A-29 Super Tucano light-attack aircraft in the AAF inventory at the time, during a training mission over Afghanistan in August 2015. Working with TAAC–Air, the AAF Super Tucano force was building up to full operational capability. (USAF)

An AAF pilot starts up his A-29 Super Tucano at Kabul for a training sortie on 16 May 2017. (USAF)

type in Afghan service. In addition to regular air force units, the Afghan Special Mission Wing (SMW) operated a further 33 Mi-17s. Established in 2012, the SMW was run directly by the Afghan Ministry of Defence to support counter-terrorism and counter-narcotics operations. Two squadrons of the SMW were based in Kabul, one squadron in Kandahar and the fourth in Mazar-e-Sharif. Since 2005, the US had acquired 63 Mi-17s from Russia for the AAF but plans to spend more than US$1 billion on even more of the helicopters were scrapped after business dealings with Russian arms manufacturers were suspended in protest at the 2014 annexation of the Crimea by Russia.

Meanwhile, security operations continued in the Paktia and Nangahar region bordering Pakistan and on 29 March 2017 a force of 65 heavily armed and well-concealed insurgents ambushed 35 US and Afghan SOF troops in the Kot Valley. An AC-130U gunship commanded by Lt Col Grant Sharpe was available for CAS and descended over the contact so that he could achieve better weapons accuracy. The aircraft was in action for 90 minutes during which it carried out 25 engagements, most of which were within the 'danger close' range where friendly forces were at risk from the aircraft weapons. Despite being low on fuel and at risk from enemy fire, the gunship remained on station until the US and Afghan troops had defeated the insurgents.

Just over a week later, on 8 April, another AC-130U was called to support SOF troops in Nangahar province. This time, a larger force of some 280 US and Afghan troops was involved in a firefight near Jalalabad with insurgents from the ISIS-K group, a fundamentalist Islamic terrorist group affiliated to Al Qaeda. When the AC-130 commanded by Capt Joseph Tomczak arrived on the scene, a number of AH-64s and F-16s were already engaging the insurgents. Tomczak[39] recalled:

> Gunship guys aren't used to packing sunscreen on deployment, that's not really something that we do, so we were a little out of our element already, just going into ... [it was] already hot when we showed up ... engagements were already taking place, and so we just kind of jumped right in ... You've got Apache helicopters that were low level, there were fighters from the 79th Fighter Squadron who were there as well, who we also developed a really close relationship with, so we started engaging ... as soon as we rolled overhead.

Co-ordinating their attacks with the F-16s and AH-64s, the gunship crew remained on station for three hours, after which they expended all of their ammunition, causing the 40mm cannon to overheat. Realizing that gunship support was still needed over the battlefield, Tomczak returned to Bagram, where another AC-130 which had already been fully armed and fuelled awaited them. Tomczak continued:

A Lockheed Martin F-22 Raptor from the 95th Expeditionary Fighter Squadron taxies past KC-10 Extender at Al Dhafra Air Base in the United Arab Emirates for an Operation *Jagged Knife* mission on 19 November 2017. The objective of the operation was to destroy the Taliban narco-insurgency and financing in Afghanistan. (USAF)

The view from a KC-10 Extender from the 908th Expeditionary Air Refueling Squadron, as it refuels an F-22 Raptor from the 95th Expeditionary Fighter Squadron during an Operation *Jagged Knife* mission on 19 November 2017. The Afghan and US combined operation struck drug production facilities and command-and-control nodes in northern Helmand province. (USAF)

Instead of having to cold-start an airplane, we co-ordinated it on the way back so that we would land, pull into parking, shut down, literally run across the ramp to the airplane that had engines running, man all of our crew positions, and then take off again. Every single person ... on that airplane knew exactly what we were going back into, and they knew that the guys on the ground needed the help, so you can imagine the hustle.

The crew took off for their second mission just 19min after landing from the first. Meanwhile, Lt Col Craig Andrle and his wingman, Capt Adam Fuhrmann, in a pair of F-16s, had already launched from Bagram with each aircraft armed with two 500lb bombs and one 2,000lb GBU-31. In short order, Lt Col Andrle had expended all of his weapons, so, leaving Fuhrman over the battleground, he returned to Bagram, swapped into a fully armed fighter and raced back to re-join the engagement. Soon both of the F-16s had used up their weapon loads but they remained overhead until the AC-130 had returned to the scene. By then the engagement had quietened down and after waiting on station the aircraft began to run short of fuel. However, at this moment the firefight erupted once again.

Tech Sgt Brett Laswell[40] took up the story:

> [We] started putting down rounds, and then we lose communication with these guys, and we're already close to minimum fuel ... And something from that day that will [live] forever with me ... you could hear the desperation in the JTAC's voice. That was one of the last transmissions ... it said we need effective immediate fire now, and that's the last thing ... so we just continued to put down rounds until we ended up Winchestering [emptying] the 40[mm cannon] again... We ended up shooting 416 rounds on the 40, and I think we shot 57 or 58 105mm rounds, with a couple thousand 25mm rounds as well in just a short period of time.

During the engagement, the gunship crew had struggled to fix numerous malfunctions with their guns. As dusk approached, the friendly forces were able to disengage and the AC-130 returned to Bagram.

In response to the continuing insurgency by the ISIS-K group in Nangahar province, the USAF dropped a GBU-43/B massive ordnance air blast (MOAB) bomb on a cave and tunnel system at the mouth of the Mahmand Valley in the Achin district of Nangarhar on 13 April 2017. The 21,600lb GPS guided weapon, which was dropped from an MC-130H Combat Talon II, obliterated much of the complex and killed 90 insurgents. This was the first time that the weapon had been employed operationally.

In yet another incident involving an AC-130 supporting US and Afghan SOF forces in Nangahar province, a gunship commanded by Maj Jarrod Judd provided CAS for a force of 378 friendly troops on 24 May. On this occasion an aircraft generator malfunctioned during the engagement, filling the flight deck with smoke and fumes. While the tactical crew continued to fire on a Taliban sniper position, the flight deck crew donned oxygen masks and tackled the aircraft emergency. The gun crew also had to cope with multiple stoppages

NEXT PAGES An F-16 Fighting Falcon from the 77th Expeditionary Fighter Squadron flying from Bagram Air Base prepares to refuel over Afghanistan from a KC-135 Stratotanker from the 340th Expeditionary Air Refueling Squadron. (USAF)

More Operation *Jagged Knife* missions were launched on the evening of 21 November 2017. Here an F-16 Fighting Falcon from the 77th Fighter Squadron takes off from Bagram Air Base. Once again, the targets were in northern Helmand province. (USAF)

with both the 25mm and 40mm guns while they maintained support for the ground forces, until reinforcements in the shape of AH-64s arrived.

Almost from the start of hostilities in Afghanistan, and in parallel with counter-insurgency operations, the Coalition nations had also been prosecuting a campaign against drug production, particularly of opium, in the country. The results had been mixed, not least because the Taliban encouraged and enforced poppy production, since taxing profits from drug manufacture was a strong source of revenue for them. The 2017 crop had produced the largest poppy harvest since the US-led intervention in 2001. Over the winter of 2017–18, US and Afghan forces carried out Operation *Jagged Knife*, a combined air operation which was aimed at destroying drug manufacturing facilities across Afghanistan. The first missions were flown on 19 November, during which the commander of US Forces in Afghanistan, Gen John Nicholson, claimed the destruction of eight drugs factories in Helmand province. The campaign opened with attacks by AAF A-29 Super Tucanos, which were followed by strikes by B-52s and Lockheed Martin F-22 Raptors. Supported by KC-10s and KC-135s, the B-52s used the conventional rotary launcher for the first time over Afghanistan to deliver 2,000lb JDAMs. The bombers were from

the 69th EBS based at Al Udeid in Qatar. The F-22s, which were making their debut over Afghanistan, flew from Al Dhafra air base in the UAE. They were chosen for the airstrikes because they could carry the GBU-39B Small Diameter Bomb (SDB) which had been selected for use in order to avoid collateral damage. Weighing only 250lb, the SDB was a precision guided munition that could be dropped 45 miles from its target. In one strike that day SDBs were used to destroy two buildings within a single compound, leaving a third building in the same compound undamaged. Operation *Jagged Knife* continued through the next months, supported by E-8 Joint STARs, with F-16s and F/A-18s also participating in airstrikes. By 12 December, 25 drugs manufacturing plants had been destroyed.

Although fewer CAS sorties were flown over Afghanistan in 2017 than in 2016, the number of weapons expended rose from 1,337 to over 4,300. By the end of 2017 it was estimated that since NATO had ceased combat operations the Taliban had either seized control of, or was contesting, at least 40 percent of the country. With the air campaign against the Taliban ramping up once more there was an obvious need for more airpower in the region and the A-10C Thunderbolts from the 303rd EFS were ordered back to Afghanistan. The aircraft landed at Kandahar on 19 January 2018

The Sikorsky UH-60 Black Hawk was chosen to replace the Mil Mi-17 in AAF service. This AAF UH-60 is at Kandahar on 18 February 2018. (USAF)

and were flying operational missions within 24 hours of arriving in theatre. Apart from providing CAS for ground troops, the A-10s were also incorporated into the tasking for Operation *Jagged Knife*. KC-135s were also deployed to Kandahar, along with MQ-9 Reapers and HH-60G Pave Hawk CSAR helicopters. The number of F-16s at Bagram had also been increased to 18 aircraft since the previous summer. The first kinetic strikes by the newly arrived A-10s were on 24 January when they provided CAS for an ANDSF patrol that had been ambushed in Helmand province. During the engagement, the target was laser marked by a RPAS operated by the US Army.

AC-130U Spooky gunships continued to work closely with SOF teams. On 25 April 2018, a joint US and ANA SOF team was directed to capture a Taliban leader who was deep inside Taliban-held territory. After the team successfully secured one compound, where they captured their target, they found intelligence material indicating that a second Taliban officer was also located nearby. The AC-130U crew made use of their night vision sensors to guide the SOF team along a stream bed from the first compound to the other compound where the second target was thought to be located. However, as they advanced, the SOF team was ambushed by enemy forces using grenades, assault rifles and belt-fed heavy machine guns. The JTAC embedded with the team, Tech Sgt Cam Kelsch, called in 40mm cannon fire from the gunship against target just 35m away from friendly positions. Rounds from the aircraft 105mm howitzer forced the insurgents back and the SOF team was able to disengage and withdraw under cover from two F-16s, which dropped 500lb bombs on any remaining enemy.

Five days later, Lt Col Michael Coloney was flying an F-16 on another task when he was diverted to assist a SOF team that was attempting to clear a village in Kapisa province, to the northeast of Kabul. The team had been ambushed by some 80 Taliban fighters and Coloney spent the next five hours carrying out GPS-guided bombing attacks and strafing passes against enemy positions, which at times were within 30m of friendly forces.

Continuing the drawdown of Coalition forces in Afghanistan, US aircraft finally left Kandahar Air Base in early May, and it was handed

over to the Afghan government on 13 May. At its height, the air base had been home to 26,000 US and Coalition personnel and was one of the busiest airports in Afghanistan. Control of the air base at Mazar-e-Sharif was also passed to the Afghan government by the German garrison the following month.

After a year-and-a-half period in which no air supply drops were made, a USAF C-17 Globemaster performed the first C-17 airdrop in country in May 2018. During the month, C-17s and C-130s also

RIGHT A Cessna C-208 Caravan of the AAF ready for a mission from Kabul on 1 June 2018, which was the first combat airdrop carried out by the AAF. Ammunition was dropped to members of the Afghan National Police (ANP) and citizens of Badakshan in northeastern Afghanistan who were fighting Taliban forces. (USAF)

airdropped more than 120 bundles weighing more than 86,000kg in support of US and Afghan ground forces. AAF Cessna C-208 Caravans also carried out their first ever combat airdrop on 1 June, delivering ammunition to ANDSF personnel and citizens who were fighting the Taliban in Badakshan province, in the northeast of the country. The AAF operated 24 of these single-engine light transport aircraft, which were well suited to the austere landing strips in the country. And, in a year that saw an almost doubling, year on year, of the number both of CAS missions and the number of weapons expended, the AAF gained the ability to drop LGBs from its A-29 Super Tucanos. The LGB capability, which greatly improved the accuracy of A-29 support to the ANDSF, had been introduced in March and over 50 LGBs were dropped in the first three months. By mid-May the A-29 Super Tucano pilots had provided CAS for approximately 30 ground missions by ANDSF troops, using their newly acquired capability. In the autumn of 2018, the first ground attack mission by a Lockheed Martin F-35B Lightning 'stealth fighter' was flown over Afghanistan. The USMC aircraft launched from USS *Essex* (LHD-2), a Wasp-class amphibious assault ship, on 27 September to strike a fixed Taliban position in Afghanistan with a precision guided weapon. The airstrike had been requested by the ground force commander in support of a ground clearance operation. After completing the mission, the F-35B landed vertically back onto the deck of the *Essex*.

OPPOSITE A USMC Lockheed Martin F-35B Lightning II from VMFA-211 of the 13th MEU launches from the amphibious assault ship USS *Essex* (LHD-2) for the first operational ground-attack mission by the type over Afghanistan on 27 September 2018. (USMC)

In late 2018, the USAF had placed an order for seven Orbital ATK AC-208 Eliminator mini-gunships for the AAF. The AC-208 was a

ABOVE A B-1B Lancer from the 34th Expeditionary Bomb Squadron at Al Udeid Air Base in Qatar is prepared for a mission over Afghanistan on 19 May 2018. The B-1B had returned to the US Central Command (CENTCOM) area of operations in April to combat Taliban and other terrorist groups. (USAF)

militarized version of the Cessna 208B Caravan and was equipped with an L3 Wescam MX-15 EO/IR sensor which included infra-red sensing, and a laser illuminator and rangefinder. The aircraft, which were delivered in February 2019, could be armed with the BAe Systems 2.75in. AGR-20 advanced precision kill weapon system (APKWS) rockets and AGM-114 Hellfire missiles. Meanwhile, by mid-2019, the four remaining Mi-35s in service with the AAF had been grounded indefinitely because they were overdue their 500-hour inspections. The AAF did not have the equipment or suitably trained tradesmen to perform the necessary checks, leaving the helicopters unusable. The story behind these helicopters originated in 2008, when five Mi-35s were supplied by the Czech Republic. These helicopters had reached the end of their fatigue life in 2015 and at that time, the US Department of Defense (DoD) had advised that the aircraft should not be sustained. The DoD recommended instead that the AAF should abandon the Mi-35 and concentrate on the US-supplied MD 530F Cayuse Warrior. However, at that point, India had responded and supplied an additional four Mi-35 helicopters, and it was these four aircraft, acquired in 2015, that were grounded in 2019.

Air operations over Afghanistan continued to expand in scope over the next year and during 2019, US offensive support aircraft employed 7,423 weapons over the country, which was more than they had during any previous year since 2009.

Nevertheless, Lt Col John Marks[41], an A-10 pilot with extensive experience over Afghanistan, commented that:

the most dramatic change in how we operated was from 2018 to 2020. We were going to strictly stay in an advisory role, so we essentially ended up being the eyes and ears for the commanders

A Bombardier E-11A battlefield airborne communications node (BACN) of the 430th Expeditionary Electronic Combat Squadron at Kandahar Airfield on 16 November 2018. Providing radio and data relay to ground forces and air units, the BACN was unique to the 430th EECS and to the Afghan theatre. (USAF)

over the battlefield, advising them on what was going on without being – except in a few rare instances – a direct participant. It was more intelligence, surveillance and reconnaissance than anything. The Afghan forces were having a hard time and we knew it. It was a situation where, well, we're doing what we can in terms of what our leaders want us to do. We would have liked to have jumped into a lot of situations, but that was not the overall strategy. That was certainly frustrating.

The USAF suffered another fatal accident on 27 January 2020 when an E-11A BACN aircraft crashed in the Deh Yak district, some 120km south of Kabul. The aircraft had experienced a catastrophic engine failure and the pilots had shut down the wrong engine, leaving them with indications of a double engine failure. The aircraft was destroyed in the subsequent attempted forced landing in open terrain.

On 29 February 2020, the US government signed a treaty with the Taliban, in which a timetable for the withdrawal of US military personnel and contractors was agreed in exchange for an undertaking that 'the Taliban will not allow any of its members, other individuals or groups, including al-Qa'ida, to use the soil of Afghanistan to threaten the security of the United States and its allies.'

Under this agreement, all US and allied military personnel would leave Afghanistan by May 2021. Although US aircraft could still operate from bases outside the country after that date, the main burden of CAS and tactical transport operations would fall on the AAF. In 2020, the AAF fixed-wing fleet comprised four C-130H Hercules (of which two were in Europe undergoing maintenance at any one time), 24 C-208 Caravans, ten AC-208 Eliminators, and 24 A-29 Super Tucanos (of which 18 were in the country, with the remainder being used for training in the USA). In addition, the helicopter fleet included 13 Mi-17s (plus another 22 aircraft allocated to the SMW), 47 MD 530 Cayuse Warriors (of which 38 were in the country), 41 UH-60A Black Hawks, and the four unserviceable Mi-35s. The US DoD[42] reported that:

the AAF relies on Contract Logistics Support [CLS] to ensure the sustainability of its fleet. CLS remains critical to platform

sustainment. Even for the Mi-17 fleet, for which the AAF and SMW can perform 90 percent of flight-line maintenance, the AAF and SMW are unable to perform overhauls required every three to four years at a cost of about $6,000,000 each. Instead, the US Army's Multinational Aviation Program Support Office manages these overhauls, and various contractors with expertise in Mi- 17 systems [mainly in Europe] perform them.

The AAF was totally reliant on contractors for the maintenance of the UH-60, since the aircraft was vastly more modern and complex than the Russian-built helicopters which formed the backbone of both engineering and piloting experience within Afghanistan. Maintenance engineers who were used to Russian language manuals found the transition to English as yet another barrier to be overcome.

Shortly after the US-Taliban treaty had been signed, the Taliban began a campaign against the ANDSF, which reached a peak between September and November 2020. Taking care not to cross the boundaries of the agreement, they set about testing the strength and will of the ANDSF. However, plans for the withdrawal of US troops were now well under way. In April, six B-52s from the 23rd EBS were detached from Minot AFB, North Dakota to Al Udeid in Qatar to cover the withdrawal. During their six-month deployment, the

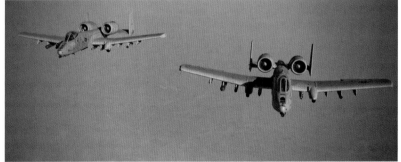

LEFT A pair of USAF A-10 Thunderbolt IIs operating from Kandahar in loose formation as they patrol the desert region of south-west Afghanistan on 15 August 2019. Predominantly used in the CAS role, the A-10 also took part in the pre-planned strikes of Operation *Jagged Knife*, targeting Taliban drug-related sources of revenue. (USAF)

aircraft flew 240 combat sorties, amounting to 3,100 hours, over Afghanistan. The aircraft carrier USS *Dwight D. Eisenhower* (CVN-65), with CVW-3 embarked, was also tasked to provide air cover for the withdrawal but was relieved on 25 June by USS *Ronald Reagan* (CVN-76), and the F/A-18E Super Hornets of CVW-5. Naval aircraft mounted regular patrols over Afghanistan, carrying out overwatch and also conducting airstrikes when tasked to do so.

By the end of June, equipment and troops making up 896 C-17 loads were flown out of Afghanistan, mainly from Bagram. The A-10s, F-16s and AC-130s were also withdrawn from the airfield. In the early hours of 2 July 2021, US forces finally left Bagram discreetly, without informing the ANDSF troops who were guarding the base at the time. Once the hub of Soviet military operations in Afghanistan,

ABOVE An A-10 Thunderbolt II, from the 303rd Expeditionary Fighter Squadron, departs a tanker aircraft after refuelling over Afghanistan on 14 November 2019 (USAF)

RIGHT A Boeing F/A-18E Super Hornet from VFA-136 operating from the USS *Harry S. Truman* (CVN-75) over Afghanistan on 14 January 2020. Naval aircraft provided air cover over the country during the withdrawal of US troops. (USAF)

and more recently the main base for US aircraft and troops, the US retreat from Bagram was deeply symbolic to the Afghans. The closure of Bagram was perceived both as a defeat for the USA and as a signal to the ANDSF that it could expect no further American assistance. ANDSF morale, which was already fragile, evaporated even further. During the month of July, the level of violence in the country increased significantly on both sides, including airstrikes by US aircraft against Taliban targets. Overwatch for US personnel on the ground was provided by F-15E Strike Eagles from the 494th EFS operating from Al Dhafra Air Base in the UAE. Because of the long distances involved in order to carry out this mission effectively, the Strike Eagles, operating in pairs, were accompanied over Afghanistan by a dedicated KC-10 Extender tanker from the 908th ERS.

While the AAF did its best to cover the shortfall in air support after the departure of US aircraft based in the country, it was too small to meet all of the needs of the ANDSF. In particular, the 15 Super Tucanos that were available for use could not satisfy the CAS demands of all seven of the corps within the ANA, as well as its SOF teams, all of which were involved in combat across the entire country. As the date for the withdrawal of the final US and Coalition troops drew closer, ANDSF resistance finally crumbled completely. Between 6 August and 5 September 2021, the Taliban carried out a complete reconquest of Afghanistan. On 15 August, Taliban forces had reached the outskirts of Kabul, at which point President Ghani fled to Uzbekistan, and his government collapsed.

A mass evacuation of non-combatant foreign nationals had already started on 13 August, after the Taliban closed all land border crossings. US and UK troops secured Kabul airport, which had by then become the only route out of the country. At this point many of the AAF aircraft were flown out of Afghanistan into neighbouring countries as AAF personnel sought to escape the Taliban. USAF C-17 Globemasters began to evacuate US nationals and other eligible foreigners, but because of the scale of the task, the ten KC-10 Extender tankers in theatre were also co-opted into the airlift fleet as transport aircraft. In addition to the ten KC-10s, the US evacuation utilized 25 C-17s, three C-130 Hercules and 61 chartered civilian aircraft. The military aircraft would deliver their passengers to a safe airfield, typically in

the Persian Gulf region, and passengers would then be transported further afield by the Civil Reserve Air Fleet (CRAF) which had been activated for the operation. The CRAF comprised 18 aircraft – three each from American Airlines, Atlas Air, Delta Air Lines, and Omni Air, two from Hawaiian Airlines and four from United Airlines.

Canada also began to extract its personnel from Kabul using chartered aircraft from 4 August. These efforts were replaced on 19 August by Operation *Aegis*, a military airlift using the CC-177 Globemaster, the CC-130J Hercules and CC-150 Polaris (a version of the Airbus A310-300) transports. The British evacuation, codenamed Operation *Pitting*, commenced on 14 August. The RAF contribution comprised five C-17 Globemasters, three Airbus A330 Voyagers, two C-130J Hercules and two Airbus A400M Atlases. The airlift gathered pace and complexity as the air

ABOVE Evacuees are silhouetted against the airfield lights as they queue to board a C-17 Globemaster III from the 816th Expeditionary Airlift Squadron at Hamid Karzai International Airport in Kabul on 21 August 2021. (USAF)

LEFT An A-10A Thunderbolt II from the 190th Expeditionary Fighter Squadron of the Idaho ANG over Afghanistan on 29 June 2020. (USAF)

ABOVE A number of nations supported the air evacuation from Kabul, including the United Kingdom. Here evacuees board a C-17 Globemaster III of 99 Sqn RAF at Hamid Karzai International Airport on 20 August 2021. (USMC)

RIGHT On 15 August 2021, a USAF Boeing C-17 Globemaster III safely airlifted some 823 Afghan citizens from Hamid Karzai International Airport. (USAF)

forces of other nations began operations. The Dutch government dispatched a KDC-10 and two C-17s, Italy provided a Boeing KC-767 and Spain used two A400Ms based in Dubai. A French Air Force A310 and an A400M shuttled between Kabul and Abu Dhabi, and a German A400M was also involved, although the Germans were heavily criticized after their aircraft left Kabul with just seven passengers on board. The Polish flew 14 civilian charter and 30 military flights from Kabul.

The RNZAF flew three evacuation flights in a C-130H Hercules, while the RAAF contribution comprised two C-130J Hercules and two C-17A Globemasters, which between them carried out 30 flights. The RAAF also provided an Airbus KC-30A (a tanker version of the A330) which flew eight sorties over Afghanistan providing fuel for the USAF F-16 Fighting Falcons, and the USN F/A-18E Super Hornets from the USS *Ronald Reagan*, which were tasked with overwatch for the evacuation. In addition to the fighter-bombers, AC-130U gunships and MQ-9 RPAS also patrolled the skies above Afghanistan to ensure that no attempt was made by terrorist or insurgent groups to interfere with the evacuation operation. 'The conditions that day were like none I had ever seen,' recalled Lt Col Dominic Calderon[43] who was flying a C-17 on 15 August. 'The airfield was breached and there were mass crowds entering the airfield.'

On average there were between 30 and 50 flights from Kabul each day, except during the period 16–19 August while the Taliban took over Kabul city, when the daily number dropped to between three and eight flights each day. It soon became clear that the air traffic controllers at Kabul airport were being overwhelmed by the numbers and diversity of aircraft using the airport, so the USAF and USMC took over the control function on 17 August. When air traffic controller Tech Sgt Benjamin Gibson[44] arrived at Kabul: 'there were literally hundreds and hundreds – possibly thousands – of refugees. There wasn't much of a direction on where to go because everything was hectic.' The combined USAF and USMC controllers set up the airfield lighting to allow 24-hour operations and divided themselves into two 12-hour shifts. Conditions at Kabul were less than ideal, with crowds of people all trying to get onto an aeroplane and the security forces having great difficulty in controlling them. On 26 August, a Taliban suicide bomb killed 170 people, including

13 US military personnel, and wounded another 150 people. Meanwhile, many Afghan civilians managed to break through the airfield perimeter fencing and surge onto the runway and the aircraft aprons.

Staff Sgt Jacob T. Crabtree[45], an air traffic controller, described how:

we had very minimal equipment to do our jobs so it was very bare bones controlling. Aircraft would call up from random positions in varying distances away from the airport. It was all just real-time decisions, doing the best we could to ensure the safety of all aircraft ... The most intense part was that there was never a moment of silence.

ABOVE 30 August 2021: The last US service member to depart from Afghanistan, Maj Gen Chris Donahue, commander of the US Army 82nd Airborne Division, boards a Boeing C-17 Globemaster III at Hamid Karzai International Airport. (US Army)

LEFT An Airbus A400M transport aircraft of the German Air Force (Luftwaffe) arrives at Tashkent Airport carrying evacuees from Kabul on 17 August 2021. (Photo by Marc Tessensohn/Bundeswehr via Getty Images)

> From the moment we got off the C-17 to the moment we left, there was gunfire in pretty much a full 360 [degrees] around us. I worked during the night hours most of the time and throughout the night you would see explosions going off in many directions, as well as tracer fire flying over aircraft that were landing or departing.

At its height, the combined air transport efforts carried 26,000 people out of the country in one day, but the average achievement was 7,500 evacuees. The normal passenger load for a C-17 was 300, but one RAF Globemaster achieved a record for the service in airlifting 436 passengers in one flight. This was exceeded a few days later by a Canadian CC-177 Globemaster which carried 506 passengers. However, even this total had already been dwarfed by the USAF C-17 crew, callsign Reach 871, of the 816th EAS, on 15 August when they transported 823 passengers (made up of 643 adults with 183 children) from Kabul.

An RAF pilot, Wg Cdr Kev Latchman[46], recalled taking off from Kabul in an aircraft loaded with 300 passengers while a bus full of Afghan refugees drove across the runway in front of him:

> they were about a thousand feet ahead of us – we wouldn't have been able to reject the take-off. If I'd tried – we'd have basically taken out the bus, that doesn't really bear thinking about. So, I had to continue the take-off and we just missed the bus by maybe 10 or 15 feet ... The conditions were stark.

While 'eligible' personnel were evacuated from Kabul, the AAF had gone into meltdown. Morale, which was already low, plummeted further because of assassinations by the Taliban of a number of their pilots. On 7 August, Hamidullah Habibi, an AAF pilot, was killed in a car bomb explosion in Kabul; other off-duty pilots had already been targeted around Mazar-e-Sharif. In addition, the AAF had become critically short of weapons and ammunition, especially since the US had earlier stopped the delivery of GBU-58 LGB bombs. In one typical incident on 15 August, Afghan security guards at Kabul airport who believed that an AAF helicopter was about to leave the country tried to board the aircraft at gunpoint, even though its actual destination was just on the opposite side of the city; in the ensuing struggle both pilot and crewman were seriously injured. Four helicopters did leave Kabul that day, carrying Afghan President Ghani and 53 other passengers, half of whom were security personnel, on a flight to Termez in Uzbekistan. In all, 46 AAF aircraft, comprising 22 fixed-wing types (a mix of A-29 Super Tucano, AC-208 Eliminator, C-208 Caravan and Pilatus PC-12) and 24 helicopters (primarily Mi-17 and UH-60 Black Hawk) were flown into Uzbekistan. A further 18 aircraft were flown to Tajikistan. Some of the AAF aircraft were already outside the country, including five Mi-17s which were being serviced in Ukraine and another 11 Mi-17s which were in storage at Davis-Montham AFB. All 16 of these Mi-17s were subsequently transferred to the Ukrainian armed forces. Meanwhile, a team from the US Army 82nd Airborne Division sought out AAF aircraft around the airfield at Kabul and sabotaged them that the Taliban could not use them. The team chose not to use explosives in case that caused panic on the airfield, so instead critical avionics systems were ripped out, instruments were smashed, and fuel leads were cut or blocked.

For most of the nations involved, the evacuation effort ended on 26 August, although the British effort lasted another two days. However, the Singapore Air Force provided an Airbus A330 MRTT to assist the US effort from 26 August. By the time of the final US flight on 30 August, nearly 124,000 people had been evacuated from Kabul by a fleet of around 85 aircraft which between them flew 2,600 sorties. While the evacuation was in progress, the US continued to strike at insurgent groups, particularly ISIS-K, using RPAS. Two ISIS-K planners were killed in a 'drone strike' on 28 August. Even after the withdrawal of all US troops from Afghanistan, the USA retained the option of carrying out further 'over the horizon' attacks using the RPAS fleet.

On 31 August, President Joe Biden announced:

Last night in Kabul, the United States ended 20 years of war in Afghanistan – the longest war in American history.

From 1985, the threat from MANPADs, such as the Stinger infra-red seeking missile, meant that all aircraft operating over Afghanistan had to be protected by decoy flares. In the case of the MiG-23 they were carried in dispensers within the over-wing strakes, which are very obvious in this view. (Grandolini)

CHAPTER 7

THE BENEFITS OF HINDSIGHT

History, with all her volumes vast, hath but one page

Lord Byron

Although this book is limited in scope to the air campaigns over Afghanistan, those campaigns can only be properly assessed in the context of the political strategies and ground campaigns that they supported.

POLITICAL STRATEGY

The often-quoted proverb 'history repeats itself' seems to be remarkably apposite in considering foreign involvement Afghanistan. As mentioned in the first chapter, the British experience in the First Anglo-Afghan War set the tone for foreign involvement in the country and both the Soviet and subsequent US/NATO interventions followed much the same course. The root causes of all of these failures to change the fundamental way of life in Afghanistan was a lack of appreciation by politicians of the size of the task, as well as a lack of long-term political will to see that task through to success. Writing in the early 1990s on behalf of the Russian general staff in their analysis of the Soviet Afghan campaign, Col Valentin Runov[47] observed:

Former First Secretary of the USSR, Mikhail Gorbachev meets President Barack Obama of the USA in July 2009; in attempting to extract their respective troops from Afghanistan within an artificially – and ultimately unrealistically – short timescale, both men had inadvertently sealed the fate of the country and the demise of the client governments there. (NARA)

during its entire sojourn, the Soviet forces in Afghanistan compellingly demonstrated the results of the lack of political support for its actions by the government of the USSR. When the highest political leaders of the USSR sent its forces into war, they did not consider the historic, religious and national particularities of Afghanistan ... It is now clear that the Afghans, whose history includes many centuries of warfare with various warring groups, could not see these armed strangers as anything but armed invaders.

Similarly, in his interim report for US Congress in May 2022 John F. Sopko[48], the Special Inspector General for Afghanistan Reconstruction (SIGAR), wrote that:

the US military has mounted four large-scale security sector assistance [SSA] efforts in the last 72 years, and three of the four have been catastrophic failures. In Vietnam and Afghanistan, the United States spent years and billions of dollars training and equipping national armies, only to see them quickly collapse in the face of far less-equipped insurgencies once US logistical, equipment enabler, and air support were withdrawn. The exception is South Korea – but the SSA effort there has taken seven decades at a cost of some $3 billion a year.

The fundamental flaw in both the Soviet and US planning was in artificially limiting the timescale in which to achieve both political aims and military objectives. The Soviet government had already begun to seek ways of disengaging from Afghanistan in 1980, shortly after it had sent troops into the country. The Geneva Accords of 1988 had defined a timescale for the withdrawal of Soviet troops, even though the security situation in the country had not been stabilized. Although the post-Soviet Najibullah regime survived the battle of Jalalabad in 1989, it was already clear that its authority had been seriously undermined by the time of the Soviet withdrawal from the country. As a result, the civil war that followed in 1983 was inevitable. Unfortunately, it seems that the lessons from the Soviet experience had not been absorbed by the US leadership; although the Obama administration had stated its public intention to with draw from Afghanistan and had started the process in 2011, the SIGAR found that:

> the single most important factor in the ANDSF's collapse in August 2021 was the US decision to withdraw military forces and contractors from Afghanistan through signing the US-Taliban agreement in February 2020 under the Trump administration, followed by President Biden's withdrawal announcement in April 2021.

Indeed, the hasty and unannounced evacuation of Bagram Air Base in July 2021 was seen by Afghans as a strongly symbolic abandonment of the ANDSF and their government, and from that moment the fate of the country was sealed.

GROUND CAMPAIGNS

Against this strategic background, both Soviet and Coalition military commanders found themselves facing a difficult task that, because of wavering political direction and support, was almost predestined to fail. Not only were they constrained by a political wish to disengage at the earliest opportunity, but they were also under-resourced to conduct successful military operations in a relatively large country with a harsh environment, extreme terrain and a hostile population. As early as 2002, former US Secretary of State and former Supreme Allied Commander Europe Alexander Haig[49] commented that 'in *Desert Storm*, we had too many troops; in Afghanistan probably not enough for the major commitment we have made.' This would appear to have been an accurate assessment, given that in the mid-1980s the Soviet OKSVA numbered somewhere between 118,000 to 150,000 troops[50] and still could not control the country, whereas in 2006 ISAF numbered just 55,000 troops[51] (including 12,000 US personnel), plus a further 20,000 US troops deployed in the country to support OEF. Furthermore, it was not until 2011 – or ten years after the intervention was launched – that ISAF reached its peak strength of 132,000. Thus, the Coalition forces were always subject to overstretch and they became reliant in airpower to 'fill the gaps' in transport and firepower. This in turn meant that air tasking tended to be reactive rather than proactive.

A Soviet T-62 main battle tank (MBT) in Afghanistan, 1987. At first the Soviet 40th Army attempted to fight a European-style war, before learning that a different approach was needed. (NARA)

When the Soviet ground campaign commenced, the OKSVA used the same tactics that it might have employed against conventional forces in Europe, but it soon became clear that a different approach was needed to fight the mujahideen. The Russian general staff noted that 'from the first day of the war, helicopters proved to be an integral asset, a true friend of the ground forces and often their sole support and salvation.'

Indeed, the use of helicopter-borne DShB troops quickly became the norm and the OKSVA began to carry out more focussed operations against specific targets, rather than employing an indiscriminate scorched earth policy. Even so, the apparent willingness of Soviet troops to inflict high collateral casualties caused great antipathy between Afghans and the invaders. Twenty years later, US Gen McChrystal noticed the same link between collateral casualties and local resentment when he assumed command of UFOR-A and ISAF, and he took action to reduce civilian casualties; unfortunately, by then much damage had already been done to Afghan-Coalition relations.

The effectiveness of Coalition efforts to secure Afghanistan was also compromised by the split lines of command and the differing missions in the US national counter-terrorist campaign (OEF and later OFS) and the NATO security, training and redevelopment

US Army soldiers from the 505th Parachute Infantry Regiment on patrol in northwestern Afghanistan in October 2004. Like the Soviets before them, US and ISAF troops did not have sufficient numbers to hold and control ground once they had driven the insurgents from it. (NARA)

campaign (ISAF and later Resolute Support). These separate campaigns were subject to different ROE and frequently had contradictory requirements. To some extent the duality of the command structure was simplified in 2008 with the appointment of Gen David D. McKiernan as the dual-hatted commander of both USFOR-A and ISAF, but nevertheless the continued presence of two simultaneous operations with differing aims that were at times mutually exclusive did not help those attempting to achieve an already difficult and complex task in Afghanistan.

In evaluating the performance of the OKSVA, analyst Alexander Alexeiv[52] noted that dominance in the air 'is of critical importance in counter-insurgency operations, since the majority of such missions depend on reliable air transportation and combat support.'

Coalition forces, too, relied on airpower for the same reason and the proper employment of airpower was critical to the success of ground operations. In Operation *Anaconda*, Coalition ground commanders did not include the proper tasking for air support into their planning and as a result the operation nearly failed in the early stages. However, the lesson was learnt and thereafter, air support tasking was integrated into ground planning.

AIR CAMPAIGNS

Against the background of flawed strategies and under-resourced ground forces, the air forces of the USSR, USA and Coalition were remarkably effective in carrying out their part of their respective missions. After Soviet forces entered Afghanistan, the VVS had to adapt quickly to an unfamiliar and inhospitable environment. The attack helicopter became a vital element in combined arms operations, but as the Russian general staff later commented, 'at the same time, analysis of combat disclosed serious shortcomings in pilot training and the capability of the aircraft to perform adequately in Afghanistan.'

This was true, too, of Soviet fixed-wing aircraft and crews, so measures were taken to improve the pre-deployment training of pilots and to give them an in-theatre orientation course prior to flying combat missions.

OPPOSITE Both the Soviet and Coalition troops came to rely heavily on airpower, and the forward air controller (FAC) (later known as the joint terminal attack controller or JTAC) was an integral member of most army patrols in Afghanistan. (USAF)

The necessity of embedding FACs into ground units was also grasped by the OKSVA, enabling aircraft to respond to the needs of soldiers and to locate their targets accurately. Ideally helicopter gunships should have escorted every convoy and other helicopters should have inserted DShB troops to seize any high ground along convoy routes, but even with four helicopter regiments in the country, there were never enough aircraft to fulfil all of these tasks. Soviet helicopter types proved to be robust machines and in particular the Mi-8/17 became the workhorse and also continued to be important all through the years of Coalition occupation.

For Soviet fighter-bomber pilots, supporting troops in a fluid and unpredictable situation brought home the need to show more initiative and responsiveness in their flying. This was not something that had previously been encouraged in the VVS. The introduction of the Su-25, as a dedicated CAS platform, also greatly increased the effectiveness of air support over what could be achieved by types such as the MiG-21, Su-17 and MiG-23. Nevertheless, the other types were still extremely useful, for, being capable of higher speeds, they

The Russian general staff considered the helicopter gunship to be 'the true friend of the ground forces' in Afghanistan. The Mi-24 certainly became an iconic symbol of the Soviet campaign in Afghanistan. (Grandolini)

could cover the distances more quickly if time was important. However, all the Soviet tactical aircraft were short-range types and the VVS had no air-to-air refuelling capability in-theatre with which to increase their time on station.

The Soviets had also quickly grasped the importance of reconnaissance: early in their campaign Yak-28R units had been deployed for photo-reconnaissance missions over Afghanistan and the task was later taken on by MiG-21P and Su-17M4 aircraft equipped with photo-reconnaissance pods. But Soviet exploitation of that reconnaissance was limited firstly by the time delay in getting photographs to the relevant commanders and secondly by the lack of an integrated system that could blend in the inputs from many different sensors to produce a single comprehensive intelligence picture. Nevertheless, the use of reconnaissance troops and a network of ground informants, coupled with the limited air-to-ground imagery from photo-reconnaissance aircraft, generated enough data to enable the intelligence-led operations by the DShB.

Perhaps the greatest challenge to the entire Soviet campaign in Afghanistan was the arrival of the MANPADS in 1984. Because of the dependence on aviation to support ground troops, any degradation of the Soviet command of the air would also adversely affect the ability of the OKSVA to carry out counter-insurgency operations. Helicopter and fighter-bomber pilots rapidly found themselves having to amend their tactics to minimize the threat from SAMs, including using IR decoy flares to distract missile heat-seeking

Along with the helicopter gunship, the dedicated CAS aircraft was a vital element of Soviet air-land operations. The Su-25 proved to be extremely effective over Afghanistan. (Grandolini)

Much of the aerial reconnaissance conducted by the Soviet Air Force was carried out by aircraft like this Sukhoi Su-17M4R (NATO: Fitter-K) which is equipped with the KKR-1 photographic reconnaissance pod on its centreline pylon. (Grandolini)

warheads and flying steep departures from and arrivals into their airfields to minimize the time spent in the SAM engagement envelope. The MANPADS threat also extended to transport aircraft, which brought everything from food, spare parts and ammunition to reinforcement troops and medical supplies into the country. Transport aircraft were also equipped with flares and adopted the steep arrival and departure profiles. Had the air bridge been broken, the OKSVA must surely have been defeated.

Despite the numerous MANPADS delivered to Afghan mujahideen in the 1980s, it seems unlikely that many of the remaining weapons would have still been serviceable 20 years later. Storage in the harsh environment, a lack of servicing and limited battery life were all factors that probably meant that there was, in fact, little threat from SAMs to Coalition aircraft. Nevertheless, learning from the Soviet experience, US and Coalition aircraft had already been equipped with decoy flares when they arrived in Afghanistan. Steep approaches and departures were also the norm as a precaution against the potential MANPADS threat. The greatest missile threat to US and Coalition helicopters was the unguided RPG. With a huge number of these weapons at their disposal, insurgents regularly fired upon helicopters, sometimes with fatal consequences to the crews.

Unlike the Soviet VVS which came to Afghanistan with no recent operational combat experience, by the time Coalition air forces were committed into the country they had flown almost ten continuous years of combat missions over Iraq and the Balkans. Not only were aircrews proficient in the roles and accustomed to working seamlessly together with Coalition partners from other nations, but the command-and-control functions of airpower had been exercised and perfected under combat conditions over the decade. Also, Coalition aircrews benefitted from the advances in technology since the 1980s. Targeting pods and precision-guided munitions, both laser-guided and GPS-guided weapons, gave the ability to carry out accurate 'surgical strikes', regardless of the weather or the time of the day. However, despite this accuracy, the use of large weapons and occasional misappreciations of the ROE did unfortunately cause unintentional casualties and collateral damage amongst civilian population of Afghanistan.

Confusion over the ROE was understandable given the two separate missions in the country and it was further complicated by the different rules issued by Coalition states to their forces. For example, in the EPAF F-16 detachment, the Danish, Norwegian and Dutch units were all working to different national rules and at one stage day and night operations had to be flown by different air forces because of clashes in the rules. Clearly, for a coalition to work together efficiently all elements need to agree a single set of unambiguous ROE.

Like the Soviets, US and Coalition forces found the helicopter to be the lynchpin of combined arms operations. The ability to transport troops quickly over long distances and across obstacles and to insert them exactly where they were needed was a vital capability for counter-insurgency operations. So, too, was the need for organic CAS provided by helicopter gunships, and in this respect the Soviet and Coalition experiences were broadly similar. It is unfortunate that like the Soviets, a chronic shortage of Coalition helicopters in

Afghanistan left occasional gaps in the provision of transport and CAS. There was a difference, however, in that US and Coalition helicopter forces also provided dedicated medical evacuation, which, along with advances in emergency trauma medicine, became a game changer for wounded soldiers. Thanks to the specifically-equipped medical evacuation helicopter, soldiers had a good chance of surviving even the severest wounds that would have proved fatal in previous years.

Also, just as in the Soviet experience, the FAC (or later JTAC) became an integral part of all US and Coalition army units. Perhaps the most technological advance was the introduction of ROVER. The ability of the JTAC to see exactly what the fighter-bomber aircrew or RPAS crew were seeing made it much simpler to direct 'eyes on' to the target. In addition, ROVER conferred a remarkable degree of situational awareness upon the ground troops. Similarly, the ability of aircrews to point out features to each other using the 'laser sparkle' facility incorporated in many targeting pods also helped them to build their situational awareness in a complex, dynamic and often unpredictable environment. In fact, the nature of the ground campaign and the targets in Afghanistan brought arguably the greatest sea change to the way that offensive support aircraft operate since World War II. Previously most offensive air support missions were pre-planned to a greater or lesser extent. In other words, before aircrew took off, they knew exactly where they were going and exactly what they would be doing when they got there; in Afghanistan things moved so quickly that more often than not, crews would get airborne with no idea where they were about to be sent and little idea of what scenario

Perhaps the greatest difference between the Soviet and US-Coalition air campaigns was the use of electronic warfare aircraft, such as the Lockheed EC-130 Compass Call, to monitor Taliban radio traffic, locate insurgent command elements and jam their communications networks. (USAF)

Just as the Mi-24 became an iconic sight in the skies over Afghanistan during the Soviet occupation, so the Boeing AH-64D Apache came to represent Coalition air power. Here, a British Army Air Corps Apache Longbow is landing at Camp Bastion airfield in October 2011. (Crown Copyright/MoD)

might greet them when they arrived on station. The ability to re-programme weapons and target coordinates in the air, as well as the crews being proficient in the role due to thorough training and practice, made this 'unplanned' approach to operations a viable one, enabling air power to react quickly to whatever eventuality they might face. This approach also depended upon the initiative and resourcefulness of the aircrew, which in turn stemmed from the practice in Western air forces of delegating tactical responsibility completely to the aircrew – something for which the Soviet VVS was not renowned. Nor did Soviet aircrew enjoy the regular flying practice and realistic training exercises afforded to NATO aircrew.

Another technological innovation that was not available to the Soviets was the RPAS. Without the need to cater for human aircrew, an RPAS could remain on station for many hours, observing points of interest on the ground, or attacking targets with precision-guided weapons. With a live feed directly into the CAOC, RPAS were also used on occasions by senior commanders to monitor developing engagements and to ensure that ROE were obeyed. This development is, however, a double-edged sword, for it opens the possibility for senior commanders to try to micro-manage individual missions, thereby compromising the very delegation of tactical control that enabled aircrew to carry out their tasks effectively. RPAS were just one part of the whole ISTAR spectrum. Where Soviet forces relied, in general, on intelligence gathered largely through ground reconnaissance or informants, Coalition forces were backed up by a network of airborne sensors. Tactical aircraft flew photo-reconnaissance missions and MPAs were also used to gather intelligence. In addition, the Afghanistan battlefront saw the debut of a number of small (and relatively inexpensive) specialized aircraft such as the US Army MARSS, USAF MQ-12 Liberty and RAF Shadow. At the opposite end of the spectrum were larger platforms such as the RC-135 Rivet Joint and E-8C JSTARS. Thanks to technology such as datalink, each of these systems could provide real-time intelligence to force commanders. Perhaps the most important point, however, was that the inputs from all of these systems could now be fused together to create a comprehensive intelligence picture of what was happening on the ground. In turn, this capability enabled the air planners to reduce the targeting cycle for airstrikes from the 24–48-hour timescale of the Cold War to almost instantaneous tasking.

The value of air-to-air refuelling was proved yet again over Afghanistan. Initially it was the only way to get ground-based aircraft into the country, until bases could be established in Afghanistan or in neighbouring countries. Later it became a means of enabling aircraft to remain on station for as long as they were needed. The integration of the tanker aircraft into the datalink network via the ROBE system also demonstrated the flexibility of the aircraft. ROBE was just one of

The Fairchild A-10 Thunderbolt II, seen here at Bagram Air Base in January 2003, reinforced the importance, demonstrated by the Sukhoi Su-25 in Soviet service 20 years earlier, of a dedicated CAS aircraft over the battlefield. (USAF)

RIGHT US and NATO forces benefitted from real time intelligence delivered by an integrated network of sensors which ranged from dedicated reconnaissance platforms to this RC-135 Rivet Joint of the 343rd Reconnaissance Squadron (seen here over Manas Air Base, Kyrgyzstan in March 2006) to targeting pods carried by tactical aircraft. (NARA)

BELOW RPAS such as the General Atomics MQ-1 Predator, shown here, assumed an increasing share of the intelligence, surveillance and reconnaissance tasking, as well as having their own hard kill capability. The number of airstrikes carried out by RPAS increased dramatically as the US-Coalition campaign in Afghanistan evolved. (USAF)

the systems that was needed to ensure full communications and data coverage across the mountainous terrain of Afghanistan. The acquisition of the E-11A BACN was an imaginative solution to the problem and one unique to the skies over Afghanistan.

Just as the Soviets had relied upon air transport to keep their forces supplied, so the Coalition depended upon a secure air bridge to do the same. In both the 1980s and 2000s, the air transport network included large numbers of heavy transport aircraft flying supplies into the main airfields and then smaller tactical aircraft distributing the loads across the country. A final helicopter-based distribution network ensured that remote

outposts were kept supplied. The USAF also frequently exercised the ability to airdrop supplies to troops in the field or in locations that helicopters could not reach. Once again, the US aircrews benefitted from technology that was not available to their Soviet forebears: GPS guided pallets could be dropped with great accuracy onto exactly where they were needed. The airlift evacuation of personnel from Kabul in August 2021 was also a remarkable achievement. Despite hostile forces surrounding the airport and the chaotic conditions within it, a multi-national fleet of transport aircraft succeeded in rescuing a huge number of people in a relatively short space of time.

One surprising development during the USAF campaign over Afghanistan was the evolution of the B-1B Lancer from strategic bomber into the CAS platform of choice. The enormous flexibility both of the aircraft and the crews, plus the introduction of precision-guided weapons, made it ideally suited to the CAS role. The long range of the aircraft, extended by AAR if necessary, plus its large weapon load meant that the aircraft could remain on station for lengthy periods and its speed gave it the ability to respond to quickly to any incidents across the country. The other

NEXT PAGES With mountainous terrain and a fragile and vulnerable ground transport infrastructure, air transport was the only viable option for moving personnel and supplies within Afghanistan. Both Soviet and later US and Coalition forces relied on a network of transport aircraft and helicopters to keep themselves reinforced and resupplied. In this typical scene in 2014, a USAF Boeing C-17 Globemaster III is taking off from Bagram Air Base with the tails of Lockheed C-130 Hercules tactical transports in the foreground. (USAF)

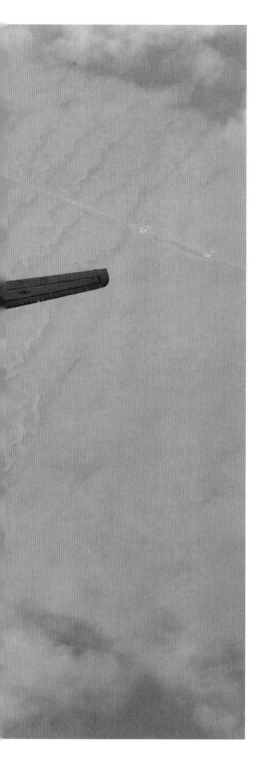

aircraft type that excelled in the CAS role was the A-10 Thunderbolt II, which like the Soviet Su-25 demonstrated the value of a highly manoeuvrable, well armoured aircraft that was designed specifically for the role.

During the Soviet occupation, the DRAAF had been equipped with the same aircraft types as their Soviet counterparts and had performed reasonably well. However, the US model for the re-formed AAF was for something altogether more modest and equipped predominantly with low-cost counter-insurgency aircraft rather than jet fighter-bombers. Furthermore, as the SIGAR observed:

> In Afghanistan and Vietnam, the United States tried to achieve similar results working with unstable and corrupt governments, and with the clock ticking on self-imposed deadlines for US withdrawal. In both places, however, the result was the creation of national armies that had a crippling dependence on US methods, combat enablers, and equipment. That, combined with corruption and failures of leadership in their own ranks, eroded the will to fight and allowed a smaller and less-equipped enemy to prevail.

One of the main failures of the US government in establishing the new AAF was to insist upon the service procuring US aircraft. For example, the decision not to progress with the Mi-17 was based upon US economic sanctions against Russia, rather than a proper analysis of

Procured as a strategic bomber, the B-1B Lancer, seen here over Afghanistan in October 2019, proved to be one of the most effective aircraft types for delivering CAS to troops during operations in Afghanistan. Operation *Enduring Freedom* brought a fundamental change in the employment of air power in counter-insurgency operations. (USAF)

what was the most practical solution for Afghanistan. The relatively simple Mi-17 was ideally suited to operations in the austere conditions in Afghanistan and moreover both aircrews and maintenance engineers were familiar with the type; on the other hand, neither had any experience of the UH-60, a far more complex type which required more attention to keep it serviceable.

It is interesting that many of the conclusions to be drawn from the Soviet and US-led Coalition campaigns are similar to those that can be deduced from the RAF experiences in 1919 and 1928. In 1919 it was the decisive use of airpower both to support ground forces and to carry out long-range airstrikes that gave Anglo-Indian ground forces the edge over their enemy, in much the same way as US airpower tipped the balance against the Taliban in 2001. In 1928, aerial reconnaissance allowed the commanders in India to monitor distant events in Kabul and the deployment of the Vickers Victoria aircraft demonstrated the reach and speed of air transport. However, the success of the 1928 airlift was chiefly due to prior planning and the proficiency and flexibility of RAF aircrews. Arrangements started to be made as soon as the possibility for the need of an evacuation became apparent, and by the time it was needed, the relevant aircraft were already alerted. Despite being normally based in the relatively flat ground of central Iraq, the

Early morning on the Afghan Air Force flightline at Kabul Air Base in November 2014. The aircraft in this view are predominantly Russian-built Mil Mi-17 helicopters which were by far the most successful aircraft to be operated by the AAF; attempts to introduce more modern American aircraft were undermined by the complexity and relative fragility of Western types. (USAF)

Victoria pilots quickly adapted to flying through mountainous terrain in challenging winter weather, thanks to their excellent training and proficiency.

In summary, the air forces of the USSR, USA and the Coalition performed admirably well during their campaigns over Afghanistan, despite the limitations placed upon them by weak political strategy and under-resourced ground forces that depended upon airpower to make up for their own deficiencies. Coalition air forces in particular were involved in every facet of the US and NATO missions in Afghanistan. The DRAAF had been a reasonably effective force in the 1980s, but the AAF of the 2010s had little chance of success given the flawed approach of the US government. In the end it might have been possible to have saved a democratically governed Afghanistan had Coalition airpower remained in the country to support the ANDSF; however, this option was jettisoned as soon as the US government entered into an agreement with the Taliban.

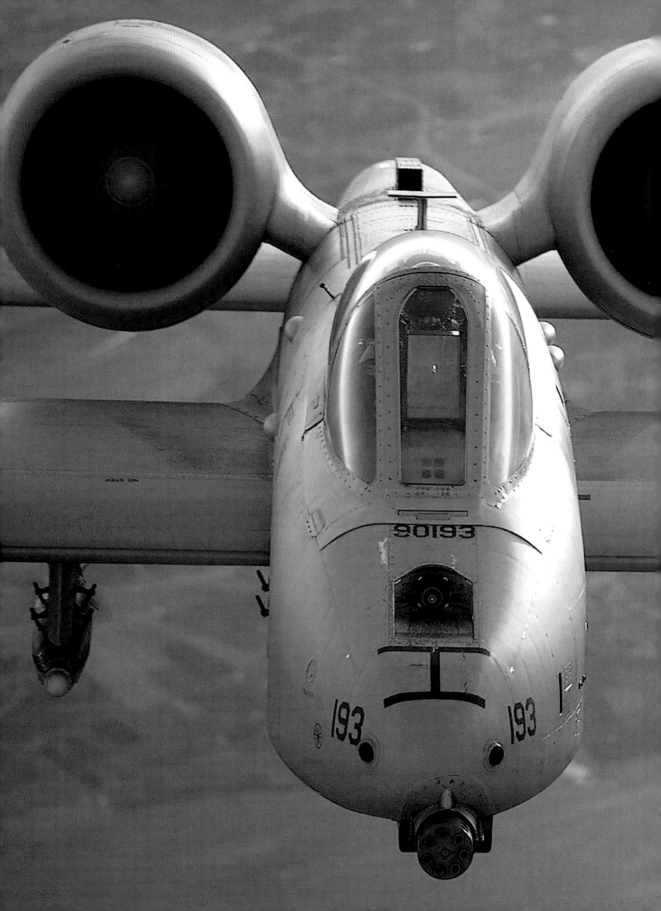

ENDNOTES

LEFT An A-10 Thunderbolt II on patrol over Afghanistan in 2006. (USAF)

Chapter 1: An Introduction to Afghanistan

1 Statistics from the United Nations Department of Economic and Social Affairs Economic Analysis

2 World Development Indicators – World Bank Databank

Chapter 2: The Soviet Experience 1979–1989

3 'Як-28Р в Афганистане' by Александр Жибров via http://www.airwar.ru

4 'МиГ-21 в Афганистане' by В. Марковский via http://www.airwar.ru

5 'Ми-8 в Афганистане' by Виктор Марковский via http://www.airwar.ru

6 'МиГ-21 в Афганистане' by В. Марковский via http://www.airwar.ru

7 'Ан-12 в Афганистане' by В. Марковский via http://www.airwar.ru

8 'Ил-76 в Афганистане' by Виктор Исаков via http://www.airwar.ru

9 'Су-25 в Афганистане' by Виктор Марковский via http://www.airwar.ru

10 *Штурмовик* by Александр Кошкин, Евгений Зубарев, Astrel publishing, 2012

11 'Истребители МиГ-23 в Афганистане' by Виктор Марковский via http://www.airwar.ru

Chapter 3: US and NATO Intervention 2001–2005

12 'CIA's Mi-17 Helicopter Comes Home', https://www.cia.gov

13 Dr. Mel Deaile, 'Inside the Longest Bombing Run Ever'

14 'Phantom of Takur Ghar: The Predator above Roberts Ridge' via https:///www.af.mil/News

15 'From the Sea – US Marines in Afghanistan', History Division USMC, 2011

16 'A-10s Ready for OEF Action' via https:///www.af.mil/News

17 'Sortie Changes Green Pilot Blue' via https:///www.af.mil/News

18 'A-10 Pods Help Track Bad Guys, Protect Friendly Forces' via https:///www.af.mil/News

19 'This Compass Call squadron was deployed in Afghanistan for 20 years. Here's their inside story', Air Force Times, June 2022
20 'Bagram A-10s Take Fight to Enemy' via https///www.af.mil/News

Chapter 4: Taliban Insurgency 2006–2008

21 Jonathan Creer, *Picking The Bone: The B-1 Bomber as A Platform for Innovation*, School of Advanced and Space Studies, Air University
22 'Paris deploys Rafales in Afghanistan', Figaro Vox, 19 March 2007
23 'Charles de Gaulle's Difficult Afghan Mission', Figaro Vox, 25 April 2007
24 'B-1 Crews Excel at Shows of Presence' via https://www.af.mil/News/
25 'A Sunday Unlike Any Other' via https://www.af.mil/News/
26 'Pilots Provide Emergency Close Air Support' via https://www.af.mil/News/

Chapter 5: ISAF Takes Back Control 2009–2014

27 'Manas KC-135s Revolutionize Combat Operations' via via https://www.af.mil/News/
28 'Tiger In Combat the French Army Experience' via https://www.australiandefence.com.au/news
29 'RAF Chinook Pilot Describes his Role in Op MOSHTARAK' via https://webarchive.nationalarchives.gov.uk/
30 'RAF support to Op Moshtarak', UK Ministry of Defence, 9 March 2010
31 'Rivet Joint Aircraft Sets Milestone: Second Time in History Aircraft Surpasses 50,000 Flight Hours' via https://www.af.mil/News/
32 'Tombé Chez Les Talibans Puis Récupéré: L'incroyable Récit Du Crash D'un Mirage 2000 Par Son Pilote' via https://www.lindependant.fr/
33 'Aviator of the Year award to 3rd MAW Marine' via https///www.marines.mil/
34 'Bagram Pilots Save 60 Soldiers During Convoy Ambush' via https://www.af.mil/News/
35 'Whiteman Pilot Reflects On 6,000 Hours in the A-10' via https://www.af.mil/News/

Chapter 6: Endgame 2015–2021

36   'Fighting not over for US F-16 pilots in Afghanistan', Stars and
     Stripes, 4 December 2015
37   'Air Force Combat Controller, AC-130 Crew Honored for Valor in
     Afghanistan', Air Force Times, 17 October 2017
38   'Afghan Air Force Gets New Helicopters, Capability' via https://
     www.dvidshub.net
39   'A Double Dose of Gunship', Air Force Magazine, 26 July 2018
40   Ibid.
41   'Meet Lt. Col. John Marks, The Airman with The Most Time in the
     A-10C "Warthog"', Air Force Times, 28 September 2021
42   'Enhancing Security and Stability in Afghanistan', US DoD, De-
     cember 2020
43   'C-17 Crew Who Saved 153 During Afghanistan Evacuation
     Awarded Distinguished Flying Cross', Air Force Magazine, 5 April
     2022
44   'Air Traffic Controllers Assist with Critical Kabul Operations' via
     https://www.af.mil/News/
45   'Eglin Airmen Control Chaos During Afghan Evacuation' via
     https://www.af.mil/News/
46   'RAF Pilots Describe "Harrowing" Scenes in Scramble to Evacu-
     ate Afghanistan' via https://www.itv.com/news

Chapter 7: The Benefits of Hindsight

47   Russian General Staff, *The Soviet-Afghan War: How a Superpower
     Fought and Lost*, 2002 (in English)
48   'Collapse of the Afghan National Defense and Security Forces: An
     Assessment of the Factors That Led to Its Demise', SIGAR interim
     report, May 2022
49   UPI interview with Haig, 7 January 2002
50   'Inside the Soviet Army in Afghanistan', RAND Corporation, 1988
51   'The International Security Assistance Force in Afghanistan',
     House of Commons Library, February 2006
52   'Inside the Soviet Army in Afghanistan', RAND Corporation, 1988

APPENDICES

APPENDIX 1

Soviet and DRA Air Forces Air Order of Battle mid-1980

Afghanistan

SOVIET AIR FORCE UNITS

Bagram	115th GvIAD	MiG-21bis	NATO: Fishbed L/N
	262nd OVE	Mi-24	NATO: Hind
Fayzabad	181st OVP	3rd AE: Mi-8	NATO: Hip
Jalalabad	292nd OVP	Mi-8, Mi-24	NATO: Hip, Hind
Kabul	50th OSAP	1st AE: An-12, An-26	NATO: Cub, Curl
		2nd AE: Mi-24	NATO: Hind
		3rd AE: Mi-8	NATO: Hip
Kandahar	136th APIB (1st & 2nd AE)	MiG-21SM	NATO: Fishbed-J
	217th APIB	Su-17M3	NATO: Fitter-H
	280th OVP	Mi-24, Mi-8MT	NATO: Hip-H
Kunduz	254th OVE		
	181st OVP (1st & 2nd AE)	Mi-6	NATO: Hook
Shindand	136th APIB (1st AE)	MiG-21SM	NATO: Fishbed-J
	302 OVE	Mi-8, Mi-24	NATO: Hip, Hind

AFGHAN AIR FORCE UNITS

Bagram	322th IAP	MiG-21PFM	NATO: Fishbed-H
	355th APIB	Su-7BMK	NATO: Fitter-A
Kandahar	366th IAP	MiG-17	NATO: Fresco
Shindand	335th SAP	MiG-17, Il-28	NATO: Fresco, Beagle

USSR

SOVIET AIR FORCE UNITS

Mary-2	39th ORAP	Yak-28R	NATO: Brewer-D
Karshi-Khanabad	64th ORAP	MiG-21R and Yak-28R	NATO: Fishbed-H, Brewer-D (deployed to Kabul in January and April 1980)

APPENDIX 2

Soviet and DRA Air Forces Air Order of Battle mid-1987

Afghanistan

SOVIET AIR FORCE UNITS

Bagram	378th OShAP (2nd AE)	Su-25	NATO: Frogfoot
	190 IAP (1st AE)	MiG-23MLD	NATO: Flogger-K
	262nd OVE	Mi-24	NATO: Hind
Fayzabad	181st OVP (det)	Mi-8 & Mi-24	NATO: Hip, Hind
Jalalabad	335 OVP (1st AE)	Mi-8MT, Mi-24V/P	NATO: Hip-H, Hind-F
Kabul	50th OSAP	An-12, An-26; Mi-24, Mi-8	NATO: Cub, Curl, Hund, Hip
Kandahar	378th OShAP (1st AE)	Su-25	NATO: Frogfoot
	976th IAP (1st AE)	MiG-23MLD	NATO: Flogger-K
	136th APIB	Su-17M4	NATO: Fitter-K
	280th OVP	Mi-24, Mi-8MT	NATO: Hind, Hip-H
Kunduz	335 OVP (1st AE)	Mi8MT, Mi-24V/P	NATO: Hip-H, Hind-F
Shindand	181st OVP (1st AE)	Mi-8, Mi-24	NATO: Hip, Hind
	190 IAP (1st AE)	MiG-23MLD	NATO: Flogger-K

AFGHAN AIR FORCE UNITS

Bagram	321st APIB	Su-7, Su-22	NATO: Fitter
	322nd IAP	MiG-21bis/PFM	NATO: Fishbed-L/N, -F
Dehdadi	393rd APIB	MiG-17	NATO: Fresco
	380th OVP (1st AE)	Mi-17	NATO: Hip
Kabul	377th SAP	Mi-17, Mi-35, An-2, An-26, Il-14	NATO: Hip, Hind-E, Colt, Curl
Kandahar	366th IAP	MiG-17	NATO: Fresco
Shindand	355th APIB	Su-7, Su-22, MiG-17	NATO: Fresco, Fitter, Fresco
	375th OVP	Mi-17, Mi-35	NATO: Hip, Hind-E

USSR

SOVIET AIR FORCE UNITS

Mary-2	156th IAP	Su-17M3	NATO: Fitter-H
Karshi-Khanabad	735 BAP	Su-24	NATO: Fencer
	87th ORAP	Su-17M3R and Yak-28R	NATO: Fitter-H, Brewer-D
Kokaydy	115th IAP	MiG-21bis	NATO: Fishbed-L/N

APPENDIX 3

US and Coalition Air Forces – Air Order of Battle October 2001

Note – Units USAF unless otherwise identified

Diego Garcia

28th BW	B-1B Lancer, B-52H Stratofortress

Kuwait

Al Jaber	16th SOS	AC-130H Spectre
	391st EFS	F-15E Strike Eagle
	466th EFS	F-16 Fighting Falcon

UAE

Al Dhafra	ERS 1/91FAF	Mirage IVP, C-135FR

Oman

Seeb	120/201 Sqn RAF	Nimrod MR2
	101 Sqn RAF	VC-10K
	216 Sqn RAF	TriStar

Qatar

Al Udeid	28th EARS	KC-135 Stratotanker
	193rd SOW	EC-130J Commando Solo
	763rd ERS	RC-135 Rivet Joint

North Arabian Sea

USN and USMC

USS *CARL VINSON* (CVN-70) – CVW-1

VF-102	F-14B Tomcat
VMFA-251	F/A-18C Hornet
VFA-82	F/A-18C Hornet
VFA-86	F/A-18C Hornet
VAQ-137	EA-6B Prowler

VAW-123	E-2C Hawkeye
VS-32	S-2B Viking

USS *THEODORE ROOSEVELT* (CVN-71) – CVW-11

VF-213	F-14D Tomcat
VFA-22	F/A-18C Hornet
VFA-94	F/A-18C Hornet
VFA-97	F/A-18A Hornet
VAQ-135	EA-6B Prowler
VAW-117	E-2C Hawkeye
VS-29	S-3B Viking

USS *KITTY HAWK* (CV-63)

160th SOAR US Army	MH-47 Chinook, MH-60 Black Hawk

USS *PELELIU* (LHA-5) – 15TH MEU

VMA-311	AV-8B Harrier
HMM-163	CH-46E Sea Knight
HMH-465	CH-53E Super Stallion
HMLA-169	AH-1W Super Cobra, UH-1N Huey

USA

Whiteman AFB	509th BW	B-2 Spirit

APPENDIX 4

US and Coalition Air Forces – Air Order of Battle mid-2009

Note – all units listed below are detachments from the named parent units; units USAF unless otherwise identified

AFGHANISTAN

Bagram	421st EFS	F-16 Fighting Falcon
	VAQ-134 USN	EA-6B Prowler
	74th EFS	A-10C Thunderbolt II
	41st EECS EC-130H	Compass Call
	336th EFS	F-15E Strike Eagle
	ED 1/33 FAF	Harfang RPAS
Camp Bastion	28 Sqn RAF	AgustaWestland Merlin HC3
	662 Sqn AAC AH-64D	Apache
	HMLA-167 USMC	AH-1W Super Cobra
	HMLA-169 USMC	AH-1W Super Cobra
Tarin Kowt	301 Sqn RNLAF	AH-64 Apache
Herat	1 Regt Av It Army	CH-47C Chinook
	5 Regt Av It Army	AH-129 Mangusta
	Esc 803 SpAF	Super Puma
	32° Stormo ITAF	MQ1 Predator
Jalalabad	2-17 Cav US Army	OH-58D Kiowa
	1-101 AV Regt US Army	AH-64D Apache
	5-101 AV Regt US Army	MH-60G Black Hawk
	6-101 AV Regt US Army	CH-47 Chinook
Kabul	Bathelico Fr Army	EC665 Tiger HAP, EC725 Caracal, AS532 Cougar, SA341/342 Gazelle

Kandahar	1 Sqn RAF	Harrier GR9
	31 Sqn BAF	F-16AM Fighting Falcon
	311 Sqn RNLAF	F-16AM Fighting Falcon
	EC2/3 FAF	Mirage 2000D
	ER 2/33 FAF	Mirage F-1CR
	430th EECS	E-11A BACN
	VMA-214 USMC	AV-8B Harrier
	VMGR-352 USMC	KC-130J
	HMH-362 USMC	CH-53D
	HMH-772 USMC	CH-53D
	42nd EAS	MQ-9 Reaper RPAS
	39 Sqn RAF	MQ-9 Reaper RPAS
	Task Force Erebus CAF	CU-170 Heron RPAS
Mazar-e-Sharif	AG 51 GAF	Tornado IDS
	6o Stormo ITAF	Tornado IDS

Arabian Sea
USN

USS *DWIGHT D EISENHOWER* (CVN-69)

CVW-7	F/A-18E Super Hornet, EA-18G Growler, E-2D Hawkeye, MH-60 Seahawk

KYRGYZSTAN

Manas	22nd EARS	KC-135 Stratotanker
	817th EAS	C-17 Globemaster III

OMAN

Seeb	120/201 Sqn RAF	Nimrod MR2
	101 Sqn RAF	VC-10K
Thumrait	9th EBS	B-1B Lancer

QATAR

Al Udeid	16th SOS	AC-130H Spectre
	99th ERS	U-2S Dragon Lady
	116th ACW	E-8C Joint STARS
	763rd ERS	RC-135 Rivet Joint

TAJIKISTAN

Dushanbe	FAF	C-135FR
	FAF	C-160

UAE

Al Dafra	908th EARS	KC-10 Extender, KC-135 Stratotanker
Al Minhad	US Navy	P-3 Orion

APPENDIX 5

US and Coalition Air Forces – Air Order of Battle mid-2014

Units USAF unless otherwise identified

AFGHANISTAN

Bagram	4th ERS	MC-12W Liberty
	4th SOS	AC-130U
	62nd ERS	MQ-1 Predator, MQ-9 Reaper
	75th EFS	A-10C Thunderbolt II
	83rd ERQS	HH-60G Black Hawk
	457th EFS	F-16 Fighting Falcon
	774th EAS	C-130J Hercules
Camp Bastion	HMH-466	CH-53E Super Stallion
	HMLA-467	AH-1W Super Cobra, UH-1Y Venom Huey
	VMM-261	MV-22B Osprey
Herat	7th Regt Av It Army	A129D Mangusta
	3-101 Av Regt US Army	AH-64D Apache
	4-101 Av Regt US Army	UH-60L Black Hawk
	7-101 Av Regt US Army	CH-47 Chinook
	1/230th Air Cav	OH-58D Kiowa Warriror
Kabul	SMW (2 Sqns) AAF	Mi-17
	Kabul Air Wing AAF	C-208 Caravan, Mi-35
Kandahar	39 Sqn RAF	MQ-9 Reaper
	904 EAW RAF	Tornado GR4
	1-52 Av Regt US Army	UH-60 Black Hawk, CH-47 Chinook
	1-229 Av Regt US Army	AH-64E Apache
	SMW (1 Sqn) AAF	Mi-17
Mazar-e-Sharif	1-227 Av Regt US Army	AH-64D Apache
	SMW (1 Sqn) AAF	Mi-17
Shindand	2-158 Av Regt US Army	UH-60 Black Hawk
	Shindand Air Wing AAF	MD-530F Cayuse Warrior

ABBREVIATIONS

AAA	Anti-aircraft Artillery
AAC	Army Air Corps (British)
AAF	Afghan Air Force
AAM	Air-to-Air Missiles
AAR	Air-to-Air Refuelling
ACW	Air Combat Wing
AE	Aviatsionnyy Eskadril'ya (Soviet Aviation Squadron)
AEW	Air Expeditionary Wing
AFAC	Airborne Forward Air Controller
AFB	Air Force Base
AG	Aufklärungsgeschwader (German Air Force Reconnaissance Wing)
AMSL	Above Mean Sea Level
ANA	Afghan National Army
ANDSF	Afghan National Defence and Security Forces
ANG	Air National Guard
APIB	Aviatsionnyy Polk Istrebiteley-Bombardirovshchikov (Soviet Fighter-Bomber Aviation Regiment)
ASOC	Air Support Operations Centre
ATGM	Anti-Tank Guided Missile
ATO	Air Task Order
Av Regt	US Army Aviation Regiment
AWACS	Airborne Warning and Control System
BACN	Battlefield Airborne Communications Node
BAF	Belgian Air Force
BCT	Brigade Combat Team
BW	Bomb Wing
CAB	Combat Aviation Brigade
CAF	Canadian Armed Forces
CAOC	Combined Air Operations Centre
Capt	Captain
CAS	Close Air Support

CBU	Cluster Bomb Units
CIA	US Central Intelligence Agency US
CJTF	Combined Joint Task Force
Col	Colonel
CRAF	Combat Search and Rescue
CVW	Carrier Wing
CWO	Chief Warrant Officer
DAP	Direct Action Penetrator
DGMAF	Dostrum-Gilbuddin Militia Air Force
DJRP	Digital Joint Reconnaissance Pod (British)
DMS	Dual Mode Seeker
DoD	Department of Defense
DRA	Democratic Republic of Afghanistan
DRAAF	Democratic Republic of Afghanistan Air Force
DShB	Desantno Shturmovaya Brigada (Soviet Air Assault Brigade)
EARS	Expeditionary Air Refuelling Squadron
EAS	Expeditionary Airlift Squadron
EECS	Expeditionary Electronic Combat Squadron
EFS	Expeditionary Fighter Squadron
EPAF	European Partner Air Force
ERS	Expeditionary Reconnaissance Squadron
FAC	Forward Air Controller
FAF	French Air Force (Armée de l'Air)
FARP	Forward Arming and Refuelling Point
Fg Off	Flying Officer
FOB	Forward Operating Base
FOD	Foreign Object Damage
Fr Army	French Army (Armée de Terre)
GAF	German Air Force (Luftwaffe)
GCAS	Ground Alert CAS
Gen	General
GvIAP	Gvardeyskiy Istrebitel'nyy Aviatsionnyy Polk (Soviet

GvTBAP   Guards Fighter Aviation Regiment)
Gvardeyskiy Tyazhelyy Bombardirovochnyy
Aviatsionnyy Polk (Guards Heavy Bombing
Regiment)

HIG   Hizb-e Islami Gilbuddin

IAP   Istrebitel'nyy Aviatsionnyy Polk (Soviet Fighter
Aviation Regiment)
IDS   Interdictor Strike
IED   Improvised Explosive Device
IR   Infra Red
ISAF   International Security Assistance Force
ISI   Pakistani Inter-Services Intelligence
ISIS-K   Islamic State of Iraq and Syria – Khorasan Province
ISTAR   Intelligence, Surveillance, Target Acquisition and
Reconnaissance
It Army   Italian Army
ITAF   Italian Air Force

JDAM   Joint Direct Attack Munition
JHMCS   Joint Helmet-Mounted Cueing System
JPADS   Joint Precision Airdrop System
JSOW   Joint Standoff Weapon
JTAC   Joint Terminal Attack Controller

L/Cpl   Lance Corporal
LDC   Least Developed Country
LGB   Laser Guided Bomb
Lt   Lieutenant
LZ   Landing Zone

Maj   Major
MANPADS   Man-Portable Air Defence Systems
MARSS   Medium Altitude Reconnaissance Surveillance System
MERT   Medical Emergency Response Team
MEU   Marine Expeditionary Unit

MOAB	Massive Ordnance Air Blast
MPA	Maritime Patrol Aircraft
MRTT	Multi-Role Tanker Transport
MSD	Motorizovannyy Strelkovaya Diviziya (Soviet Motor Rifle Division)
NATO	North Atlantic Treaty Organization
NTISR	Non-Traditional Intelligence Surveillance and Reconnaissance
ODA	Operational Detachment Alpha
OEF	Operation *Enduring Freedom*
OFS	Operation *Freedom's Sentinel*
OKSVA	Ogranichennyy Kontingent Sovetskikh Voysk v Afganistane (Limited Contingent of Soviet Forces in Afghanistan)
ORAP	Otdel'nyy Razvedyvatel'nyy Aviatsionnyy Polk (Soviet Independent Reconnaissance Regiment)
OSAP	Otdel'nyy Smeshannyy Aviatsionnyy Polk (Soviet Independent Mixed Aviation Regiment)
OShAP	Otdel'nyy Shturmovoy Aviatsionnyy Polk (Soviet Independent Assault Aviation Regiment)
OVE	Otdel'nyy Vertoletnyy Eskadril'ya (Soviet Independent Helicopter Squadron)
OVP	Otdel'nyy Vertoletnyy Polk (Soviet Independent Helicopter Regiment)
PAF	Pakistan Air Force
PDPA	People's Democratic Party of Afghanistan
PRT	Provincial Reconstruction Team
RAAF	Royal Australian Air Force
RAF	Royal Air Force
RAPTOR	Reconnaissance Airborne Pod for Tornado
RC–S	Regional Command – South
RDAF	Royal Danish Air Force
RIO	Radar Intercept Officer

RNLAF	Royal Netherlands Air Force
RNoAF	Royal Norwegian Air Force
ROBE	Roll On Beyond Line Of Sight Enhancement
ROE	Rules of Engagement
ROVER	Remotely Operated Video Enhanced Receiver
RPAS	Remotely Piloted Air System
RPG	Rocket Propelled Grenade
SAM	Surface-to-Air Missiles
SAS	Special Air Service Regiment
SDB	Small Diameter Bomb
SEAL	Sea Air and Land (USN Special Forces)
SIGAR	Special Inspector General for Afghanistan Reconstruction
SLAM-ER	Standoff Land Attack Missile-Extended Range
SMW	Special Mission Wing
SOF	Special Operations Forces
SOS	Special Operations Squadron
SOW	Special Operations Wing
SpAF	Spanish Air Force (Ejército del Aire)
Sqn Ldr	Squadron Leader
SSR	Soviet Socialist Republic
STARS	Surveillance Target Attack Radar System
TARPS	Tactical Airborne Reconnaissance Pod System
TIALD	Thermal Imaging Airborne Laser Designation
TIC	Troops in Contact
TLAM	Tomahawk Land Attack Missile
UAE	United Arab Emirates
UAV	Unmanned Aerial Vehicle (see also RPAS)
UN	United Nations
USFOR-A	US Forces Afghanistan
USMC	US Marine Corps
USN	US Navy
USSR	Union of Soviet Socialist Republics

VVS	Voyenno-Vozdushnye Sily – Soviet Air Force
VVS-DA	VVS Dal'naya Aviatsiya – Soviet Air Force Long-Range Aviation
WO	Warrant Officer
WSO	Weapons System Operator

BIBLIOGRAPHY

Books

Alexeivich, Svetlana, *Boys in Zinc*, Penguin Random House, 2017

Baker, Anne, *Wings Over Kabul*, William Kimber, 1975

Braithwaite, Rodric, *Afghansty*, Profile Books, 2011

Franzak, Michael, *A Nightmare's Prayer,* Threshold Editions, 2010

Loveless, Anthony, *Blue Sky Warriors*, Haynes Publishing, 2010

Orchard, Ade, *Joint Force Harrier*, Michael Joseph, 2008

Ripley, Tim, *Air War Afghanistan,* Pen & Sword Books, 2011

Russian General Staff, *The Soviet Afghan War*, University Press of Kansas, 2002

Tremelling, Paul, *Harrier – How to Be a Fighter Pilot*, Penguin Random House, 2022

Articles and Papers

Agnard, Bernard & Wodka-Gallien, Philippe, 'The Mirage 2000D In Afghanistan: An After-Action Report; The Mission: Close-Air-Support and Reconnaissance Missions in Support of US Ground Forces', *Journal of Electronic Defense*, 2003

Anon, *A Good Ally: Norway in Afghanistan 2001–2014*, Norwegian Ministry of Foreign Affairs and Ministry of Defence, 2016

Anon, *Afghanistan: Two Italian AMX Aircraft Destroy a Taliban's Powerful Radio Communication Transmitter*, Italian Ministry of Defence, 2014

Anon, *Agreement for Bringing Peace to Afghanistan between the Islamic Emirate of Afghanistan which is not recognized by the United States as a state and is known as the Taliban and the United States of America,* US Government, 2020

Anon, *Enhancing Security and Stability in Afghanistan December 2020*, US DoD, 2020

Anon, *Enhancing Security and Stability in Afghanistan June 2019* - US DoD, 2019

Anon, *International Border Study Afghanistan-USSR Boundary*, Office of the Geographer, Bureau of Intelligence and Research, 1983

Anon, *Op HERRICK (Afghanistan) Aircraft Statistics*, UK MoD, 2015

Anon, *Operation Enduring Freedom and the Conflict in Afghanistan: An*

Update, House of Commons Library, 2001

Anon, *Operations in Afghanistan – Memorandum from the Ministry of Defence,* House of Commons Select Committee on Defence, 2010

Anon, *The Air Force Approach to Irregular Warfare*, RAAF Air Power Development Centre, 2011

Anon, *The Canadian Armed Forces in Afghanistan*, Veterans Affairs Canada, 2011

Anon, 'The Commitment of French Land Forces in Afghanistan', *Doctrine Magazine*, Commissariat de l'armée de terre de Saint-Etienne

Anon, *The UK Deployment to Afghanistan – Fifth Report of Session 2005–06*, HMSO, 2006

Anon, 'Tombé Chez les Talibans puis récupéré – l'incroyable récit du crash d'un Mirage 2000 par son pilote', *L'Indépendant*, 2015

Anon, *U.S. Military Withdrawal and Taliban Takeover in Afghanistan: Frequently Asked Questions,* Congressional Research Service, 2021

Anon, *UK Operations in Afghanistan Thirteenth – Report of Session 2006–07*, HMSO

Anon, *Wanat Combat Action in Afghanistan, 2008*, US Army Combat Studies Institute Press, 2010

Anon, *Australia's Military Involvement in Afghanistan Since 2001: A Chronology*, Australian Parliamentary Library Research Publications, 2010,

Anon, *Dutch Contribution to Operation Enduring Freedom in Afghanistan*, Netherlands Ministry of Defence, undated

Anon, *Operation Anaconda: An Air Power Perspective*, Headquarters United States Air Force, 2005

Anrig, Christian F., *The Quest for Relevant Air Power*, Air University Press, 2011

Belasco, Amy, *Troop Levels in the Afghan and Iraq Wars, FY2001–FY2012: Cost and Other Potential Issues*, Congressional Research Service, 2009

Bereiter, Gregory, *The US Navy in Operation Enduring Freedom, 2001–2002*, Naval History & Heritage Command, 2016

Bolkcom, Christopher, *Operation Enduring Freedom: Potential Air Power Questions for Congress*, CRS Report for Congress, 2001

Brooke-Holland, Louisa, *In Brief: UK Troop Withdrawal from Afghanistan*, House of Commons Library, 2013

Camporini, Vincenzo et al, *The Role of Italian Fighter Aircraft in Crisis*

Management Operations: Trends and Needs, Instituto Affari Internazionali, 2014

Cohen, Rachel S., '*Inside The B-52s' Deployment to Support the Afghanistan Withdrawal*', *Air Force Magazine*, 2021

Cohen, Rachel S., 'This Compass Call Squadron is Coming Home After 20 Years of Hacking and Jamming Enemies in CENTCOM', *Air Force Times*, 2022

Cordesman, Anthony H., *US Airpower in Iraq and Afghanistan: 2004–2007*, Center for Strategic and International Studies, 2007

Cordesman, Anthony H. & Allison, Marrisa , *The U.S. Air War in Iraq, Afghanistan, and Pakistan*, Center for Strategic and International Studies, 2010

Cross, Michael A., 'Operation *Mountain Lion*: CJTF in Afghanistan, Spring 2006', *Military Review*, 2008

Darack, Ed, 'The Final Flight of Extortion 17', *Smithsonian Air & Space Magazine*, 2015

Darak, Ed, 'The Drone that Stalked Bin Laden', *Air & Space Magazine*, 2016

De Lespinoi, Jérôme, *Adaptation in The Air Force. A Case Study of The French Air Force in Afghanistan*, Institut de récherche strategique de l'école militaire, 2018

Deaile, Mel, *Inside the Longest Bombing Run Ever*, United Service Organization, 2014

Degen, Edmund J. & Reardon, Mark J., *Modern War in an Ancient Land – The United States Army in Afghanistan 2001–2014 Volume II*, US Army Center of Military History, 2021

Donnelly, Thomas & Schmitt, Gary J. 'Musa Qala: Adapting to the Realities of Modern Counterinsurgency', *Small Wars Journal*, 2008

Dressler, Jeffrey, *Operation Moshtarak: Preparing for The Battle of Marjah*, Institute for the Study of War, 2010

Dunham, Mike, 'The Teeth of Bulldog Bite', *Air Force Magazine*, 2011

Everstine, Brian W., 'B-52s, F-22s Continue Hitting Taliban Drug Dens in Afghanistan', *Air Force Magazine*, 2017

Everstine, Brian W., 'Kabul Evacuation Flight Sets C-17 Record With 823 On Board', *Air Force Magazine*, 2021

Feickert, Andrew, *US Military Operations in the Global War on Terrorism: Afghanistan, Africa, the Philippines and Columbia*, Congressional

Research Service, 2006

Feickert, Andrew, *U.S. and Coalition Military Operations in Afghanistan: Issues for Congress,* Congressional Research Service, 2006

Grant, Rebecca, *Airpower in Afghanistan: How a Faraway War is Remaking the Air Force*, Mitchell Institute, 2009

Grant, Rebecca, 'An Air War Like No Other', *Air Force Magazine*, 2002

Grant, Rebecca, 'The Airpower of *Anaconda*', *Air Force Magazine*, 2002

Haffa, Dr Robert P. Jr. & Datla, Anand, 'Joint Intelligence, Surveillance, and Reconnaissance in Contested Airspace', *Air & Space Power Journal*, 2014

Haulman, Daniel L., '44 Hours', *Air Force Magazine*, 2017

Hayward, Joel (ed.), *Air Power, Insurgency and the 'War on Terror'*, Royal Air Force Centre for Air Power Studies, 2009

Henriksen, Dag, *Airpower in Afghanistan 2005–10 The Air Commanders' Perspectives*, Air University Press, 2014

Hirsch, Steve, 'A Double Dose of Gunship', *Air Force Magazine*, 2018

Jonathan Creer, *Picking the Bone: The B-1 Bomber as A Platform for Innovation*, Air University 2010

Kummer, David W., *U.S. Marines in Afghanistan, 2001–2009 Anthology and Annotated Bibliography*, History Division USMC, 2014

Lambeth, Benjamin S., *Air Power Against Terror: America's Conduct of Operation Enduring Freedom*, RAND Corporation, 2005

Lambeth, Benjamin S., *American Carrier Air Power at the Dawn of a New Century*, RAND Corporation, 2005

Lowrey, Nathan S., *US Marines in Afghanistan, 2001–2003: From the Sea*, USMC History Division, 2011

Maass, Citha D., *Afghanistan's Drug Career – Evolution from a War Economy to a Drug Economy*, Stiftung Wissenschaft und Politik, 2011

Machi, Vivienne, 'NATO Scrambles to Complete Afghanistan Evacuations "As Soon As Possible"', *Defense News*, 2021

Malkasian, Carter, Meyerle, Jerry & Katt, Megan, *The War in Southern Afghanistan 2001–2008*, Center for Naval Analyses, 2009

Marion, Forest L., 'Building USAF 'Expeditionary Bases' for Operation ENDURING FREEDOM-AFGHANISTAN, 2001–2002', *Air & Space Power Journal*, 2005

Marion, Forrest L., *Air Advising for Civilian Casualty Avoidance: Afghanistan, 2015–2020*, Air Force Historical Research Agency, 2022

Marion, Forrest L., 'Ten Seconds to Impact: The Strike at Bagram

Afghanistan November 12, 2001', *Air Power History*, 2014

Meyerle, Jerry & Malkasian, Carter, *Insurgent Tactics in Southern Afghanistan 2005–2008*, Center for Naval Analyses, 2009

Mills, Claire, *The Withdrawal of Military Forces from Afghanistan and its Implications for Peace,* House of Commons Library, 2021

Neumann, Brian F. & Williams, Colin J., *The U.S. Army in Afghanistan Operation Enduring Freedom May 2005–January 2009*, US Army Center of Military History, 2020

Nichol, Jim, *Kyrgyzstan and the Status of the U.S. Manas Airbase: Context and Implications*, Congressional Research Service, 2009

Perkins, Robert et al, *Air Power in Afghanistan – How NATO Changed the Rules, 2008–2014*, Government of Norway, Ministry of Foreign Affairs, 2014

Perry, Walter L. & Kassing, David, *Toppling the Taliban – Air-Ground Operations in Afghanistan October 2001–June 2002*, RAND Corporation 2015

Quilliam, Rebecca, 'From Afghanistan to Aotearoa', *NZ Air Force News*, 2021

Roe, Andrew, 'Evacuation by Air: The All-But-Forgotten Kabul Airlift of 1928–29', *Air Power Review*, 2012

Sand, Ivan, *Challenges and Lessons Learned from the Projection of French Airpower in Afghanistan*, Air University, 2021

Schaub, Gary Jr, *Learning from the F-16*, Center for Militære Studier Københavns Universitet, 2015

Schultz, Karsten, *Forsvarets Luftmilitære Engagement i Afghanistan*, Det Krigsvidenskabelige Selskab, 2020

Schumacher, Benjamin F., *Alternative Airpower for Afghanistan: Unmanned Aircraft Systems*, Air University, 2021

Shapiro, Jeremy, *The Role of France in the War on Terrorism*, Brookings Institute, 2016

Sinterniklaas, Rob, *Information Age Airpower in Afghanistan*, Universiteit van Amsterdam, 2019

Sopko, John F., *Collapse of the Afghan National Defense and Security Forces: An Assessment of the Factors That Led to Its Demise*, Special Inspector General for Afghanistan Reconstruction, 2021

Sopko, John F., *G222 Aircraft Program in Afghanistan: About $549 Million Spent on Faulty Aircraft And No One Held Accountable*, Special Inspector

General for Afghanistan Reconstruction, 2021

Spidahl, Seth D., *The Once and Future Air Support Operations Center: A Critical Reflection on Developments in Air-To-Ground Command and Control*, Air University, 2016

Suhrke, Astri, *Faithful Ally – The UK Engagement in Afghanistan*, Peace Research Institute Oslo, 2011

Taylor, Claire, *Military Campaign in Afghanistan*, House of Commons Library, 2010

Taylor, Claire, *Military Campaign in Afghanistan*, House of Commons Library, 2010

Taylor, Claire, *The International Security Assistance Force in Afghanistan*, House of Commons Library, 2009

Teeple, Nancy, *Canada in Afghanistan: 2001–2010 A Military Chronology*, Defence R&D Canada, CORA, 2010

Thomas, Andrew, 'An Overview of the Medical Emergency Response Team (MERT) in Afghanistan: A Paramedic's Perspective', *Journal of Paramedic Practice*, 2014

van der Vegt, Quirijn, 'Joining Forces Over Afghanistan: The EPAF "Experiment"', *Scandinavian Journal of Military Studies*, 2021

Vecchi, Gian Carlo, 'AMX in Afghanistan', *Air Forces Monthly*, 2019

Welsh, Kyle, 'Task Force Erebus – Providing Essential Support to Canada's Mission in Afghanistan', *Canadian Air Force Journal*, 2010

Whitcomb, Darrel D., *Good Friday Medevac*, US Army Center of Military History, 2011

Wiltenburg, Ivor & Leeuwenburg, Lysanne, *The Battle of Chora*, Dutch War Studies Research Centre, 2021

Wood, David, 'Holding Fire in Afghanistan', *Air Force Magazine*, 2010

Wright, Donald P. et al, *A Different Kind of War: The United States Army in Operation Enduring Freedom (OEF), October 2001– September 2005*, Combat Studies Institute Press US Army Combined Arms Center, 2010

Russian language articles

As listed in Endnotes.

Various short news releases/articles from:

UK MoD, US Air Force, US Army, US Navy, US Marine Corps, US DoD, AFCENT, Netherlands Government, Canadian Government, Australian Government, BBC, Reuters, *Washington Post*, *Flight Global*, *The Guardian*.

INDEX

References to images and maps are in **bold**.